Actions and *Reactions*

Arnold Toutant
Senior Author

Sharon Sterling   Anita Chapman

Caren Cameron   Sharon Jeroski

Kathleen Gregory

Toronto
Oxford University Press Canada
1998

Oxford University Press Canada
70 Wynford Drive Don Mills Ontario M3C 1J9
www.oupcan.com

Oxford New York
Athens Auckland Bangkok Calcutta
Cape Town Chennai Dar es Salaam Delhi
Florence Hong Kong Istanbul Karachi
Kuala Lumpur Madrid Melbourne
Mexico City Mumbai Nairobi Paris
Singapore Tapei Tokyo Toronto Warsaw

and associated companies in
Berlin Ibadan

OXFORD is a trade mark of Oxford
University Press

Canadian Cataloguing in Publication Data

Main entry under title:

Actions and reactions

(Identities; 7)
ISBN 0-19-541362-8

Readers (Elementary). 2. English language—
Problems, exercises, etc.—Juvenile
literature. I. Toutant, Arnold, 1938- . II.
Series: Identities (Toronto, Ont.); 7.

PE1121.A24 1998   428.6   C97-932555-2

Design and Electronic Assembly:
Pronk&Associates
Cover Illustration: Doug Martin

Since this page cannot accommodate all
the copyright notices, the following page
and page 296 constitute an extension of
the copyright page.

Printed in Canada

2 3 4 5—02 01 00 99 98

Acknowledgements

The publisher and authors would like to
thank the following people for their valuable
insights and for their contributions to the
development of this manuscript.

Graham T. Foster
Language Arts Supervisor
Catholic School Centre
Calgary, Alberta

Irene Heffel
Alberta Educator
Alberta

Rudi Engbrecht
English Consultant
Winnipeg School Division #1
Manitoba

Lori Rog
Language Arts Consultant
Regina School Division #44
Regina Public Schools
Saskatchewan

Al Mouner
Happy Valley Elementary School
Victoria, British Columbia

Rosemarie Harrison
St. Nicholas Catholic Junior High School
Edmonton, Alberta

Ann Naymie
Director Professional Development
BC Principals and Vice-Principles Association
Vancouver, British Columbia

Christine Giese
Learning Resources Consultant
C.C. Carrothers School
London, Ontario

Literary Acknowledgements

Every reasonable effort has been made to trace the original source of reprinted material in this book. Where the attempt has been unsuccessful, the publisher would be pleased to hear from copyright holders to rectify any omission.

Zlata Filipovic, translated by Christina Pribichevich-Zoric, excerpts from *Zlata's Diary: A Child's Life in Sarajevo* (London: Penguin Books, 1994)

Gip Forster, excerpt from 'The Man' from *'Gip' Forster's Collected Ramblings*

'Local Hero' and 'A View from the Mound' from *The Last-Place Sports Poems of Jeremy Bloom* by Gordon Korman and Bernice Korman. Copyright © 1996 by Gordon Korman and Bernice Korman. Reprinted by permission of Scholastic Inc.

'Manon Rheaume' printed with permission from *Celebrating Excellence: Canadian Women Athletes* by Wendy Long. Published by Polestar Book Publishers, Victoria, BC.

Excerpts from *My Left Foot* by Christy Brown (London: Martin Secker & Warburg, 1954). Reprinted by permission of Random House UK Limited.

'Tuk: The Heroic Polar Bear' from *More Animal Heroes* by Karleen Bradford, Scholastic Canada, 1996. Reprinted by permission of the publisher.

'Kindest Cut' from *People*, 1994

Mike Wesley, 'Unsung Hero' from *Courageous Spirits: Aboriginal Heroes of Our Children*, J. Archibald, V. Friesen, and J. Smith, eds. (Penticton, BC: Theytus Books, 1993)

Excerpts from Taming the Tube by permission of its creator, Dalia Naujokaitis <pugglers@ottawa.net>.

'Virginie's Story' by Max Paris from *Adbusters*, Vol. 3, No. 1, Winter 1994. Reprinted by permission.

'The Granddaughter' from *Tales from the Brothers Grimm and the Sisters Weird*, copyright © 1995 by Vivian Vande Velde, reprinted by permission of Harcourt Brace & Company.

'The Visitor' by Christine Pinsent-Johnson from *Notes Across the Aisle* (Thistledown Press Ltd., 1995).

'The Defender' by Robert Lipsyte from *Ultimate Sports* by Donald R. Gallo. Copyright © 1995 by Donald R. Gallo. Used by permission of Bantam Doubleday Dell Books for Young Readers.

Gish Jen, 'The White Umbrella' copyright © 1994 by Gish Jen. First published in *The Yale Review*. Reprinted by permission of the author.

'Warrior's remains found' from *The Vancouver Sun*, 24 April 1997. Reprinted by permission of Associated Press.

Notes: Bodies and Bones—The Tales They Tell' from *Mysteries of Time* by Larry Verstraete, Scholastic Canada, 1992. Reprinted by permission of the publisher.

Excerpts from *Tales Mummies Tell* by Patricia Lauber. Copyright © 1985 by Patricia G. Lauber. Used by permission of HarperCollins Publishers.

Eve Bunting, excerpts from *I Am The Mummy Heb-Nefert* (Toronto: Tundra Books, 1997)

Text by Shelley Tanaka © 1996 The Madison Press Limited, from *I Was There: Discovering the Iceman*, a Scholastic/Madison Press Book.

Excerpt from *Frozen Man* by David Getz, © 1994 by David Getz. Reprinted by permission of Henry Holt and Company, Inc.

Excerpts from *The Bone Detectives* by Donna Jackson. Text Copyright © 1996 by Donna M. Jackson; Photographs Copyright © 1996 by Charlie Fellenbaum. by permission of Little, Brown and Company and Charlie Fellenbaum.

'Convicted by a cat' from *Maclean's*, 5 May 1995. Reprinted by permission of Maclean's Magazine.

'How We Got the Word Mummy' reprinted by permission of Carolrhoda Books, Inc., from *Mummies and Their Mysteries*. Copyright © 1993 by Charlotte Wilcox.

'The Mystery of the Stone Statues' from *Whatever Happened to Uncle Albert & Other Puzzling Plays* by Sue Alexander. Copyright © 1980 by Sue Alexander. Reprinted by permission of Clarion Books/Houghton Mifflin Company. All rights reserved. Permission to perform this play must be cleared with the publisher.

Text by Shelley Tanaka © 1996 The Madison Press Limited, from *I Was There: On Board The Titanic*, a Scholastic/Madison Press Book.

Taken from *A Child in Prison Camp* © 1971 Shizuye Takashima, published by Tundra Books.

Arnold Adoff, 'Though The Afternoon Was Freezing Cold' and 'Sometimes In Center Field On A Hot Summer Evening' from *Sports Pages* (Toronto: Fitzhenry & Whiteside, 1986)

'The Sidewalk Racer or On the Skateboard' and 'Photo Finish' from *The Sidewalk Racer and Other Poems of Sports* and Motion by Lillian Morrison. Copyright © 1965, 1967, 1968, 1977 by Lillian Morrison. Used by permission of Marian Reiner for the author.

Edwin Hoey, 'Foul Shot' from *Read Magazine* (Xerox Education, 1962)

'High Jumper' copyright Don Welch, 1997. Reprinted by permission of the author.

Reprinted by permission of Farrar, Straus & Giroux, Inc.: 'flies' from *Small Poems Again* by Valerie Worth. Copyright © 1986 by Valerie Worth.

'Mosquito' from *Austin Says and Other Stories* by Veronica Eddy-Brock. Reprinted by permission of the author.

Judith Nicholls. 'Whalesong' from *Dragonsfire and Other Poems* by Judith Nicholls (London: Faber and Faber, 1990). Reprinted by permission of Faber and Faber Ltd.

Iglukik, 'Polar Bear' from *Eskimo Poems*, Tom Lowenstein, trans., Allison & Bus by

Reprinted by permission of Farrar, Straus & Giroux, Inc.: 'cat' from *Small Poems* by Valerie Worth. Copyright © 1972 by Valerie Worth.

'Lone Dog' from *Songs to Save a Soul* by Irene McLeod (London: Chatto & Windus). Reprinted by permission of Random House UK Ltd.

Dorthi Charles, 'Concrete Cat' from *Knock at a Star: A Child's Introduction to Poetry*, X.J. Kennedy and Dorothy M. Kennedy (Boston: Little, Brown and Company, 1982)

David McCord, 'So You Found Some Fresh Tracks in the Snow?' from *Speak Up* by David McCord. Copyright © 1980 by David McCord. by permission of Little, Brown and Company.

'Life Lesson' from Like Haiku by Don Raye ([city]: Charles E. Tuttle Co., [year]). Reprinted by permission of Charles E. Tuttle Co., Inc.

Sharon Lange, 'My room is a mess' from *An Ice Cream Cone Feeling In the Dark of December*, Emma E. Plattor and Jack R. Cameron, eds., The English Council of the Alberta Teachers' Association. Reprinted by permission of the Alberta Teachers' Association.

Robert Bennett, 'Young and Old' from *I can never get the first pickle out of the jar*, North York Board of Education

Dale McMechan, 'Depression' from *Action English 1*

Brian S. Powell, 'Desert' from *Making Poetry* (Toronto: Collier Macmillan, 1973)

Jamaal Haidar, 'A Vision of the Coming Revolution of the Earth' is reprinted by permission of the author, a self-educated writer.

The Evergreen Foundation website is reprinted by permission of The Evergreen Foundation, a registered non-profit organization, dedicated to connecting people with nature through the enhancement of healthy natural environments in schools and communities across Canada.

New Brunswick Environmental Network website reprinted by permission.

Excerpts from Worm Composting brochure reprinted by permission from *City Farmer*, G.V.R.D., C.R.D.

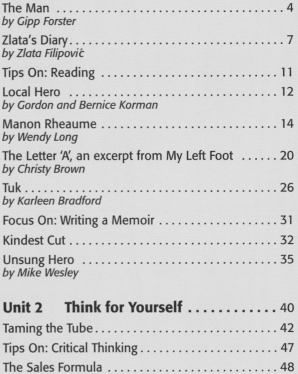

TABLE OF CONTENTS

Unit 1   Heroes Gallery 2

The Man 4
by Gipp Forster

Zlata's Diary 7
by Zlata Filipović

Tips On: Reading 11

Local Hero 12
by Gordon and Bernice Korman

Manon Rheaume 14
by Wendy Long

The Letter 'A', an excerpt from My Left Foot 20
by Christy Brown

Tuk 26
by Karleen Bradford

Focus On: Writing a Memoir 31

Kindest Cut 32

Unsung Hero 35
by Mike Wesley

Unit 2   Think for Yourself 40

Taming the Tube 42

Tips On: Critical Thinking 47

The Sales Formula 48
by Sharon Sterling

Does It Really Hurt? 53

Focus On: Debate 60

The Language of Film 64
by Sharon Sterling

Unit 3   Actions and Reactions 74

Tips On: Reading Short Stories 75

The Granddaughter 76
by Vivian Vande Velde

Focus On: Interpreting Fiction 86

The Visitor 88
by Christine Pinsent-Johnson

The Defender 100
by Robert Lipsyte

The White Umbrella 112
by Gish Jen

Unit 4   Reconstructing Past Lives 124

Warrior's remains found. 126

Bodies and Bones The Tales They Tell 128
by Larry Verstraete

Tips On: Reading for Information 133

How to Make a Mummy Talk?...............134
by James M. Deem

I Am the Mummy Heb-Nefert................142
by Eve Bunting

Discovering the Iceman....................145
by Shelley Tanaka

Frozen Man............................152
by David Getz

Focus On: Writing Historical Fiction.........154

Skeletal Sculptures......................156
by Donna M. Jackson

Convicted by a Cat......................162

Unit 5   It's Showtime! 166

It Takes Many People 168
by Sharon Sterling

Tips On: Nonverbal Communications..........173

The Mystery of the Stone Statues 174
by Sue Alexander

Focus On: Making Decisions in a Group 190

The Back Flip 192
by Kathy Vanderlinden

Unit 6   Young People in History......198

Tips On: Viewing.......................199

On Board the Titanic 200
by Shelley Tanaka

Focus On: Representing Using Visual Forms.....212

A Child in Prison Camp 214
by Shizuye Takashima

Unit 7   Imagined Worlds...........234

Tips On: Reading Poetry..................234

Sports..............................235

Though the Afternoon Was Freezing Cold 236
by Arnold Adoff

Photo Finish 237
by Lillian Morrison

Foul Shot   237
by Edwin A. Hoey

Sometimes in Centre Field on a Hot Summer Evening . 238
by Arnold Adoff

The Sidewalk Racer or On the Skateboard 239
by Lillian Morrison

A View From the Mound 239
by Gordon and Bernice Korman

High Jumper   239
by Don Welch

Animals 242

Mosquito.............................242
by Veronica Eddy Brock

Polar Bear 243
by Iglukik

Cat 243
by Valerie Worth

Whalesong............................244
by Judith Nicholls

Lone Dog.............................245
by Irene McLeod

Something Told the Wild Geese 245
by Rachel Field

Flies 245
by Valerie Worth

Form................................248

My Room is a Mess 248
by Sharon Lange

Life Lesson 248
by Don Raye

Kite 249

Concrete Cat 249
by Dorthi Charles

Young and Old 250
by Robert Bennett

Galaxies and Atoms 250

A Lady from near Lake Louise...............251

So you found some fresh tracks in the snow 251
by David McCord

Desert 251
by Brian Powell

Depression 251
by Dale McMechan

Focus On: Revising Your Poem 253

Unit 8   Making Things Happen.......256

Tips On: Understanding Communications.......257

A Vision of the Coming Revolution of the Earth . . 258
by Jamaal Haidar

Food Fun.............................262

Worm Composting......................269

Focus On: Meetings.....................272

Correspondence........................274

Help Yourself 278

Heroes Gallery

When you think of a hero, what comes to mind? Who are your heroes? What attributes or characteristics do they share? Do you share the same view as others about what makes a person a hero?

Many people have faced and overcome obstacles to become famous. These are the heroes you read about in books, newspapers, magazines, and Internet articles. You watch these heroes as they relive their accomplishments on television or in movies about their lives.

Not all heroes achieve great fame. This unit is about ordinary individuals who have lived their lives in heroic ways. The selections are portraits in words of people who have met challenges and persevered. They overcame obstacles, persisted in things that mattered to them, and cared about others.

SETTING GOALS

In this unit you can:

■ Learn ways to compare your ideas and views about heroes with those of others.

■ Learn about techniques authors use to help you picture their heroes.

■ Practise strategies to use while you read to help you become a better reader.

■ Use a variety of ways to represent your ideas about heroes.

The Man 4
by Gipp Forster

In this memoir, the author remembers a personal hero, a soldier who returned from World War II.

Zlata's Diary 7
by Zlata Filipović

A young girl, Zlata, who lived in Bosnia during wartime, kept a diary to record her observations and feelings about the war going on around her.

Local Hero 12
by Gordon and Bernice Korman

In this poem, a local sports hero explains reasons for being admired.

Manon Rheaume 14
by Wendy Long

This article describes Manon, the first women in Canada to play in a National Hockey League game.

The Letter "A" 20
taken from My Left Foot
by Christy Brown

This is an autobiography of a man with cerebral palsy who tells about the challenges he meets while growing up.

Tuk 26
by Karleen Bradford

This article explains how a polar bear becomes a hero in the eyes of people in Vancouver.

Kindest Cut 32

In this magazine article, students support a heroic friend.

Unsung Hero 35
by Mike Wesley

A boy recalls in a memoir why his grandfather is his personal hero.

The Man
by Gipp Forster

Before You Read

Around 1944, many soldiers returned to Canada from the war in Europe. In those days, people went to movie theatres to watch newsreels that showed what was happening around the world. In *The Man*, the writer recalls a time when he was young and met a soldier who had returned from the war.

Think of someone who was special to you when you were younger. Recall things you enjoyed doing together. Do you remember a favourite time? Was there a place that you liked to go or topics you discussed together? What pictures come to mind when you think of this person?

Try This

When you see ✳ take a moment to pause and think about the questions or statements in the margin.

Once, a very long time ago, there was a man who was a hero in a young boy's eyes. He was not a man of renown, of great achievements, of spectacular looks, of exciting adventures. He was simply a man with peppermints in his pocket, a bag of bread crumbs in his hand to feed pigeons, and the time to tell a child stories he could not understand, but who hung on his every word. ✳ The child simply called him "The Man" and he would search him out on a bench, in Somerset Park.

The little boy knew the man had been a soldier because the man had told him so, but that did not overly excite the child, for in 1944 there were many soldiers and war was a living game that came out of a radio, or out of older people's mouths at the supper table or on the news reels at a Roy Rogers movie on Saturday afternoons. No, he wasn't a hero because he had been a soldier. He was a hero because he treated the little boy like a person, to talk to about pain and squirrels and candy floss clouds and growing up and a place called "over there." ✳✳

But little boys must grow up and heroes grow down as years take moments and place them in a box called memory. But that older man never died. He just faded away into the country of the past with his peppermint-filled pockets and bread crumbs and misty eyes and stories of here and "over there."

✳ Pause and Think
What do you think the writer means by the expression "hung on his every word"?

✳✳ Pause and Think
"Over there" is referring to Europe where the war took place.

First Reaction

1. What pictures formed in your mind as you read *The Man?* Draw these pictures and give them a title.

Look More Closely

2. Go back to the selection and find words and phrases that illustrate how important this man was to the young boy. Record these in a web.

3. The writer uses a number of techniques to help you see the picture of what he remembers. Locate examples where the author:

   • Explains what the boy and the man did together.

   • Describes how the boy feels.

   • Describes the scene in detail.

Develop Your Ideas

4. Write a memoir about a person who was important in your life when you were young. Try the techniques used by the author of *The Man* to create images of this person in the minds of your readers.

Zlata's Diary

Before You Read

Zlata is a young girl who kept a diary during wartime in Bosnia. She wrote about the war from September 1991 to October 1993. During that time, she couldn't go to school because it was too dangerous to walk on the streets. She had to stay in her own home and wasn't able to see her friends.

Zlata and her parents were allowed to leave Bosnia in 1993. They fled to Paris. There her diary was translated into English and published throughout the world. It records chilling events — deaths, mutilations, and suffering.

Think about the words *birthday* and *war*. Draw a circle on a page in your notebook and put the word *war* in the centre. Record all the words and phrases that come to mind when you think of war. Draw a second circle on your page and print the word *birthday* in the centre. Record all the words that come to mind when you think of birthdays. Can you think of a situation where the words might be used together?

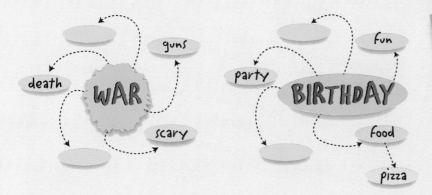

Try This

Zlata has been keeping a diary since September, 1991. This entry was made on her birthday, Thursday, December 3, 1992. Read Zlata's diary to find out what it was like for her to have a birthday during wartime.

Zlata's Diary

by Zlata Filipovič

Life changed quickly in the spring of 1992. Within a couple of months of Zlata's first diary entry, Serbian artillery positions were set up on the hills directly above her house. The family had to move all their possessions into the front room, which was protected from shrapnel by sandbags. Soon, there were no more windows left in Zlata's

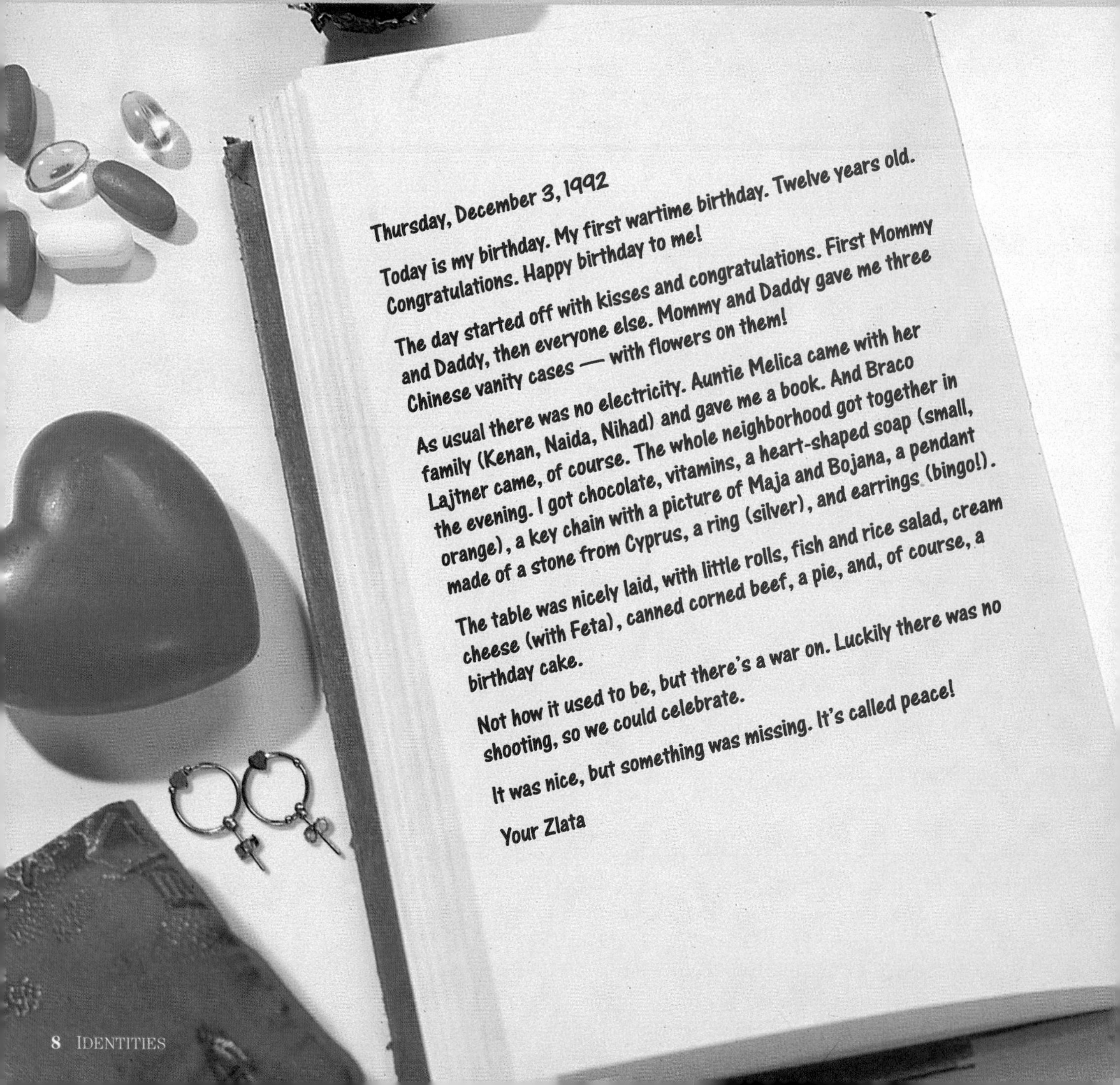

Thursday, December 3, 1992

Today is my birthday. My first wartime birthday. Twelve years old. Congratulations. Happy birthday to me!

The day started off with kisses and congratulations. First Mommy and Daddy, then everyone else. Mommy and Daddy gave me three Chinese vanity cases — with flowers on them!

As usual there was no electricity. Auntie Melica came with her family (Kenan, Naida, Nihad) and gave me a book. And Braco Lajtner came, of course. The whole neighborhood got together in the evening. I got chocolate, vitamins, a heart-shaped soap (small, orange), a key chain with a picture of Maja and Bojana, a pendant made of a stone from Cyprus, a ring (silver), and earrings (bingo!).

The table was nicely laid, with little rolls, fish and rice salad, cream cheese (with Feta), canned corned beef, a pie, and, of course, a birthday cake.

Not how it used to be, but there's a war on. Luckily there was no shooting, so we could celebrate.

It was nice, but something was missing. It's called peace!

Your Zlata

apartment — they were all blown out by the impact of shells. At that point, Bosnians who could leave the city fled; others refused to go, not really believing that their city would be reduced to rubble. Zlata watched with disbelief as her friends and relatives tried desperately to flee before it was too late. "I'm all alone here," she wrote.

Friday, December 4, 1992

It's awful in Otes. The place is in flames. We can hear the thunder of the shelling, which is constant, even here, and we're ten kilometres away. Lots of civilians have been killed. We're worried about Braco, Keka, Mikica, and Dačo. Mommy keeps listening to the radio. Braco called from the press center last night. What's going to happen to them? Until now, everything down there was fine. There was no shooting, they had food, as if there was no war. You never know where or when this war is going to flare up.

Zlata

Sunday, December 6, 1992

Sad, sad news. The whole of Otes has been destroyed and burned down. Everything went up in flames. People were killed, they fled and were killed as they ran, they were trapped in the ruins and nobody could help them. Parents were left without their children, children without their parents. Horrible. More horror.

Luckily, Braco, Keka, Mikica, and Dačo managed to get out in one piece. Keka, Mikica, and Dačo drove out and Braco fled on foot. He ran with his injured leg, falling and hiding, he swam across the Dobrinja river and managed to make it to the radio and television center.

He fled with Mišo Kučer (his best friend, they reported from Otes together). At one point Mišo was hit, he fell and that was the end of him. Braco barely managed to drag him to a house and then went on running, to save his own life. It's terrible. Terrible when you're powerless to help a friend.

Your Zlata

First Reaction

1. What pictures or thoughts formed in your mind as you read Zlata's diary? What sights, sounds, and feelings did you think of as you read the selection? Divide a page into three columns to record your thoughts. Label the columns *Sights*, *Sounds*, and *Feelings*.

Sights	Sounds	Feelings

Look More Closely

2. Zlata lets you know how she feels about the events she describes in her diary. Find statements that show when Zlata felt upset, frightened, confused, and happy.

Develop Your Ideas

3. What else do you know about Zlata from reading the selection? Do you think she is heroic? Why or why not? Tell your ideas to a partner.

4. Today Zlata is safe in Paris. She published her diary to inform others about war and to remind everyone that wars continue to be a part of daily life for many people in the world. Find information on wars that are currently taking place and how they affect people today. Record and illustrate your findings on a poster.

Think About Your Poster

5. Use the following checklist to guide your work as you plan, draft, and revise your poster.

- ☑ The message is clear and understandable.
- ☑ The colours, shapes, and design create a mood.
- ☑ The poster includes interesting and accurate details.
- ☑ The presentation is organized and easy to read.
- ☑ Spelling, punctuation, and capitalization are correct.

Tips On Reading

Effective readers select strategies to fit the type of material they are reading. If one strategy doesn't work, they try another. To remember the choice of strategies, you can think of the Five Ps: pick a purpose, predict, practise using prior knowledge, pose questions, and picture the scene.

Pick a Purpose

Decide why you are reading the selection. Do you want to find specific information? Are you reading for enjoyment? Are you reading to confirm predictions?

Predict

Start by thinking about the illustrations and title. What clues do they give? Make predictions about characters, setting, and possible conflicts.

Practise Using Prior Knowledge

Make connections with your experiences, thoughts, and feelings. Ask yourself, "Does what I'm reading remind me of anything? Has this happened to me or to someone I know? Have I read something like this before?"

Pose Questions

Ask yourself questions to help you understand confusing parts. When you come to a word you don't know, ask yourself, "What other word makes sense here?" When you are confused by a part, ask yourself, "Do I need to reread this part? Should I ask someone for help before I go on?"

Picture the Scene

Visualize what or who is being described — the hero, the setting, the action. Use the descriptive words, the sounds, and the conversations of the characters to picture what is taking place.

Before You Read

When writers want to emphasize a certain point of view or an idea, they sometimes say the opposite of what they mean. This writing technique is called *irony*.

Write down the name of someone you consider to be a *hero* or a *star* in a particular sport. This person could be someone you know, someone you've read about, or someone you've watched on television. List words and phrases to describe the person.

Try This

Read the poem to yourself to find out how the hero is the same or different from the hero you wrote about.

LOCAL HERO

by Gordon and Bernice Korman

The local paper says I'm great;
I fear I must agree.
Of all the players on the team,
There's no one good as me.

I dribble like a wizard, and
My jump shot is pure art.
The way I crash the boards is like
Raw talent à la carte.

My passing is so delicate,
The coaches swoon and sigh.
In all this town no player is
As masterful as I.

I point with pride to all this praise,
And I puff out my chest.
Of all my qualities, they like
My modesty the best.

First Reaction

1. What pictures of the local hero came to your mind as you read the poem? Do you like the hero? Is the hero similar to the one you wrote about? Why or why not?

Look More Closely

2. Reread the poem. List the words and phrases from the text that describe the talents of the local hero.

3. Reread the last four lines of the poem. What is the idea the poets want to leave you with?

Develop Your Ideas

4. Work with a partner to decide how you could present *Local Hero* to an audience. Think about the different ways that poems can be read. For example, each person can read a section, lines can be read together, and props and actions can be used. Plan how you and your partner will read the poem. Practise and present it to another pair or to a small group.

Think About Your Oral Presentation

5. Before you present your poem to an audience, read the following criteria for an oral presentation. You might want to ask your audience to write comments on how well you were able to meet these criteria.

   • Easy to hear (words were loud and clear).

   • Audience is interested (unique and humorous ways to present the poem).

   • Teamwork (both partners shared the presentation).

Manon

by Wendy Long

Before You Read

As far back as the 1800s, there are records of women in long skirts playing hockey. In the 1960s, women's hockey became highly organized in Ontario. In 1982, the Female Hockey Council was formed. Manon Rheaume was the first woman to play for a Canadian Junior Team and the first woman to play in the National Hockey League.

Have you or someone you know or heard about ever wanted to be part of a team, group, or organization, but were not allowed to take part? Talk to a partner about the experience. What did it feel like to be excluded? What were the reasons for not being able to be a part of the group?

Try This

Read the article about Manon Rheaume to find out who she is, what she accomplished, and why she persisted in spite of frustration.

Rheaume

Trailblazer. Role model. Rebel. Phenomenon. Celebrity. Oddity. Publicity Seeker.

Manon Rheaume has been called many things since she suited up to play her first league hockey game in 1977. She would prefer most of the labels used to describe her be forgotten, except a basic one that often gets buried under glitzier, more controversial titles —Goaltender.

"**P**eople ask: 'Do you play hockey for the money?'" bristled Rheaume. "'For the publicity?' I think: Are you crazy? I really love the sport. I have to get up early every morning, train hard. If I do it for the publicity, it's crazy. I enjoy doing it. I'm happy doing it. I find it hard when people say things like that."

Rheaume also knows the comments come with the territory — uncharted and wild country she forged by becoming the first woman to play in the prestigious Quebec International Peewee Tournament in Quebec City; the first woman to play in an official game for a Canadian major junior hockey team; the first woman to play in a National Hockey League game.

Her compass? A love of hockey coupled with determination, athleticism, and a willingness to learn the nuances all good netminders must master. Her map? A largely blank piece of paper that she filled in along the way — a collection of dead-ends, exciting peaks, and disappointing valleys she encountered and conquered, leaving a hint of a trail that others might follow.

Her sustenance? Love of family and friends, support of teammates, and a fierce will that keeps her going with each smack of a puck blasted by a player who doesn't want her there, with each disparaging remark made by just about anyone who says she doesn't, and shouldn't, belong.

Manon Rheaume was born February 24, 1972, the middle child of three and the only daughter. Her earliest memories are of serving as goaltender to brothers' shots parlayed on a makeshift rink in the family backyard at Lac Beauport, Quebec. She was good at many sports, including skiing, and even dabbled in figure skating, but from an early age the challenge of staring a breakaway forward in the eye and stopping a slapshot cold exerted the strongest pull of all.

It's a great sport, a great feeling when you stop the puck, when you win a game.

"It's a great sport, a great feeling when you stop the puck, when you win a game," she said. "Sure, you also have lots of pressure. I love the speed, the action. For me the goal is always the same. I need to stop the puck, whether it's guys or girls shooting. Just stop the puck, whatever it takes."

Rheaume started her first game at age five, wearing white figure skates and playing for the team coached by her father, flanked by her teammate brothers and neighbourhood friends who were so accustomed to testing her netminding skills in street hockey and scrimmages they weren't surprised to see her between the pipes. Adults, particularly parents of other players, proved a different matter. Even as a youngster, Rheaume and her parents would be criticized for her participation on boys' teams, taking the place of a budding NHLer when she would go nowhere. The reality was if she wanted to play hockey the only opportunity was to crack the lineup on a boys' squad. Rheaume resolved to go as far as she could in the sport.

She went farther than most people, except herself, thought possible, netminding through atom, peewee, and bantam AA levels until a decision not to invite her to midget AAA training camp forced her to quit the sport in frustration. She played on the Sherbrooke women's team in 1990-91, but the lure of challenges yet unmet proved too strong and she accepted an invitation to train with the Trois Rivières junior A team.

In fall 1991 she attended the Trois Rivières Draveurs training camp, becoming the team's third-string goalie while playing for Tier II Louisville. In November of that year she was called to dress for the Draveurs when their starter injured a collarbone. On November 26, 1991,

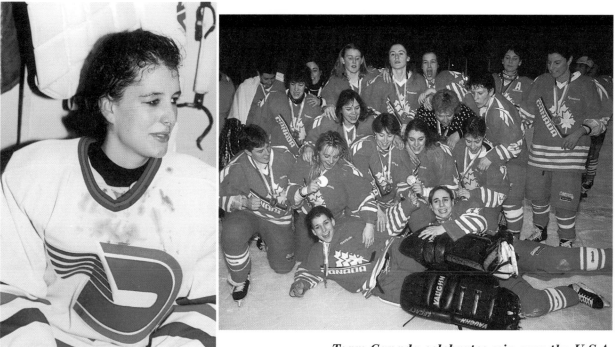

Team Canada celebrates win over the U.S.A.

Manon Rheaume: first woman to play a National Hockey League game.

with the Draveurs and Granby Bisons tied 5-5, nineteen-year-old Rheaume came off the bench at 12:28 of the second period to replace shell-shocked starter Jocelyn Thibault, who had earlier in the game enjoyed a 4-1 Draveurs lead. Rheaume let in three goals from twelve shots, and after seventeen minutes in the net she was forced to leave the game after being hit by a shot on the mask that gave her a gash above her right eye that required three stitches. The Draveurs lost the contest 10-6.

"My starting goalie wasn't playing well," Draveurs coach Gaston Drapeau told a Canadian Press reporter after the game. "She's the backup and I used her like I would any backup goalie. We don't look at her as a woman, we look at her as a goalie."

Her seventeen minutes of major junior experience earned Rheaume plenty of publicity but mixed reviews. Some observers felt the move was just a publicity stunt. They said the same when, after tending goal for the Canadian women's team that won the world women's hockey championship, Rheaume was invited to attend 1992 training camp for the NHL Tampa Bay Lightning. The howls of derision reached a crescendo when general manager Phil Esposito announced Rheaume would start in the September 23, 1992, exhibition game against the St. Louis Blues.

A woman, with just seventeen minutes game experience in major junior hockey, starting an NHL game? She hadn't paid her dues, she didn't belong, what a publicity stunt.

Rheaume saw the situation differently.

"I worked hard in training camp, why shouldn't I get a chance to show what I can do in a game situation?" she said. "Publicity stunt? That's a big risk. If I don't play well, perform well, they don't look very good. And do I turn down the chance, the challenge? No way!"

A standing ovation from the more than eight thousand spectators greeted her when she stepped on the ice, nervous beneath her mask but exuding quiet confidence to the outside world. She neatly blocked the first shot that came her way forty seconds into the game, then Blues' Jeff Brown scored at 2:21 with Brendan Shanahan scoring fourteen minutes later. The score was tied 2-2 at the end of the first period. Wendell Young took over the Lightning netminding duties for the next two periods, with St. Louis winning the contest 6-4.

I am realistic. There are still ways I can improve.

"I was preparing myself for just a normal game," recalled Rheaume. "Everyone on the ice was playing for a job, trying to show what they could do. After the game I felt there were twenty pounds less on my shoulders. I knew I had done a good job."

Rheaume was signed to play and develop her skills in the Tampa Bay minor league system. She also had to cope with a flood of interview and appearance requests.

Her professional hockey career in the Tampa Bay system took her to the Eastern Hockey League's Knoxville Cherokee. In February 1994 she was reassigned to the EHL Nashville Knights, which was a promotion of sorts in that she was the third-string netminder in Knoxville but would be the second goalie for the Knights. She finished the EHL season with a 5-0-1 record and a 3.64 goals against average.

Rheaume also returned to the national women's team in 1994 to contribute to another world championship win at Lake Placid, New York, looking ahead to compete for Canada at the 1998 Winter Olympics in Japan, where women's hockey will debut on the Olympic program. She also opted to continue working on her skills in the summer, signing with the New Jersey Rockin' Rollers of the Roller Hockey International League. In September 1994, she signed a contract with the Las Vegas Thunder of the International Hockey League.

"I am realistic. There are still ways I can improve," she said of playing as a professional. "You need to play a lot to make a team at that level. I'm playing, working on improving. My goal is just to go as far as I can in this game. That's all I've ever wanted."

First Reaction

1. Did you know about Manon before you read this article? What do you think of what she has accomplished?

Look More Closely

2. Manon faced many challenges, persisted in things that mattered to her, and cared about others. Reread the article to find evidence of each of these heroic qualities. Explain the evidence in your own words and record the page numbers where you found the information.

3. Compare Manon to the local hero in the poem on page 12. How are they the same? How are they different? Record your ideas in a diagram similar to this.

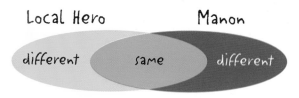

Local Hero   Manon

different   same   different

4. The author begins the article with words describing Manon. Choose four words and write a sentence for each one that explains why the word is appropriate for Manon.

Develop Your Ideas

5. Manon did not make the team for the next national women's championship. Is she still a hero? Write a paragraph explaining your opinion and your reasons.

6. Write a draft of a bio-poem on Manon Rheaume using the following outline:

First Name
Four traits that describe the character
Lover of (list three things)
Who feels (list three things)
Who needs (list three things)
Who fears (list three things)
Who gives (list three things)
Who would like to see (list three things)
Last Name

Think About Revising Your Bio-Poem

7. Use the following questions to revise and proofread your first draft of a bio-poem about Manon.

- Were you able to follow the outline? Are there lines you still need to complete?

- Is the information about Manon accurate?

- Does it capture her heroic qualities? Have you missed any key points about her?

- Are spelling, punctuation, and capitalization correct?

Before You Read

The book *My Left Foot* is the autobiography of a man, Christy Brown, who was born in 1932 with cerebral palsy. Cerebral palsy is caused by an injury to the brain before or at birth. The injury makes it difficult for individuals to speak and control their bodies' actions. Christy overcame his physical disability with the help of his family and his doctor. Before his death in 1981, Christy Brown published a number of successful books.

> Think of something difficult you have learned to do. What were you trying to learn? Did you learn by yourself? Did someone help you to learn? How were you feeling at the time?

Try This

When you see ✶ take a moment to pause and think about the questions or statements in the margin.

The

Letter "A"

from "My Left Foot"
by Christy Brown

I was now five, and still I showed no real sign of intelligence. I showed no apparent interest in things except with my toes — more especially those of my left foot. Although my natural habits were clean I could not aid myself, but in this respect my father took care of me. I used to lie on my back all the time in the kitchen or, on bright warm days, out in the garden, a little bundle of crooked muscles and twisted nerves, surrounded by a family that loved me and hoped for me and that made me part of their own warmth and humanity. I was lonely, imprisoned in a world of my own, unable to communicate with others, cut off, separated from them as though a glass wall stood between my existence and theirs, thrusting me beyond the sphere of their lives and activities. I longed to run about and play with the rest, but I was unable to break loose from my bondage. *

* Pause and Think
Another word for bondage is prison.

Then, suddenly, it happened! In a moment everything was changed, my future life molded into a definite shape, my mother's faith in me rewarded and her secret fear changed into open triumph.

It happened so quickly, so simply after all the years of waiting and uncertainty that I can see and feel the whole scene as if it had happened last week. It was the afternoon of a cold, gray December day. The streets outside glistened with snow; the white sparkling flakes stuck and melted on the windowpanes and hung on the boughs of the trees like molten silver. The wind howled dismally, whipping up little whirling columns of snow that rose and fell at every fresh gust. And over all, the dull, murky sky stretched like a dark canopy, a vast infinity of grayness.

Inside, all the family were gathered around the big kitchen fire that lit up the little room with a warm glow and made giant shadows dance on the walls and ceiling.

In a corner Mona and Paddy were sitting huddled together, a few torn school primers before them. They were writing down little sums onto an old chipped slate, using a bright piece of yellow chalk. I was close to them, propped up by a few pillows against the wall, watching.

It was the chalk that attracted me so much. It was a long slender stick of vivid yellow. I had never seen anything like it before, and it showed up so well against the black surface of the slate that I was fascinated by it as much as if it had been a stick of gold. ✳

Suddenly I wanted desperately to do what my sister was doing. Then — without thinking or knowing exactly what I was doing, I reached out and took the stick of chalk out of my sister's hand — *with my left foot.*

I do not know why I used my left foot to do this. It is a puzzle to many people as well as to myself, for, although I had displayed a curious interest in my toes at an early age, I had never attempted before this to use either of my feet in any way. They could have been as useless to me as were my hands. That day, however, my left foot, apparently on its own volition, reached out and very impolitely took the chalk out of my sister's hand.

✳ Pause and Think
What pictures come to mind when you read this scene?

I held it tightly between my toes, and, acting on an impulse, made a wild sort of scribble with it on the slate. Next moment I stopped, a bit dazed, surprised, looking down at the stick of yellow chalk stuck between my toes, not knowing what to do with it next, hardly knowing how it got there. Then I looked up and became aware that everyone had stopped talking and were staring at me silently. Nobody stirred. Mona, her black curls framing her chubby little face, stared at me with great big eyes and open mouth. Across the open hearth, his face lit by flames, sat my father, leaning forward, hands outspread on his knees, his shoulders tense. I felt the sweat break out on my forehead. *

My mother came in from the pantry with a steaming pot in her hand. She stopped midway between the table and the fire, feeling the tension flowing through the room. She followed their stare and saw me, in the corner. Her eyes looked from my face down to my foot, with the chalk gripped between my toes. She put down the pot.

Then she crossed over to me and knelt down beside me, as she had done so many times before.

"I'll show you what to do with it, Chris," she said, very slowly and in a queer, jerky way, her face flushed as if with some inner excitement.

Taking another piece of chalk from Mona, she hesitated, then very deliberately drew, on the floor in front of me, *the single letter "A."*

* Pause and Think
Imagine the pressure Christy feels with everyone watching. Can you relate to his feelings?

"Copy that," she said, looking steadily at me. "Copy it, Christy."

I couldn't.

I looked about me, looked around at the faces that were turned toward me, tense, excited faces that were at that moment frozen, immobile, eager, waiting for a miracle in their midst.

The stillness was profound. The room was full of flame and shadow that danced before my eyes and lulled my taut nerves into a sort of waking sleep. I could hear the sound of the water tap dripping in the pantry, the loud ticking of the clock on the mantelshelf, and the soft hiss and crackle of the logs on the open hearth.

I tried again. I put out my foot and made a wild jerking stab with the chalk which produced a very crooked line and nothing more. Mother held the slate steady for me.

"Try again, Chris," she whispered in my ear. "Again."

I did. I stiffened my body and put my left foot out again, for the third time. I drew one side of the letter. I drew half the other side. Then the stick of chalk broke and I was left with a stump. I wanted to fling it away and give up. Then I felt my mother's hand on my shoulder. I tried once more. Out went my foot. I shook, I sweated and strained every muscle. My hands were so tightly clenched that my fingernails bit into the flesh. I set my teeth so hard that I nearly pierced my lower lip. Everything in the room swam till the faces around me were mere patches of white. But — I drew it — *the letter "A."* There it was on the floor before me. Shaky, with awkward, wobbly sides and a very uneven centre line. But it *was* the letter "A." I looked up. I saw my mother's face for a moment, tears on her cheeks. Then my father stooped down and hoisted me onto his shoulder.

I had done it!

Christy Brown

First Reaction

1. Write your first impressions about *The Letter "A."* You may want to use the following words to start your sentences.

   • I liked . . .

   • I was surprised . . .

   • I was confused . . .

Look More Closely

2. It could be said that everyone in this story is heroic. What is your opinion? Who do you think is heroic and who is not? Give your reasons.

3. What helped Christy learn to write? Record your answers and the page numbers where you found them. Be prepared to read those parts of the story to the class.

Develop Your Ideas

4. A *found poem* is made up of words and phrases you have found in other places. Review the story to find words and phrases that describe Christy Brown. Record these on strips of paper and arrange the strips of paper in a poetic form to create your poem about Christy Brown.

Think About Your Found Poem

5. Reread your found poem and see how well you were able to:

   • Arrange ideas in a poetic form so that it reads like a poem.

   • Select words and phrases that present a clear description of Christy.

Tuk is the story of a bear that lived at the Vancouver Zoo until he died in December 1997. Tuk became a hero.

How can a polar bear become a hero? What animal heroes do you know about from real life, books, and movies? What makes each animal heroic?

Try This

When you see ✳ take a moment to pause and think about the questions in the margin.

Tuk

by Karleen Bradford

Tuk is an old bear, about thirty-four years old. He has lived far longer than any polar bear would in the wild, and almost the longest of any polar bear in captivity. He spends most of his time lying in the sun sleeping, nose twitching at the occasional fly. Looking at him, you would never imagine that years ago, when he was a young bear, he saved a life.

He was brought as a cub to the Stanley Park Zoo in Vancouver in 1961, along with three other polar bear cubs. A special Polar Bear Grotto was built just for them at the zoo, and they settled in. ✳ It was the best Polar Bear Grotto the zoo could build at that time. Mike Mackintosh, the head of Wildlife Services for the City of Vancouver, came to work at the zoo as a student volunteer when the bears were about five years old, and he's been there ever since. He got to know them very well. There were two other males besides Tuk, Old Man and Grump, and a female, Lady.

✳ Pause and Think
Picture in your mind a polar bear grotto. What is the size? What is inside? What is it made of?

When the bears were young, they used to play together. They were in and out of the pool all the time, running around, diving in, tumbling all over, and shoving each other. When they slept, they would lie together in one big ball in the central den.

"But they all had their own unique personalities," Mike says. Grump was the biggest, weighing nearly 500 kilograms, but Old Man was the boss. Old Man was bothered for much of his life by arthritis, and was quite a bit slower than the others, but there was no doubt that he was in charge.

Grump was Mike Mackintosh's personal favourite. "He was all roar and no action," Mike says. "He was a very active bear and in outstanding physical condition. He could stand and touch his nose to the top of the Bear Grotto, which was almost four metres high. Kids watching him would just gasp in awe. We'd toss fish to him, and when he stood and put his feet up against the sides to support himself while catching them, it was incredible how much space those feet would cover."

"As big as dinner plates," Graham Ford, the assistant manager at the zoo, describes Grump's feet.

"He was a very, very interesting bear," Mike says. "I was really fond of him."

Lady was the most predatory of the group. "Of all the bears, I considered her the most untrustworthy," Mike says. "I used to think that in spite of the fact that she was the smallest of the bears, if any one of them was going to eat me, it would be her." She was quite aggressive. When she wanted something, she didn't hesitate to tell the others off, even Old Man.

Mike describes Tuk as the "serendipity bonzo" of the group, a bit of a prankster and rather a free spirit by polar bear standards. ✶ "One of his favourite jokes was to lunge at people coming into the feeding den. Standing quietly off to one side, he would wait until someone had walked up close to the bars. Then he'd suddenly leap forward, rather like a dog might." Mike and his co-workers played along. They would bring visitors, especially kids, in to watch the bears feeding, and smile as Tuk made them gasp and jump away.

"He still does it," Graham says. "Even though he's old. I call them play charges." It may be play, but the keepers are glad there are bars between them and the bear. "We sometimes pat him through the bars, but you have to be careful," Graham continues. "You never know when you're going to lose a finger. Polar bears can't be trained. You'll never see one in a circus. They're more ferocious than other bears." Tuk has lived in a zoo nearly all his life, but he is not tame. He is not a pet.

✶ Pause and Think
What other animal do you know or have you read about with a personality similar to Tuk's?

One sunny summer day, there was the usual crowd of people, mostly children, around the Bear Grotto. The bears had just been let out for the morning, after being fed. Tuk was lying on the parapet overhanging their big pool. He was sprawled out on his stomach, dozing lazily in the sun. Suddenly two young men came running by. As they ran past, one of them reached underneath his jacket, pulled something out, and threw it into the pool. To the horror of everybody around, a young kitten hit the water with a splash and sank below the surface. Everyone screamed.

Tuk woke up. He opened one eye and looked over the edge of the pool. The kitten was just a small blob under water. Tuk stood up and stretched, and the people around the grotto held their breath. Did the little kitten look like dessert to the massive bear? Tuk yawned, then he slid into the water. Children screamed again. A few seconds later, Tuk surfaced. The tiny cat was pinned delicately between Tuk's front teeth by the nape of its neck, just the way a mother cat would carry her kitten. Tuk swam to the edge of the pool and hauled himself out, dripping water. Still holding the kitten carefully in his teeth, he lumbered back up onto the parapet. Then he lay down. He flattened the kitten with his enormous paws, opened his huge mouth — and began to lick the tiny creature dry. ✳

The other bears were beginning to take notice, and they didn't look as friendly as Tuk. The zookeepers frantically tried to get the bears separated. It took well over an hour, but finally they got all except Tuk inside. It took a while longer to convince Tuk to leave the kitten and go inside the pen as well, but at last they succeeded. The little kitten was fetched out of the grotto and taken home by one of the volunteer workers.

Tuk is still living at the Stanley Park Zoo. He's the last one left of the four bears. Polar bears are by nature very solitary animals, and Tuk doesn't seem to mind being alone. In fact, he seems happier without Lady bossing him around. The zoo is going to be closed soon, and the other animals relocated, but not Tuk. He's too old to be moved someplace new. So, the grotto will stay as long as Tuk lives. In the meantime, he has "the best we can give him," Mike Mackintosh says. The best medical care and the best food. Chicken, fish, horsemeat, whole salmon, animal meals, oils, vitamins, carrots, beef, herring, minerals, and bones — Tuk eats everything.

"He has as good a life as we can afford him," Mike says. "And he deserves it."

✳ Pause and Think
Why do you think Tuk rescued the kitten?

First Reaction

1. Divide a page in your notebook into four parts as shown in this chart. In point form, record some ideas under each heading.

Favourite Parts of the Story	Things That Surprised Me	Questions I Have	Other Books	Films	Characters I'm Reminded Of

Look More Closely

2. Reread *Tuk* and list the five or six main events that took place. Sketch each event and arrange them in the order they occurred. Use the sketches as cue cards to retell the story to a partner. If you find there is an important part of the story missing, add a sketch for that event.

3. Record three or four phrases from the story to show Tuk was well cared for at the zoo. Make a list of the things the zoo could not provide for Tuk.

Develop Your Ideas

4. Develop a list of four or five questions you can use to interview people about their animal heroes. Use your questions to interview a partner or someone else you know. Summarize what you learn in the interview and present the information to others.

Think About Your Interview Questions

5. Before you conduct your interview, check that your questions:

☑ Focus on the topic of animal heroes.

☑ Cannot be answered with a simple *yes* or *no*.

☑ Are asked in a logical order.

Writing a Memoir

A *memoir* is a personal account of a true experience. In a memoir, you tell more than what happened. You also tell what you were thinking and feeling at the time. A memoir focuses on the importance of the experience in your life.

Getting Started

Start by deciding on a memory that you want to write about. Some people think they have nothing to write about. "I can't remember anything." "Nothing important has ever happened in my life!" If you feel that way, you might want to try some of these suggestions.

- *Bring some mementos from home.* Your mementos may be photos of you when you were younger, a special gift someone gave you, an object from home that you had when you were younger, a souvenir, or anything that triggers a memory.

- *Talk with others.* Work with a partner or in a small group and share some memories. You might talk about a favourite place, a time you'll never forget, a holiday to remember, or a pet. You could ask each other questions such as, "What is the most surprising thing that has happened to you? Why? Was there a moment in your life that caused things to change forever? Describe it."

- *Sketch and web.* Think of a special time when you were younger. What were you doing, wearing, and thinking about? Sketch a picture of yourself at that time. Make a web of your thoughts and feelings; sights, sounds, and smells you recall; and any words that capture this moment.

The First Draft

When you've decided on a memory and collected some ideas, you're ready to write a first draft. When you write, focus on describing what is special about this memory. At this stage, don't worry about spelling, punctuation, or neatness!

Revising

After you have completed a first draft of your memoir, you might want to read it to someone you think would be interested in your memory. You might decide to leave it for a period of time and work on it later. When you revise, here are some things to check for.

- ☑ I tell the reader what I was thinking and feeling at the time.

- ☑ My descriptions include sights, sounds, and smells.

- ☑ I include interesting details about the time and place.

The article you are going to read is about a young boy with cancer. Many people who have cancer need to undergo chemotherapy treatments. A side effect from having this treatment is that some people lose their hair for a short time.

What is the most unusual thing that you have done to help a friend? Write a brief description of your experience.

Try This

Read the title and predict two things you think the story might be about. Read the story to find out if your predictions are confirmed.

Kindest CUT

IT WAS A BOLD AND BALD-FACED — OR RATHER, BALD-headed — act of friendship: On March 11, 13 boys lined up to have their pates shaved. Valuing substance over style, the boys embraced the full-sheared look because their classmate Ian O'Gorman, about to undergo chemotherapy for cancer, would soon lose his hair.

Says Ian's pal Erik Holzhauer, "You know, Ian's a really nice kid. We shaved our heads because we didn't want him to feel left out.

If compassion were a subject, the Bald Eagles, as the boys now call themselves, would clearly get As. They took notice in early February that Ian was starting to lose weight. Then on February 18, doctors removed a tumor the size of an orange from Ian's small intestine. The diagnosis was non-Hodgkin's lymphoma, which has a 68 percent survival rate after five years for children under the age of 15. Two days later, Ian's best friend, Taylor Herber, came to the hospital. "At first I said I would shave my head as a joke, but then I decided to really do it," says Taylor. "I thought it would be less traumatizing for Ian." At school he told the other boys what he was planning, and they jumped on the *baldwagon*.

"Soon," says Erik, "just about everyone wanted to shave their heads." That included a few girls, who never went through with it, much to Erik's relief — "I don't think Ian wanted to be followed

---

pate Top of the head.

around by a bunch of bald girls," he observes — and Jim Alter, their teacher, who did. "They did all this by themselves," he says. "They're just really good kids. It was their *own* idea. The parents have been very supportive."

Ian, who completes his chemo in May, is already well enough to be playing first base on his baseball team. "What my friends did really made me feel stronger. It helped me get through all of this," he says gratefully. "I was really amazed that they would do something like this for me."

And they won't stop until it's over. "When Ian gets his next CAT scan," vows Erik, "if they decide to do more chemotherapy, we'll shave our heads for another nine weeks."

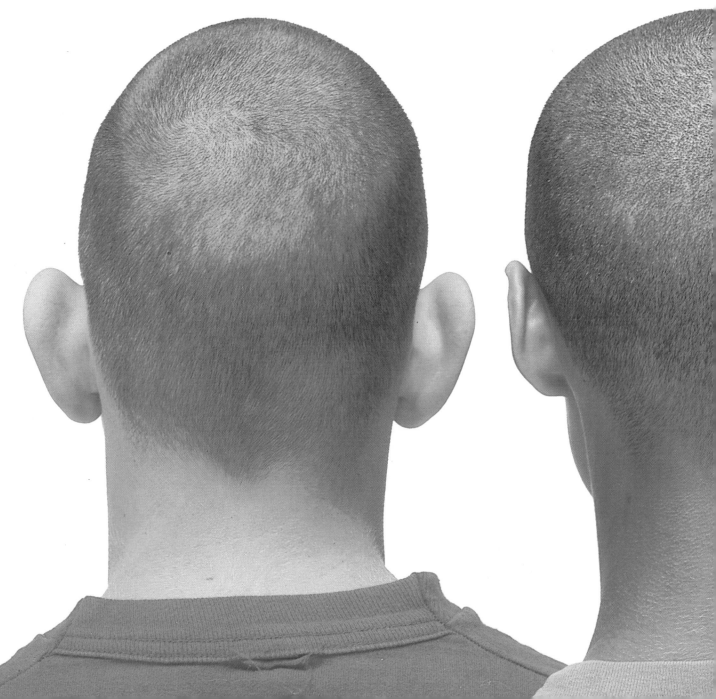

First Reaction

1. What do you think about *Kindest Cut*? About Ian's friends? About what they did for Ian? Tell a partner what you are thinking.

Look More Closely

2. Why do you think the author selected *Kindest Cut* as the title of the article? Can you think of another title?

3. What word or phrase captures the meaning of the story? Complete the following sentence frame.

   The word or phrase I chose is . . . because . . .

Think About Your Reading

4. Copy the italicized words below and beside each word describe how often you use the strategy by recording *usually, sometimes,* or *not yet.* Select one strategy that you use the most and explain how it helps you become a better reader.

   How often do you:

   - *Predict* what you think will happen?

   - *Reread* parts you do not understand?

   - *Ask yourself* questions that help you understand confusing parts?

   - *Make connections* with ideas you already know?

   - *Substitute* a familiar word when you don't understand a word?

   - *Visualize* what is being described?

Before You Read

In this selection, the unsung hero is a Cree elder. An elder is a *keeper of the knowledge* in aboriginal cultures. The author of this memoir listens to and respects the knowledge his elder has to share.

What qualities do you admire in an adult? What characteristics does an adult need to have to be a hero in your eyes? What do you think the title *Unsung Hero* means? Write your own definition of *unsung hero*.

Try This

Read the story to find out if the unsung hero in the story matches your definition.

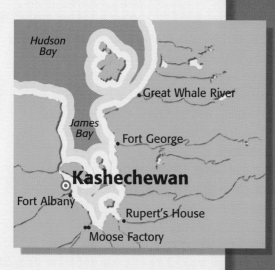

Hudson Bay

Great Whale River

James Bay

Fort George

Kashechewan

Fort Albany

Rupert's House

Moose Factory

Unsung HERO

by Mike Wesley

A hero is a person who does great and brave deeds and is admired for them, according to the *Canadian Dictionary* definition. A hero can be dead or alive. A hero can be honoured or unsung; known or unknown.

In my case, my hero is not alive. He is unknown and unsung, but to me he is a great man. His name is James Wesley, my great Grandpa. He was born in the bush, somewhere in James Bay, on September 12, 1905. He lived up to July 11, 1991. He had 11 children, all living. He took care of his family. He was helpful, smart, brave, and kind.

He helped the poor people in Kashechewan by giving moose meat, goose stew, ducks, and snow geese after a good hunt. He was an excellent hunter and trapper. He used to bring lots of animals for the fur and the meat. He shared the meat with the people. He showed how smart he was by teaching younger boys, including me, how to select a good place to set up traps. He also taught us cultural things such as making bows and arrows, snowshoes, sleds, blinds, slingshots, and moose and goose calls. He took us to the bush to learn all these activities. He was an excellent teacher.

He was brave even when he was young. He went hunting alone in the bush. He wasn't afraid of wild animals like wolves, bears, snakes, and foxes and he wasn't afraid of getting lost. His strong Indian spiritual beliefs made him brave.

Bravery, kindness, helpfulness, and smartness are the qualities I admired in my great grandfather. Because of these things, he is my hero. I want to develop the same qualities.

First Reaction

1. Work with a partner to have a written conversation about your reactions to the story. Write your thoughts or feelings about the story. Exchange papers and read your partner's reaction. Respond to the written comments by adding additional thoughts, questions, and feelings. Exchange your papers a few times to discuss your views.

Look More Closely

2. Now that you have read the story, revise the definition you wrote of an *unsung hero* before you read the story. You might want to change what you wrote, add new ideas, and provide examples to make your ideas clearer.

3. The author admires "bravery, kindness, helpfulness, and smartness." Reread the text and find examples of each of these qualities in the hero. Record these on a chart.

Qualities	Examples From the Story
bravery	
kindness	
helpfulness	
smartness	

Develop Your Ideas

4. Using the pattern set by the author, write your own story about an unsung hero. Think of an elder you know. Consider writing a story about an aunt, an uncle, a grandparent, a parent or step-parent, or a friend. You might want to use the following outline.

- A hero is . . .
- In my case, my hero is . . .
- He/she . . .
- . . . are the qualities I admire in . . .

Think About Your Story

5. After you complete the first draft of your story, ask a partner to read it and give you a response. You might want to use some of the statements below, as well as adding your own ideas.

After reading my story, tell me:

- What I believe a hero is.
- The images you thought about when you read my story.
- How I feel about my hero.
- One thing I could change to improve my story.

Make Connections

Now you can demonstrate what you've learned in *Heroes Gallery*. Read and think about the questions below.

Ask Yourself . . .

 Have you compared your ideas and views about heroes with those of others?

 Have you learned about some of the techniques authors use that help you picture their heroes?

 Did you apply strategies while you read to help you become a better reader?

 Have you represented (shared and presented) your ideas about heroes in a variety of ways?

The following activities can help you think about your work in this unit and plan how to use what you've learned in the future. Each activity is keyed to the questions in *Ask Yourself* . . .

Look Back . . .

1. Skim through the selections in the unit to recall the characters. Make a chart showing which characters are heroes in your eyes and which are not. Give reasons for your decisions. Compare your chart with a partner's chart. ❶

2. Look through the selections in this unit and choose an author who developed a clear picture of their hero for you by:

   • Using vivid words and details.

   • Including characters' thoughts, feelings, and actions.

   • Appealing to the senses and emotions.

   List the techniques that helped you picture the hero. ❷

3. Tell a partner how you used the ✳ icons to help you pause and think about the questions or statements in the margin. When and how did you use them? Record what worked well for you and what did not.

   List other strategies you used to help you read the selections in this unit. For ideas, refer to *Tips On: Reading*, page 11. ❸

4. Think about the different ways you shared and presented your ideas about heroes, and respond to the following.

- My favourite way to share and present ideas is . . . because . . .

- One way to represent my ideas that I have never tried before is . . .

- I learned . . .

- I wish I had the chance to . . . because . . .

- One way of representing that I still need to work on is . . .

- Next time, I plan to . . . ❹

Show What You Have Learned . . .

5. Write your own piece about a hero. You might decide to write a poem, article, story, biography, or memoir. Use several of the techniques that published writers use to help others picture your hero. ❶ ❷

6. Find an article, story, poem, memoir, diary, or biography about a hero that could be added to this unit.

- Mark with the icon any places that you suggest a reader might want to pause and think. Include questions or statements that you think are worth considering. For ideas, refer to *Tips On: Reading*, page 11.

- Explain why, in your view, this character is a hero.

- Choose a way to represent your ideas about the hero. Complete your representation and share it with others. ❶ ❸ ❹

Think for Yourself

"Watching TV is bad for you."

"Watching TV is a fun way to expand your view of the world."

Do you agree with either of these statements? Whether these statements are true or not, they raise some interesting questions. The main question is whether or not your actions and beliefs are influenced by what you see and hear in the *media* — newspapers, television, movies, radio, and the Internet.

In *Think for Yourself*, you'll have a chance to collect information about this issue and form your own opinions. You'll also have a chance to experiment with the creative side of filmmaking.

SETTING GOALS

In this unit you can:

- Investigate television-viewing habits of kids worldwide, including your own habits.

- Learn persuasive techniques used in television programs to get and keep your attention.

- Practise critical thinking and forming your own opinions when you read, view, and listen to entertainment, sports, and news.

- Learn the basics of filmmaking and apply what you learn by developing ideas for a film sequence.

Taming the Tube 42
by the students of St. Elizabeth School in Ottawa

Statistics and information on television-viewing habits around the world.

The Sales Formula 48
by Sharon Sterling

This article gives you the inside scoop on why television is so entertaining.

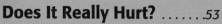

Does It Really Hurt? 53

Magazine articles, statistics, and reports on the subject of violence in television.

The Language of Film 64
by Sharon Sterling

A reference article that explains how the camera is used to influence the viewer's thoughts and feelings.

Before You Read

Taming the Tube tells you about an Internet-based research project run by students of St. Elizabeth School in Ottawa. Each year, students at St. Elizabeth invite their peers all around the world to participate in a *survey* about their television-viewing habits.

In a survey, each person answers the same questions by giving simple *yes* or *no* answers, or by providing figures in a preset range. All the answers are then collected and sorted to create *statistics*.

For the *Taming the Tube* project, the information is collected electronically or on paper, then the results are posted on the Internet for anyone to see.

How many hours of television per week do you think the average Canadian student your age watches? Make a prediction of hours per week for boys and hours per week for girls. What is your prediction based on?

Try This

Statistics may be presented in numbers or in various types of charts and graphs. Some of the information in *Taming the Tube* is presented in *bar graphs*.

How to Read a Bar Graph

1. Read the title or description for a general idea of what the graph is about.

2. Look for a legend to explain the colours or shading for the different bars on the graph.

3. Look along the side (*y*-axis) and along the bottom (*x*-axis) to determine what the units of measurement are and the range. In this sample graph, the unit of measurement on the *y*-axis is the percentage of students. The range is 0 to 100 percent. Also notice that the measurements are evenly spaced. There are no units of measurement on the *x*-axis.

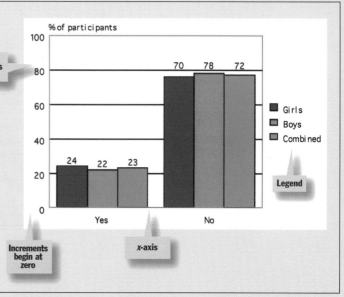

Taming the Tube is an annual Internet event that has run from January to May each year since its launch in 1994. A call for participation is posted on various educational listservers and on the St. Elizabeth School web site.

Participating

Classes register with the *Taming the Tube* coordinator and are then sent information about how to collect the raw data for the project. Each student in a participating class keeps a television-viewing logbook for the seven-day period agreed upon for the project.

- The student records television-viewing time for each day, rounded to the nearest five minutes. The logbook must show whether the person recording the information is a boy or a girl.

- The week's total is added up at the end of the seven days. The information for the class is collected and submitted to the project coordinator.

For this survey, television watching does not include video games or rented movies. Movie specials or television programs that have been taped directly and watched later are included.

Students are also asked to name their favourite television programs. Separate lists are recorded for boys and for girls.

Let's dial up and find out what the results were one year when 4,000 responses were received from around the world.

THE RESULTS *(next page)*

listserver An electronic mailing list on the Internet about a particular topic. If you add your name to the list, you will be sent any information that is posted to the listserver.

web site The address of a computer that delivers web pages. A web page is one or more screens of information about a person or group.

raw data Basic figures before they are interpreted.

dial up To use a modem to connect one computer to another.

average A number reached by adding each person's television-viewing time and dividing by the number of people surveyed.

range The numbers between the lowest and highest numbers in a group.

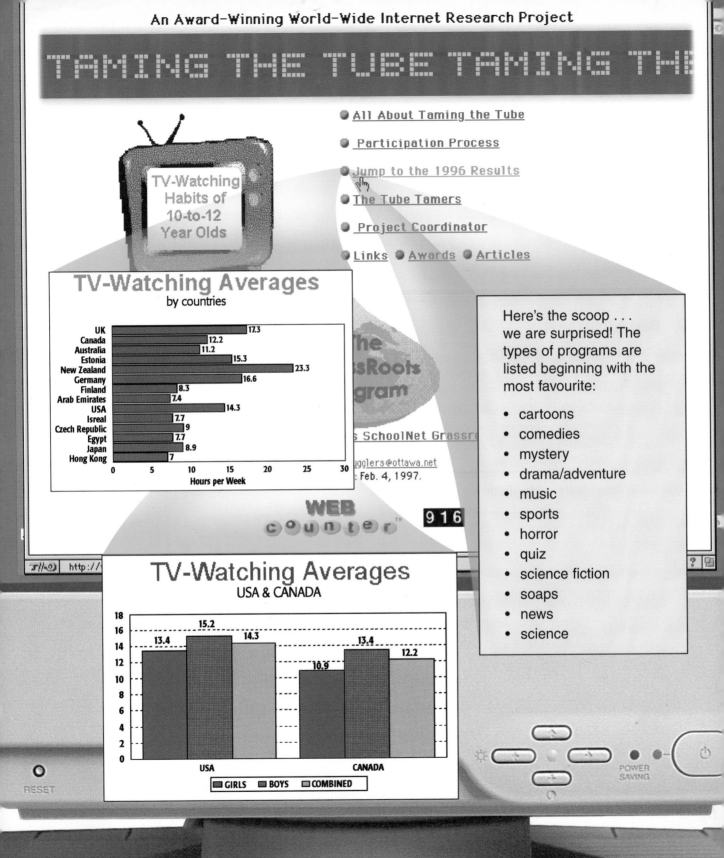

An Award-Winning World-Wide Internet Research Project

TAMING THE TUBE TAMING TH

TV-Watching Habits of 10-to-12 Year Olds

- All About Taming the Tube
- Participation Process
- Jump to the 1996 Results
- The Tube Tamers
- Project Coordinator
- Links ● Awards ● Articles

TV-Watching Averages
by countries

Country	Hours per Week
UK	17.3
Canada	12.2
Australia	11.2
Estonia	15.3
New Zealand	23.3
Germany	16.6
Finland	8.3
Arab Emirates	7.4
USA	14.3
Isreal	7.7
Czech Republic	9
Egypt	7.7
Japan	8.9
Hong Kong	7

Hours per Week: 0, 5, 10, 15, 20, 25, 30

SchoolNet Grassr

ugglers@ottawa.net
: Feb. 4, 1997.

WEB
counter™   9 1 6

Here's the scoop . . . we are surprised! The types of programs are listed beginning with the most favourite:

- cartoons
- comedies
- mystery
- drama/adventure
- music
- sports
- horror
- quiz
- science fiction
- soaps
- news
- science

TV-Watching Averages
USA & CANADA

USA: GIRLS 13.4, BOYS 15.2, COMBINED 14.3
CANADA: GIRLS 10.9, BOYS 13.4, COMBINED 12.2

GIRLS ■ BOYS ■ COMBINED

http://

RESET

POWER SAVING

First Reaction

1. Do any of the results of the *Taming the Tube* survey surprise you? Why or why not? How close was your prediction?

Look More Closely

2. Read *Tips On: Critical Thinking*, page 47, before you start this activity.

   Here's how to use two of the tips to analyse the survey results.

   • *Decide whether or not you trust the source of the information.*

     What is the source of this information? Is it St. Elizabeth School or the students who completed the survey? Or is it both? Decide what the source is and give your opinion, with reasons, of why this is or is not a reliable source.

   • *Decide how accurate you think this information is.*

     Another survey on this topic concluded that Canadians watch an average of 24.2 hours of television per week. Give a possible reason, besides an arithmetic error, that could explain the difference in these two numbers.

3. Suggest one or two possible reasons for the difference between Canadian viewing habits and Egyptian viewing habits. Write questions you would ask Egyptian students to find out if your reasons were correct.

4. Recently published statistics are often used by news media as the beginning point for a news story. The same statistics, however, can be interpreted in different ways. Write two different newspaper headlines for news stories about the results of the *Taming the Tube* survey. In one headline, present the number of hours of television watched by Canadian young people as good news. In the second headline, make it sound like bad news.

About Newspaper Headlines

The title of a newspaper story takes the form of a short sentence. It begins with a capital letter but has no punctuation at the end.

Snowstorm stalls traffic

Monster spiders invade city

5. How many hours of television a week do you estimate you watch? Write down an estimate. To check your estimate, keep a logbook of your television viewing habits for a seven-day period. Record the number of hours you watch television, which programs you watch, ratings of the programs, and your reasons for watching television. Make a chart as shown here. Keep your chart with a pen near the television.

Rating Key

T=Terrific
O=Okay
W=Waste of Time

Date	Hours	Program Name	Type	Rating	Reasons for Watching

At the end of one week, compare your estimate with the actual figures. These questions will help you think critically about your viewing habits. Answer each in one or two sentences.

- Do you watch more or less television than you estimated?
- Do you watch more or less television than the average given in *Taming the Tube?*
- What's your most common reason for watching television?

Add up the hours you'd have free if you eliminated the *okay* and *waste of time* programs for a week. Make a list of the hobbies, sports, and other pastimes you could do instead.

Think About Your Critical-Thinking Skills

6. In Activity 2, you used critical thinking skills to analyse the source and accuracy of the *Taming the Tube* information.

Look again at the *Tips On: Critical Thinking*, page 47. Select the tip on this list that seems the most useful to you and think of three or four ways you can use it to make sure you really understand what you watch, hear, or read.

Completing these sentences might help you think of ideas.

- When I watch a television program, I can . . .
- When I read newspapers or magazines, I can look for examples of . . .
- When I discuss ideas with my friends, I can remember to . . .

Tips On Critical Thinking

Another term for thinking for yourself is *critical thinking*.

Whenever you watch television, surf the Internet, or read magazines, you are collecting information about the world and making decisions about what you see, read, and hear. You might not be thinking about that when you're enjoying your favourite comedy or watching hockey. The people who create the programs are thinking about it, though, and doing everything they can to keep your attention and make you think and behave in certain ways.

Here are some tips to help you take charge of the situation.

Sort the Facts From the Opinions

Statements with no evidence, sentences that begin with *I think*, and generalizations are often signs of opinions.

Decide Whether or Not You Trust the Source of the Information

Is the information from an organization or person you know something about and trust? Is the source of the facts clearly stated?

Decide How Accurate You Think This Information Is

Based on your knowledge of how the information was collected, decide whether you think it is accurate.

Look for Facts to Back Up Claims

If a claim is made, such as "boys watch more TV than girls," look for facts to back up the statement.

Identify the Point of View

Everything you read, view, or hear is created by a person or group who has some personal opinions about the subject. This is the person's or group's *point of view*. Take the point of view into account when you read, view, and listen. Also identify your own point of view.

Look for Hidden Messages

Hidden messages are often trying to persuade you to do something, want something, or feel a particular way. Images that don't match the facts are often signs of hidden messages.

Before You Read

Why would kids with a choice of dozens of things to do spend twelve hours a week in front of the television?

Television has some obvious attractions. It's an easy thing to do, no matter what the weather. It's not expensive and doesn't require any special skills. It shows you places, people, and things you'd never get to see in your everyday life, and it gives you something to talk about when you meet your friends.

What about the not-so-obvious attractions? *The Sales Formula* will let you in on some of the ways scriptwriters get and keep your attention, and the reason why they are eager to do this.

Name your favourite television program. Make a web that shows:

• The general mood of the program.

• What type of program it is.

• How you feel when you're watching it. Try closing your eyes and remembering the last time you watched the program.

• What the main characters are like.

• The usual situations shown in the program.

• The reasons why this is your favourite program.

Try This

When you read *The Sales Formula*, think about how understanding the techniques described in the article can help you think critically when you watch television. Ask yourself, "How would I know if I was seeing this technique used?"

The Sales Formula

by Sharon Sterling

The goal of commercial television is to sell things to the viewer. The entertainment, sports, and news programs are designed to keep you watching the television until the next commercial.

A television scriptwriter has three elements to work with when writing a show: image, sound, and story. This is a powerful combination. When you see and hear things, you take in a lot of information at once — sometimes even more information than you realize at the time. Some sounds and images can give you very strong feelings, much stronger than if you read a written description of the same events.

ANY CHANGE IN AN IMAGE CREATES A MOMENT OF EXCITEMENT AND GETS THE VIEWER'S ATTENTION. THE TELEVISION INDUSTRY CALLS THESE MOMENTS OF EXCITEMENT *JOLTS*. . . .

Images

Film technology can do amazing things with images. The camera can move in on a subject, give you the distant view, fade out to a new scene, or rapidly cut to a completely different image. With computer imaging a zebra can suddenly appear on the roof of a skyscraper a woman's aged skin can become miraculously smooth.

Any change in an image creates a moment of excitement and gets the viewer's attention. The television industry calls these moments of excitement *jolts* and carefully plans out how many *jolts-per-minute* a television show will have. A sudden movement on the screen, a quick cut to a new scene, an unexpected image, or a scene of violence are all common techniques used to keep the viewer tuned in until the commercial.

Jolts have another effect on the viewer besides getting her or his attention. A jolt leaves a person feeling slightly uneasy. In this emotional state, you are more likely to accept advice. Advice such as "buy this brand of soap and your whole life will be better."

Sound

Eerie organ music — must be a mystery. Loud rock music — no need to guess who the audience is for this program. The *sound track* is used to create mood and to tell the audience right away which age group the program will appeal to.

A *tension track* is a short segment of music or a special sound effect used to give you a feeling of anticipation. For example, news programs often begin with the urgent, tight sound of a wire-service machine clacking.

Volume is another tool in the scriptwriter's toolbox. If people are shouting, the music is loud, and there are lots of sound effects such as gun fire and squealing tires, the viewer will pay more attention.

---

sitcom A short form for situation comedy, a comedy series featuring the same cast of characters in each episode.

melodramatic Exaggerated drama that appeals to the emotions, usually involving a romantic situation.

cliffhanger An ending that leaves an exciting situation unresolved.

authority figure A person who is presented as being in charge and knowing what is going on.

anchorperson The main host of a television news show.

The Story

Television programs are predictable — you always know what to expect. The predictability of television programs encourages the viewer to tune in each week, sure of what will happen.

Television programs also offer escape. The world of television is a glamorized version of our daily lives. Real police officers come in a variety of shapes and sizes. They spend a large part of their day on routine tasks. Television police officers, however, are good-looking and always in the middle of some exciting case. People like to see scenes of rich, attractive people to forget problems in their own lives.

The whole time the viewer is watching the program, there are also other questions raised in his or her mind: "Why aren't I as attractive as these people? Why isn't my life as exciting and fun?" A question that a commercial is happy to answer with "Because you don't have this wonderful product!"

Want to write a television script?

Just make sure you've got the right formula for the type of program.

- likable characters + amusing misunderstanding + happy ending = SITCOM

- bad guys + heroic acts by good guys + good wins out in the end = CRIME DRAMA

- puzzle to solve + several suspects + clever detective + solution = MYSTERY

- sports event + excited commentator + interviews with experts = SPORTS

- glamorized ordinary people + melodramatic events + cliffhanger every episode = SOAP OPERA

- recent events with lots of jolts + authority figure anchorperson + some lighter events + weather + sports reports = NEWS

- film clips of real events + more information from authority figure = DOCUMENTARY

First Reaction

1. What new ideas did this article give you about ways to think of television?

Look More Closely

2. Use the information in *The Sales Formula* to figure out why the following program features are used in television.

- Commercials are recorded at a higher volume than the programs they are shown with.

- In a book or movie, the plot usually has rising action, a climax, and a resolution. In television stories, there are many mini-climaxes all through the program.

- The jolts-per-minute in a television program increase just before the commercial breaks.

- Characters in television programs tend to be stereotypes.

3. Reconsider your favourite television program. Write out the formula for it. Does it fit one of the television script formulas in *The Sales Formula?*

Develop Your Ideas

4. Create a Venn diagram showing similarities and differences between watching a mystery movie and reading a mystery novel.

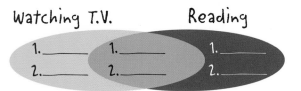

Before You Read

One of the most frequently used jolts in television and movies is violence. From cartoons to the latest hot drama, images of beatings, murder, and car crashes are used to get your attention and keep it.

Is this just fun and entertainment that nobody takes seriously? Or does violence on television encourage people to be violent in real life? *Does It Really Hurt?* contains articles to help you think critically about this issue and form your own opinion.

Students participating in the *Taming the Tube* survey may also complete an optional set of questions about their opinions of the influence of television on their attitudes and lifestyles. Here are the questions the survey asks about violence. What is your opinion?

Try This

Does It Really Hurt? includes six separate articles, each with a slightly different point of view. As you read, identify the point of view of each. Also think how your own point of view affects the way you read the articles. Try to keep an open mind to new ideas.

Do you think that violence on television is a big problem?

(a) yes _____   (b) no _____

Do you think violence on television affects your behaviour?

(a) yes _____   (b) no _____

Do you think violence on television should be:

(a) reduced _____   (b) left as it is _____
(c) completely eliminated _____

Your gender: (b) female _____

(a) male _____

DOES IT REALLY HURT?

VIRGINIE'S STORY

by Max Paris

Virginie Lariviere holds a plaque commending her efforts in initiating a petition against violence on television.

Here are a couple of violent scenes:

Scene One:

A young girl is walking back to her relative's house after buying bread at the store. On her way back she is accosted by a man who robs her of six dollars and then kills her.

Scene Two:

A maverick police officer catches a suspect criminal. He throws him to the ground, places his foot on the suspect's chest, and levels a shotgun at his head.

Both of these scenes could easily be portrayed on television. Scene two is a movie trailer for Bruce Willis' latest action flick. Scene one is what happened to Virginie Lariviere's sister, Marie-Eve — a real life violent scene.

Experts debate the connection between real-life violence and that on TV, but for Virginie, there is no debate. "My sister and I liked to watch violent movies like *Terminator* and *Robocop*, and I thought that might have something to do with her murder," Virginie contends. "I was so mad my sister was killed. I had to do something."

What did she do? She petitioned, asking for support in her campaign against violence. While the petition was circulating she made speaking appearances on TV, radio, and at media conferences all over the country to publicize her campaign. Finally, in November 1992, Virginie presented then Prime Minister Brian Mulroney with the signatures of 1.3 million Canadians who believed, like her, that there was far too much violence on TV.

To other activist-minded teens, Virginie offers this advice:

"Do what you believe in. And always follow your convictions, no matter what your cause."

THE VIOLENCE CODE

Virginie's petition was one of the events that prompted the Canadian Association of Broadcasters to revise their violence code. Here are some of the highlights of that code:

- An outright ban on the broadcast of gratuitous violence and programming that encourages people to act violently or makes it look glamorous.

- No violence unsuitable for children shown before 9:00 P.M.

- Sensitivity to violence against vulnerable groups, such as women and minorities.

- Classification of programs by their level of violence.

The code also has some rules especially for children's programming:

- Violence will not be shown as a preferred way of solving problems.

- The consequences of acting violently will be shown.

- Violence will not be the central theme of cartoons.

- Violence shown in cartoons will not be actions that children might be tempted to imitate.

If you think a television program is breaking any of these rules, you can send a complaint to the Canadian Broadcast Standards Council.

Here's what students participating in the 1996 *Taming the Tube* survey reported as their opinions of violence on television.

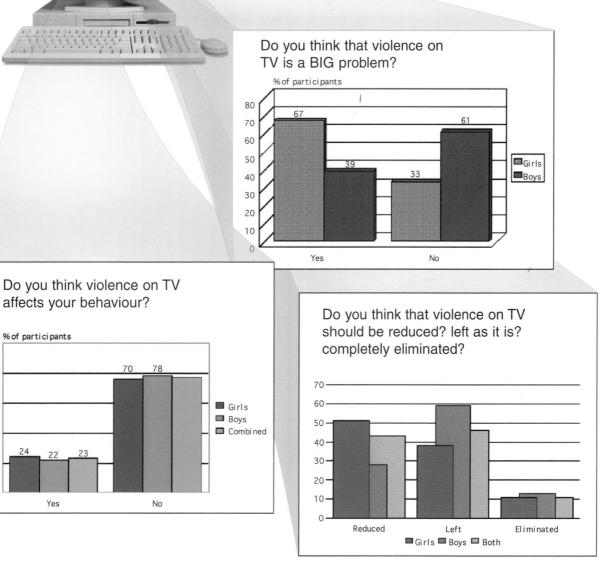

Do you think that violence on TV is a BIG problem?

% of participants

- Yes: Girls 67, Boys 39
- No: Girls 33, Boys 61

Do you think violence on TV affects your behaviour?

% of participants

- Yes: Girls 24, Boys 22, Combined 23
- No: Girls 70, Boys 78

Do you think that violence on TV should be reduced? left as it is? completely eliminated?

Girls, Boys, Both (Reduced, Left, Eliminated)

CENSORSHIP

Making rules about what people can and cannot watch on television, read in magazines, and watch at the movies is called *censorship*. Some people believe that censorship is an important way to make sure that society is fair and safe for everyone. Other people think that individuals should be allowed to make up their own minds about what they read or view. One of the tricky questions about censorship is: "Who gets to decide what is bad and what is good?"

EVIDENCE

There's no direct evidence to prove whether or not a person who watches a violent act on television will then go out and commit the same act.

After researching the topic by reading over two hundred scientific papers, the Canadian Radio-Television and Communications Commission (CRTC) decided that a high rate of violence in television programs is likely to increase the general amount of violence in society. At the same time as they were conducting this report, they found out about Virginie Lariviere's petition, which told them that many Canadians were coming to the same conclusion based on their personal experiences.

As a result of public opinion and their own research, the CRTC has been working with the television industry, parents, and anyone else interested in the issue to come up with guidelines for the type and amount of violence that should be allowed on television.

THE V-CHIP

The CRTC and broadcasters have developed a set of classification codes for television programs similar to movie ratings. For example:

CTR-C-FAM [Violence is] minimal, infrequent. May contain comedic, unrealistic depictions. Contains no frightening special effects not required by the storyline.

CTR-C-18+ Contains depictions of violence which, while integral to the development of plot, character, or themes, are intended for adult viewing, and thus are not suitable for audiences under 18 years of age.

The rating for a particular program can be encoded into the transmission signal.

Professor Tim Collings of Simon Fraser University in British Columbia has invented the V-chip. This is an electronic device that can be installed on a television set, channel converter, or decoder box. The viewer can set the V-chip to select only programs of a particular rating. If a program of a higher rating comes along, the screen goes blank.

The intended use of the V-chip is to allow parents to program their televisions to filter out television shows they don't want their children to watch.

First Reaction

1. Has reading *Virginie's Story* changed your opinion about violence on TV? Why or why not?

Look More Closely

2. Review the six articles in *Does It Really Hurt?* to find at least one example of each of the following: a fact, an opinion, a strongly stated point of view, a claim that is not proven, evidence of an effort to ensure accuracy, and a hidden message.

3. These questions will get you thinking about the V-chip.

- What problem do you think the V-chip is trying to solve? Quote from one of the articles in *Does It Really Hurt?* to support your idea.

- In your opinion, is this a problem we need to think about? Explain why or why not, quoting from *Does It Really Hurt?* or other articles to support your opinion.

- If you agree this is a problem we need to think about, do you think the V-chip is the right solution? Give reasons for your opinion. If you don't think it is the right solution, suggest something that you think would work better.

Develop Your Ideas

4. Virginie Lariviere thought about television, came to an important conclusion, and acted on it by creating a petition. A petition is a piece of paper that explains a problem and proposes a solution. People who agree with the solution sign the petition.

Canadian filmmakers are talented people who produce fine work, but most of the films available at the media centre are American. We, the undersigned, would like to see more Canadian films available for student viewing. At least 50% of the films at the media centre should be Canadian productions. The remaining 50% should represent filmmakers from all over the world, not just American films.

Name	Address	Signature

Think about something that you'd like to write a petition about. It might be about what you see on television, or something else entirely. Write a statement explaining the problem and a second statement explaining your solution. You might want to see how many of your classmates would be willing to sign your petition. You might also want to create a colour poster to draw attention to the issue.

Debate

What is a debate?

A debate is a formal oral argument. In a debate, there are always two sides, each side speaking for or against a *resolution*. Here's a sample resolution:

Resolved:
Violence on Television Increases Violent Behaviour in Society

In a debate, you are trying to win the argument — you are not aiming for a compromise the way you might when discussing an issue with a friend. The side that agrees with the resolution is the *affirmative* side. The side that disagrees with the resolution is the *negative* side. In most debates, there are two team members on each side.

How do I prepare for a debate?

Find all the information you can about both sides of the resolution. The best way to poke holes in another team's strong points is to think of them first!

Because debating is done in teams, you have to work with your partner at all stages. Together, you must decide the main issues and identify key points. Although you might research the topic independently, you will have to get together to decide what evidence you have found for and against the resolution. It's a good idea to use separate index cards to record evidence for and against each key point. You might also want to note a rebuttal idea right on the card. Make sure you record the source of the information on the card — you might want to go back to the original.

What happens during a debate?

There are rules about who gets to speak and when in a debate. Here's one pattern to follow.

Who	Type of Speech	Length of Time
Opening (Constructive)		
First Affirmative *The first team member for the affirmative presents the team's reasons for agreeing with the resolution.*	constructive	three minutes
First Negative *The first team member for the negative presents the team's reasons for being against the resolution.*	constructive	three minutes
Argument (Rebuttal)		
Second Affirmative *The second team member for the affirmative explains why specific points raised by the negative are wrong.*	rebuttal	two minutes
Second Negative *The second team member for the negative explains why specific points raised by the affirmative are wrong.*	rebuttal	two minutes
Conclusion (Constructive and Rebuttal)		
Final Affirmative *The first team member for the affirmative summarizes the team's main arguments and flaws in the negative argument.*	constructive and rebuttal	three minutes
Final Negative *The first team member for the negative summarizes the team's main arguments and flaws in the affirmative argument.*	constructive and rebuttal	three minutes

In a *constructive* speech, you present your ideas and the evidence to support them. In a *rebuttal*, you try to disprove your opponent's ideas.

Debate

Affirmative

Key point: Some people say they are influenced by what they see on television.

Evidence: Survey results from Taming the Tube say that 23% of kids ages 10 to 12 believe violence on television influences their behaviour. This small percentage adds up to a lot of actual people.

Rebuttal: These statistics are only people's opinions. They don't tell us if they really are influenced, or how they are influenced. Do these kids actually go out and commit crimes?

Source: Identities, page 62.

Negative

Key point: Most people say they are not influenced by what they see on television.

Evidence: Survey results from Taming the Tube say that 77% of kids ages 10 to 12 believe violence on television does not influence their behaviour.

Rebuttal: These statistics tell us what people think, not how they actually behave.

Source: Identities, page 62.

What goes into my speeches?

Only use the best points and best evidence you found during your research. You don't have a lot of time to get your ideas across, so stick to the topic. In a debate your personal opinion does not matter at all. The best debaters sound totally convinced of their arguments, no matter which side they are asked to defend.

Each speech should build on key points that come together for a final, strong summary statement.

How do I give my speech?

When you have completed your research, prepare a final set of index cards containing the notes you will use to help you remember your speech. Each index card should include one key point and evidence in point form.

Practise giving your speech by standing in front of a mirror and speaking to your own image. You should glance down at your index cards to refresh your memory, but try not to read your speech word-for-word. Most people make the mistake of speaking too quickly, so slow down. Time yourself to keep within the limits allowed for your speech.

When you give the actual speech, speak with enthusiasm and use gestures and facial expressions to help you look as though you really mean what you are saying.

How do I prepare my rebuttal?

This is the hard part of debating! While the other team members are speaking, you and your teammate must take notes and quickly come up with ideas and evidence against the other team's points.

It will be easier to give a good rebuttal if you and your teammate prepare a list of the points you think your opponents are likely to make. Prepare some responses in advance. Take the list with you to the debate.

What do I do about my nerves?

It's normal to feel excited about making a formal presentation in public. One good technique for staying focused on the job is to breathe in and out slowly while you are waiting for your turn to speak.

Types of Arguments

Here are some common strategies people use to present their ideas.

Inductive

Present your evidence, then draw a conclusion that states your key point.

Deductive

Present your key point, then provide the evidence to support it.

Concede a Point

If your opponent has made a good point, admit that it has some value, but immediately go on to explain that there are other sides your opponent hasn't considered.

Signs that a debating team has done a good job:

☑ Arrives at the debate with both their own and rebuttal ideas prepared.

☑ Clearly states and maintains a position on the issue.

☑ Provides evidence to support position taken.

☑ Organizes ideas so others can understand them.

☑ Listens to opponent's position and refers to it in rebuttal.

☑ Speaks clearly without too much reading of notes.

☑ Shows interest and enthusiasm through voice and gesture.

☑ Shows respect for other debaters and rules of the debate.

Now Practise

Here are some resolutions to debate with members of your class.

- Television Programs are Exciting and Creative Examples of Filmmaking

- Images of Thin Women in the Media Cause Teenage Eating Disorders

- Sitcom Families Show the Way We Really Live

- News Programs are Designed to Entertain, Not Inform

- The Internet is a Reliable Source of Information

- Watching Sports on Television is a Waste of Time

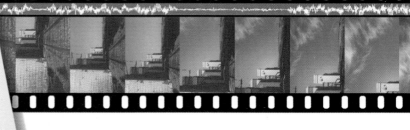

The Language

by Sharon Sterling

Before You Read

Television programs are filmed in the same way movies and home videos are filmed. In *The Language of Film*, you'll learn how filmmakers use camera techniques to get the viewer to think and feel certain ways. This will help you to understand what you're watching on television and in movies. It might also give you ideas for making your own film sequences.

Good writing often has two layers of meaning. In a written story, this is called the *plot* and the *theme* — the plot is what's going on, the theme is the "hidden message."

In film, each shot also has two layers of meaning. The *content* is the people and objects in the picture. The way the objects and people are shown, combined with the sound track, gives the picture its hidden message.

Make a few notes on what you already know about the ways television programs communicate hidden messages. You might want to look again at *The Sales Formula*. Beneath the list of what you know, write one or two questions about topics or techniques you have seen and wondered about.

Try This

The Language of Film is a reference article that describes techniques scriptwriters use to communicate their ideas, defines the vocabulary needed to write a script, and shows an example of one way to create a script. You might want to read the entire article word-for-word to learn about filmmaking. You might want to skim through to see what information is available, then refer back to the article as you need to do the activities.

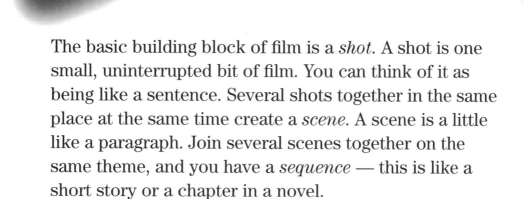

of *Film*

The basic building block of film is a *shot*. A shot is one small, uninterrupted bit of film. You can think of it as being like a sentence. Several shots together in the same place at the same time create a *scene*. A scene is a little like a paragraph. Join several scenes together on the same theme, and you have a *sequence* — this is like a short story or a chapter in a novel.

Types of Shots

Any of the following shots can be exterior (EX) or interior (INT) shots. Exterior shots are filmed outdoors. Interior shots are filmed indoors.

Close-Up (CU)

In a close-up shot, the camera is close to the subject. You might see part of a body, or a close view of an object. This type of shot suggests that you are being let in on something private. It also focuses the viewer on exactly what the filmmaker wants to emphasize. A close-up is often used in commercials when an actor wants to "let you in on a secret new product." You don't get to see much in a close-up, so the feeling becomes the most important part of the shot. An extreme close-up (XCU) is so close to an object or part of a person that the image may be distorted.

Medium Shot (MS)

In a medium shot, the camera is a little further away from the subject. A medium shot will show the full human figure and some of the setting. In a medium shot, the viewer gets much more information about the subjects — how they look, the way they are dressed, and body language. Where the subjects are also becomes part of the story.

Long Shot (LS)

In a long shot, the camera is far from the subject. In fact, the setting may be the subject, rather than any people in the picture. Long shots are often called *establishing shots* because they literally give the viewer the big picture of what is going on. A long shot showing a small figure in a landscape can make the figure look lonely and unimportant. With the right music, the same figure can seem brave.

Camera Angle

Low Angle

In this angle, the camera is below the subject, looking up at it, which gives the viewer a sense of looking up as well. The person or object in the shot looks big and powerful. Depending on the sound effects and the story being told, a person shown from this angle can look dangerous, important, or powerful. In the classic horror movie spoof *The Attack of the Killer Tomatoes*, camera angle is used to make tomatoes look menacing!

High Angle

In this angle, the camera is above the subject, looking down. This makes the subject look less powerful and more vulnerable. Depending on the other messages in the shot, the viewer might feel protective toward the person shown, frightened for the person, or dismiss the person as unimportant.

Straight-On Angle

In this angle, the camera and the subject are looking at each other eye-to-eye. The viewer sees the subject as an equal. If an object is being shown, the viewer is likely to consider the object as something that is easy to get. Depending on the other information in the film, a straight-on angle can make it seem as though the subject is challenging the viewer.

Lighting

The amount and angle of lighting in a shot has a great effect on the mood.

High Key Lighting

The scene is brightly lit from all angles. This gives a happy, open feeling and is often used in comedies.

Low Key Lighting

There is less light and perhaps only from certain angles, which creates shadow. This type of lighting gives an uneasy feeling and is often used for mysteries, or crime or horror stories.

Camera Movement

This is the actual or imagined movement of the camera in relation to the subject.

Pan

This is a slow steady movement across the scene from the same point of view — the camera doesn't actually move.

Tracking

The camera moves steadily to follow the subject's movement.

Zoom

The image gets larger or smaller as the camera lens is adjusted.

Transitions

To create a film, different shots must be selected and joined together to build scenes and sequences. The movement from one scene to the next is the *transition*. Different types of transitions have different effects on the viewer.

Cut

This is an immediate change from one shot to the next. With the right music and a clear connection between shots, this type of edit will get the viewer's attention but not be unsettling. If the cut is a jarring change from shot to shot or scene to scene, it is called a *jump cut*. A jump cut will certainly get the viewer's attention and may be unsettling. A sequence of unrelated images that together make up a message is called a *montage*.

Fade

Fade-in is when the screen gradually changes from black to an image. *Fade-out* is when the image is gradually replaced by black. A *dissolve* combines the two — one image fades in while another fades out. Fades give the viewer lots of warning about a change and can be used to suggest that time has passed.

Putting it Together: The Storyboard

A storyboard is a common way to work out a film sequence. In a storyboard, a sequence in a film will be shown as a series of frames, one for each scene. Each frame in a storyboard has three types of information:

- A sketch or a still photograph of the most important shot in the scene.

- Information about the image, including camera angle, distance of the shot, camera movement, and lighting.

- Information about the sound, including sound effects, music, and dialogue.

Before doing a storyboard, it's a good idea to write a synopsis that includes a general description of the type of program, the action in the sequence, the intended audience, and the mood you want to create.

The House on The Hill

Synopsis:

The House on the Hill is a one-hour mystery program for teens. In the opening sequence, Lee and Marcie seek refuge at the house of Dr. Munro, who is trying to find the secret of eternal youth. The atmosphere is tense and threatening.

1. Fade In:

Ext. Long Shot Mansion on a Hill — Night
It is raining heavily. From time to time, bolts of lightning highlight the scene, casting heavy shadows. The road leading past the mansion is wooded, no other houses to be seen. Colours are grey, black, and blue.

(Sound) Heavy rain. Thunder.

2. Cut To:

Int. Medium Shot Library in Mansion — Night Dr. Munro, a middle-aged woman neatly dressed in a grey suit, is reading a large dusty book.

(Sound) Rain outside. Ticking clock. Crackling fire.

3. Slow Zoom To:

Int. Close Up Dr. Munro in Library — Night
Dr. Munro closes a large dusty book and looks straight at the viewer. Her eyes are bright and intense.

(Sound) Rain outside, ticking clock, crackling fire fade as Dr. Munro speaks.
DR. MUNRO: That's the answer, then. The only solution.

4. Cut To:

Ext. Long Shot Road Leading to Mansion — Night
A car approaches, headlights bright through the dark night, then suddenly stops.

(Sound) Heavy rain, but faint sound of car radio tuned to a rock station. A loud bang as the car gets a flat tire.

5. Slow To Zoom:

Ext. Medium Shot Interior of Car Seen Through Windshield — Night
Lee, 17, and Darlene, 15. Darlene is driving. The wipers keep moving throughout the scene.

(Sound) Heavy rain, windshield wipers, car radio.
LEE: Great.
DARLENE: I'm not getting out in this weather to change it.
LEE: No problem there. (They look at each other and he shrugs with a grin.) No spare.

6. Dissolve To:

Ext. Long Shot, High Angle Front of Mansion — Night
Darlene and Lee on the front porch, ringing the bell. Nobody answers.

(Sound) Rain, thunder, and slowly building tense music.

7. Pan To:

Ext. Close Up, Direct Angle One Window in the Mansion — Night
Dr. Munro's face is in the window, lit from below left. Her gaze is down, toward the porch. She smiles.

(Sound) Rain, thunder crash, and intense music as Dr. Munro smiles.

First Reaction

1. Which techniques described in *The Language of Film* are familiar to you? Where have you seen them used?

Look More Closely

2. Use the information in *The Language of Film* to analyse *The House on the Hill* storyboard.

   Read the storyboard and find one example of each of the following.

   - Lighting used to create mood.

   - Lighting used to make someone seem dangerous.

   - Camera angle used to make characters seem to be in danger.

   - Camera distance used to let the viewer in on something the characters don't know.

   - Sound used to create mood.

3. For each of the following situations, select the type of shot, camera angle, and lighting you think would work best for the purpose. Briefly explain your choices.

   - A nature program wants to show the viewer how a barn swallow builds its nest. The shot shows a bird bringing straw to a partially completed nest.

   - In a soap opera, one of the main characters has just heard some bad news. The shot shows his reaction to the news.

   - In a crime drama, a detective is looking for the suspect in an abandoned warehouse. This shot shows the villain appearing suddenly behind the detective.

Develop Your Ideas

4. Form a group to do some camera work. If you don't have a video camera to work with, you can still experiment with camera angles and movement. In this case, you'll need to cut a frame from a piece of cardboard.

   This piece of cardboard becomes your camera viewfinder. Looking through the viewfinder will give you a picture similar to what you would see if you used a camera. Here are some ways you can use the viewfinder as a camera.

Long Shot: Stand far enough away from the performers so you can see their entire bodies. Hold the viewfinder close to one eye.

Close Up: Move the viewfinder away from your eye until only the head and shoulders of one person shows in the frame.

High Angle: Stand on a chair and look down at the group.

   As a group, decide on a sequence to perform. You might want to do a part of a play or short story, or invent a short role-play for the purpose. Keep your story simple.

   Work together to figure out the most effective way to *film* the sequence. Members of the group can take turns being performers and camera operators. See how many different ways you can film the various scenes. Record your final decisions for the sequence in the form of a storyboard.

5. Write a checklist for a well-developed storyboard. List five to ten elements you would look for.

Make Connections

Now you can demonstrate what you've learned in *Think for Yourself*. Read and think about the questions below.

Ask Yourself . . .

 Did you learn about ways to investigate television-viewing habits of kids worldwide, including your own habits?

 Have you learned about the persuasive techniques used in television programs to get and keep your attention?

 Did you practise critical thinking and forming your own opinions when you read, viewed, and listened to entertainment, sports, and news?

 Have you learned some basics of filmmaking, and did you apply what you learned by developing ideas for a film sequence?

The following activities can help you think about your work in this unit and plan how to use what you've learned in the future. Each activity is keyed to the questions in *Ask* . . .

Look Back . . .

1. Describe one thing you learned in this unit about your own television-viewing habits. ❶

2. Describe the most interesting technique you learned in this unit to get across a hidden message in a television program. Explain how the technique works and why it interests you. ❷ ❹

3. Did the information you read in this unit about television change your opinion of whether or not violence on television influences people's behaviour? In a two- or three-paragraph essay, explain your opinion and why it did or did not change. Alternatively, you might want to write your opinion on one of the topics for debating listed in *Focus On: Debate*, page 60. ❸

4. Explain one way preparing for a debate is a good way to practise using your critical-thinking skills. ❸

Show What You've Learned . . .

5. Design a brief survey to find out how much time teenagers spend on the Internet and what sites they like to visit. In your design, include an explanation of how you would collect raw data, a description of how you would present the results of your survey, and the actual questions you would ask. ❶

6. Use *Tips On: Critical Thinking*, page 47, as a guide to create a list of *Tips On: Critical Viewing* that people could use when they watch television. Exchange tips with a partner and discuss any similarities or differences. You might want to revise your tips after this discussion. ❶ ❷ ❸ ❹

7. Find a newspaper, magazine, or an Internet article and:

- Analyse the reliability of the source.

- Identify two facts and two opinions.

- Describe the point of view of the person who wrote the material.

Summarize the results of your analysis in a paragraph. ❸

8. Create a synopsis and a storyboard for a film sequence for either the teaser for a sports program, a scene from a story, or poem in this book or another book. Before you create your storyboard, sketch out some rough ideas and discuss them with a partner. You might find it helpful to experiment with the cardboard viewfinder again to get your shots just right.

After you have created your storyboard, ask a partner to read your synopsis and storyboard. Have your partner give her or his opinion of whether the camera would create the mood you intended. If you made a checklist for a well-developed storyboard, use it to help you with your work. ❷ ❹

Actions and Reactions

Reading *fiction* — novels and short stories — gives you opportunities to experience people, places, and events outside your everyday life. You can meet characters who entertain you, reveal their feelings and motivations, and help you learn more about yourself.

As with all fiction, each short story in this unit develops out of a *conflict*. The author places the *characters* in a situation where they face a problem. Sometimes the *setting* — where the story takes place — is an important part of the conflict. The *plot* is made up of a series of events that happen as the characters try to resolve the problem. The interesting part of reading stories is finding out how the characters act and react to the events.

This unit is about the actions and reactions of characters in the stories. It's also about your *actions* as you practise using reading strategies, and your *reactions* as you meet and respond to the characters, settings, and conflicts presented.

SETTING GOALS

In this unit you can:

- Learn how short stories develop from the actions and reactions of characters as they encounter a variety of challenges.

- Practise using a variety of strategies to help you understand, respond to, and interpret stories.

- Learn some techniques authors use to create interesting stories and use these techniques to create new works of your own.

- Create charts, illustrations, webs, cartoons, diagrams, journal entries, and found poems to share your ideas about the stories you have read.

The Granddaughter *76*
by Vivian Vande Velde

In a new twist on an old story, Grandmother and her friend the wolf have a problem with an obnoxious Little Red Riding Hood.

The Visitor *88*
by Christine Pinsent-Johnson

A Newfoundland town comes back to life when an unusual visitor brings excitement and hope.

The White Umbrella *112*
by Gish Jen

A young girl struggles with her feelings about her mother.

The Defender *100*
by Robert Lipsyte

A high-school student defends his title in a sport of the future.

Tips On Reading Short Stories

The first time you read a short story is a bit of an adventure. Here are some tips to guide you.

- **Set the Scene**
  Look at the title and the illustrations for a general idea of what the story might be about. Read the opening paragraphs slowly and carefully. Try to visualize the setting and the characters. Predict what might happen next.

- **Empathize**
  Try to put yourself in the story. Look at the events from the main character's point of view.

- **Follow the Conflict**
  Ask yourself questions about the conflict. Who wants what? What *actions* are they taking to solve their problems? Who or what is getting in the way? How does the main character react to new events? How is the main conflict resolved?

- **Pause and Think**
  As you read, pause from time to time to think back over what has happened. Make a mental summary, then predict what will happen next.

- **Use Your Word Skills**
  When you encounter a word you don't know, don't panic! You can often make a good judgment about the meaning of one word or phrase by thinking about the meaning of the rest of the sentence and reviewing what you already know.

Before You Read

Have you ever read or heard a parody of a fairy tale?

Vivian Vande Velde has written parodies of many fairy tales. In *The Granddaughter*, she tells a somewhat different story about what happened when Little Red Riding Hood went to visit her grandmother.

In the traditional story *Little Red Riding Hood*, a kind little girl takes a basket of presents to her grandmother in the woods. A wicked wolf attacks the grandmother, puts on her clothes, and tries to persuade Red Riding Hood to come close enough to be eaten. Red Riding Hood is saved by a brave woodcutter.

Brainstorm ways that the story of Little Red Riding Hood could be changed to make it more interesting. What if Little Red Riding Hood wasn't a very nice little girl? What if the wolf was kind and brave?

Try This

As you read, notice how *The Granddaughter* follows the pattern of *Little Red Riding Hood*. Try to predict what will happen next.

parody A humorous imitation of an existing story or work of art.

Once upon a time in a land and time when animals could speak and people could understand them, there lived an old woman whose best friend was a wolf. Because they were best friends, they told each other everything, and one of the things that Granny told the wolf was that she dreaded visits from her granddaughter, Lucinda.

The Granddaughter

by Vivian Vande Velde

"I'm afraid my son and his wife have spoiled her," Granny said to the wolf as they shared tea in the parlor of the little cottage Granny had in the woods.

"Children will be children," the wolf said graciously. He had no children of his own and could afford to be gracious. "I'm sure she can't be all that bad."

"You'll see," Granny told him. "You haven't seen Lucinda since she was a tiny baby who couldn't even talk, but now she's old enough that her mother has said she can come through the woods on her own to visit me."

"Lucky you," the wolf said with a smile.

End of
Scene #1 "Lucky me," Granny said, but she didn't smile.

The wolf didn't visit Granny for nearly a week, being busy with wolf business in another section of the forest where he was advising three porcine brothers on home construction. After he came back, though, he was walking near the path leading from the meadow to Granny's house when he saw a little girl with a picnic basket. He recognized her right away from the picture Granny kept on her mantel.

"Hello," he said, loping up to the child. "You must be Lucinda."

"Don't call me that," the girl snapped. She stopped to glare at him. "I'm Little Red Riding Hood."

The wolf paused to consider. "A little red riding hood is what you are wearing," he said. "It's not a name."

"It's my stage name," the girl said. She swirled her red cape dramatically. "I'm going to be a famous actress one day, and I'm going to travel all around the world, and when I do, all my clothes will be red velvet. It'll be my trademark."

The wolf nodded and opened his mouth, but before he could get a word out, Little Red continued: "Madame Yvette — she's my acting instructor — Madame Yvette says every great actor or actress needs a trademark. Mine will be red velvet because Madame Yvette says I look stunning in red velvet. Not everybody can carry off such a dramatic color, you know, but I have the coloring and the flair for it."

The wolf nodded and opened his mouth, but before he could get a sound out, Little Red continued: "I played Mary in our church's Easter pageant, and my performance was so touching everyone in the congregation wept — they actually wept. Even the priest had tears in his eyes, and you've got to believe he's seen an Easter pageant or two in his time, so you *know* I must have been stunning, even though they told me Mary had to wear white linen and not red velvet."

The wolf nodded, but before he could get his mouth open, Little Red continued: "When I go on tour, I'm going to demand that all the theaters I perform in must have red velvet seats, and I'll travel in a coach with red velvet

"Hello," he said, loping up to the child. "You must be Lucinda."
"Don't call me that," the girl snapped.

cushions, and kings and queens and emperors and popes will stand in lines by the roads, waiting for hours for a chance to catch a glimpse of me."

Little Red paused for a breath.

The wolf was pretty sure there was only one pope, and that — since there was only the one — he probably wasn't permitted to stand on roadsides, waiting for actresses to pass by. But he didn't want to waste his opportunity to speak and decided he'd better say something important. He said: "Well probably I should introduce myself —"

"Oh I know who you are," Little Red interrupted. "You're that wolf who is my grandmother's friend. Yes, I noticed the scratch marks your claws left on her hardwood floors. I told her, I said, 'I don't know how you put up with it. I mean, having a nonhuman friend, is one thing,' I told her, 'but scratches and dings on the floors and furniture, which just make the whole house look shabby, is another. After all, I have an image to maintain for my fans.'"

Little Red leaned forward to lay her hand on the wolf's shoulder. She didn't seem to notice that his eyes were beginning to glaze over. She said, "I know I can speak frankly with you because you've been a friend of the family, so to speak, for ages, so you've got to know I'm only telling you this for your own good, but you really should consider meeting my grandmother outside in the garden. She could sit in a nice comfy lawn chair, and then you wouldn't have to worry about scratch marks or shedding or fleas or anything like that."

Fleas? The wolf thought. *Fleas?*

But Little Red continued on. "'And meanwhile,' I told Granny, 'have you ever tried Professor Patterson's Wood-Replenishing Cream? Madame Yvette uses it to polish the stage. It's great for bringing out the natural shine of wood.' Granny had never heard of it — which, of course, I'd already guessed by the state her furniture was in — but I told her I was sure my mother would be willing to spare a jar of hers, since Granny's floors were in such obviously desperate need."

Little Red stopped for another breath, but by then the wolf's head was spinning. He was just opening his mouth to protest that he did not have fleas, but he wasn't fast enough. Little Red started telling him about other products that her mother used around the home, and once she started, he wasn't able to get a word in edgewise.

> "Oh I know who you are," Little Red interrupted. "You're that wolf who is my grandmother's friend."

After a few minutes that felt like an hour or two, the wolf was thinking that he was in serious danger of being bored to death.

The next time Little Red paused to inhale, he pointed to the sun overhead and exclaimed, all in one rush so Little Red couldn't interrupt, "My goodness, look at the time, I had no idea it was so late, I'm late for an appointment, it was real nice meeting you, good-bye!"

End of scene #2

He also had the sense to start moving as soon as he started talking.

Which was a good thing, because Little Red started telling him, even as he left, about the clock her father had bought, which had been made in Switzerland, and it had a dial to show the phases of the moon and you could set it to any one of three different kinds of chimes, and it was carved with something-or-other—but by then the wolf had speeded up and was out of earshot.

He felt ready to collapse with exhaustion. The only thing that kept him going was the thought of poor Granny, and the knowledge that she had to be warned.

Luckily, he knew a short cut.

Racing ahead, he got to Granny's house and pounded on the door.

Though it was midmorning, Granny came to the door wearing her nightie and slippers, with a shawl wrapped around her shoulders.

Before she could get a word out, the wolf said: "I met her, I know what you mean, she's on her way — quick, get dressed, there's still time to escape out the back door."

Granny sneezed. Twice. Three times. The wolf thought Little Red would probably blame him for giving her grandmother allergies, but Granny said, "She gave me her cold, and now I'm too sick to leave. I hoped her mother wouldn't let her come again today. What am I going to do? I'm not up to one of her visits."

"Tell her she can't come in," the wolf suggested.

"You can't say that to family," Granny said. She blew her nose in her hankie. "I can't face her. She'll tell me it isn't a cold and that I'm sneezing because of all the dust in my house. Can you believe she told me my house is one huge dust trap and that her mother wouldn't stand for it?"

"Yes," the wolf said, "I believe it." Looking out the window, he added, "here she comes up the walk."

"She's sure to have all sorts of remedies and advice," Granny said. "Well, I'm hiding in the closet. Call me when it's safe to come out again."

She stepped into the closet and pulled the door closed behind her.

Something has to be done about that little girl, the wolf thought, *or she'll never leave*. He grabbed a spare nightie and nightcap out of the chest at the foot of the bed and leapt into Granny's bed, pulling the covers up to his chin just as Little Red walked in without knocking or waiting for an invitation.

End of scene #3

"I got the most beautiful azaleas out of our garden for you to cheer you up," Little Red said, reaching into her basket, "along with the regular cakes and bread and jams and other goodies my mother usually packs for you. I'll bet you thought it was too early in the year for azaleas, but we have the very first ones, because what we do is we force them by putting burlap bags on the ground to . . ."

Little Red stopped talking, and it was the first time the wolf had heard such a thing.

"What are you doing here?" she demanded.

"Why, dear," the wolf said, trying to sound like Granny. "I'm your grandmother, I live here."

> "If you're Granny," she said, and jabbed the wolf's front leg with the spoon, "why do you have such big, hairy arms?"

"You're not Granny," Little Red said, "You're that rude wolf."

Rude! the wolf thought. "No dear," he insisted in a high, shaky voice. "I'm Granny, I'm feeling much better today, but very contagious. Why don't you leave the basket of goodies on the night table and go back home?"

Little Red put the basket down on the floor, but she picked up a wooden spoon with which Granny had been eating a bowl of oatmeal, and she approached the bed. "If you're Granny," she said, and jabbed the wolf's front leg with the spoon, "why do you have such big, hairy arms?"

The wolf winced but ignored the oatmeal, which stuck to his fur. He forced himself to speak gently and lovingly. "The better to hug you with, my dear," he said.

"And if you're Granny, why do you have such big, hairy ears?" She poked him on the side of the head with the spoon, leaving behind another glob of oatmeal.

"Ouch! The better to hear you with, my dear." He forced himself to smile.

"And if you're Granny, why do you have such big, sharp teeth?"

She smacked him on the muzzle with the spoon — which hurt a lot.

The wolf lost his temper. "The better to eat you with!" he yelled. He didn't mean it, of course. He was angry, but not angry enough to eat his best friend's granddaughter.

But as he jumped out of bed, intending only to frighten Little Red a bit, his back leg caught on the blankets and he half fell on her.

Landing heavily on the floor, she began to scream.

Loudly.

Very loudly.

End of scene #4 Extremely loudly.

She scrambled backward, knocking Granny's chair over, and continued screaming, all the while whacking away at the wolf with the wooden spoon.

The wolf, still caught in the bed linens, flailed about, shredding the sheets with his claws, and began to howl.

Granny, hearing all the commotion, tried to open the closet door, but the tipped chair was in the way. She was sure an intruder had come into the house and was killing both her best friend and her granddaughter. "Help!" she began to scream, knowing that there were woodcutters working nearby, "Help!"

And one of the woodcutters, a neighbor man named Bob, heard her.

Bob shifted his ax to his left hand and swept up his hunting musket as he took off running across Granny's yard.

Throwing open the front door, he saw the snarling wolf dressed in Granny's clothes, and he saw Little Red, still on the floor screaming. He assumed the worst and fired the musket . . .

. . . just as he stepped into Little Red's basket of goodies.

The bullet missed the wolf and shattered the bowl of oatmeal on the night table.

"What idiot's shooting guns off in my house?" Granny yelled, but nobody could hear her because of Little Red's screaming.

Bob dropped the musket, which was only good for one shot before it needed to be reloaded, and switched the ax back to his right hand, all the while trying to shake the basket off his foot at the same time he was approaching the bed. Dragging Little Red out of the way, he swung his ax at the wolf . . .

. . . just as Granny heaved herself against the closet door, scraping the fallen chair across the floor.

The ax embedded itself in the edge of the door.

Granny looked from the ax head, three inches away from her nose, to Bob.

There was a moment of stunned silence. The wolf stopped struggling against the tangled bed-sheets. Even Little Red stopped screaming.

"What in the world did you do that for?" Granny demanded.

"I thought the wolf ate you," Bob said. "I was trying to rescue your granddaughter."

Too shocked for words, the wolf shook his head to indicate he'd never eat Granny.

"Well!" Little Red said. "Some rescue! First you barge in here, tracking your muddy boots all over the floor" — Bob opened his mouth to apologize, but Little Red continued — "which I know wasn't in very good shape to begin with, Granny being the indifferent housekeeper she is — I know she doesn't mind my saying that because I only mention it for her own good, and believe me, when I'm a famous actress I'll hire a maid to give her a hand, because heaven knows, she isn't getting any younger." The wolf saw that Bob's eyes were beginning to bulge as his hand slipped from the handle of his ax, but Little Red continued: "But even leaving Granny's messy habits out of it, you come in here trailing big globs of mud and grass, shoot a hole through the bowl, which *my family* bought Granny for Christmas last year, gouge a perfectly fine door with your ax, not to mention pulling my hair, and look at this — *look at this*!" Everybody looked. "You are

Too shocked for words, the wolf shook his head to indicate he'd never eat Granny.

stepping in the goodies my mother made and which I brought here for my sick Granny, never mind that I had to walk for hours to get here and that I'm even now missing a class with Madame Yvette to be here, inhaling wolf dander and catching a chill from sitting on this floor, which no doubt will ruin my stunning speaking voice. And you call this a rescue?"

Bob shook the basket off his foot.

The wolf saw that the azaleas were crunched, but the food was surprisingly undamaged. He straightened the nightcap, which had fallen to cover one eye. He, Granny, and Bob looked at one another. They looked at the basket of goodies. They looked at Little Red.

There was only one thing they could do.

They locked Little Red in the closet, then they went out in the backyard and had a picnic.

The Granddaughter

First Reaction

1. Sketch or describe the scene in *The Granddaughter* that is the most interesting or humorous to you.

Look More Closely

2. Write three words or phrases that describe Lucinda. For each word or phrase, support your choice with quotations from the story.

Develop Your Ideas

3. Imagine that you are Lucinda's grandmother. Write a postcard or a note to your daughter (Lucinda's mother) thanking her for the basket of goodies and telling her about Lucinda's visit. Remember, be polite! Use your imagination.

4. Choose a fairy tale or other children's story and create your own parody. You can present your story in writing, as a series of storyboards, through cartoons that show what the characters are thinking as well as what they are saying, as a picture book, or by acting it out. Use a chart such as the one shown on this page to plan your story.

Story: Hansel and Gretel		
Characters	**Original**	**My Version**
Hansel	good brother	good; kind to everyone
Gretel	good sister	hates her stepmother; thinks Hansel is a goody-goody
Stepmother	wants to get rid of children	loves children; spoils them
Witch	wicked; wants to bake children in her oven	lonely; wants new friends
Plot		
Beginning	children go to forest to gather wood; they leave a trail of breadcrumbs	
Events		
Ending		

Think About What Makes an Effective Parody

5. Before you begin working on your story, think and talk to others about what makes an effective parody. For example, you might decide that it should:

   - Follow the basic pattern of the original.
   - Change parts of the original story in interesting or surprising ways.
   - Include funny or unusual details.
   - Be clear and easy to understand.

   After you have finished your first draft, check your work to see how well it meets the criteria you listed.

Interpreting Fiction

When you interpret fiction you use your ideas and experiences to help you make sense out of what the author has written. In order to interpret a story you must first figure out your own *response*. You then *reread* to more clearly understand the author's message and your reaction to it.

Responding to What You Read

Here are some things to make notes on after your first reading.

- *Start with your first reactions.* What stands out in your mind? Sketch or write about the part that seems most vivid to you. Ask yourself, "Did I like the story? How did it make me feel? What did it make me think about?"

- *Build connections.* How does the story connect with other things you've read or experienced? How do the characters, ideas, and events connect to the things you know and care about?

- *Ask questions.* Is there anything you don't understand? Are there parts that seem confusing? Parts that you want to think over?

- *Talk it over.* Talking will help you clarify and develop your ideas about the story. Listen to others and compare your views to what they have to say. Don't be afraid to disagree!

Rereading for a Purpose

Rereading helps you learn more about the characters and the *theme* of the story — the author's main message. When you reread, it's important to decide your purpose in advance. Ask yourself, "What am I looking for when I read this time?"

- *Look for the key events.* Choose an effective way to summarize the events of the story. You might use a story map, create a series of sketches, list the main events, or make a chart. Summarizing the story helps to make it clear in your mind. You'll be able to remember the stories you summarize.

- *Look for details*. When you're asked a question or given an assignment, don't try to answer immediately. Look for specific evidence or examples that the author has included. For example, if you're asked to describe the mood, don't just say "it's scary." Find the words and phrases that the author uses to scare you!

- *Read between the lines*. Try to get *between the lines* of the story. What's really going on here? Why are these people behaving this way? What are they thinking? Sometimes it's helpful to imagine the story as a cartoon with thought bubbles letting you in on the character's thoughts.

- *Search out the author's ideas*. Authors give you a lot of clues about the ideas and themes they are trying to convey through their stories. Ask yourself these questions. Which character does the author seem to favour? Which character is described in the most positive way? Are there ideas, words, or phrases that are emphasized or repeated? What pictures stand out in your mind? If you listen to the story in your mind's ear, what tone is the author using? Does it change for different people or events?

Before You Read

Many Canadian communities were created because of nearby resources that provided work. Mines, lumber mills, or fisheries attracted workers who then brought their families and developed strong communities. Today, many of those towns have disappeared because the resources have run out. People have left to look for work in other places. This story tells about a Newfoundland mining community that is slowly dying.

> Imagine that your community was slowly disappearing — that every day when you came to school there were fewer and fewer students. Think about how you would feel. Write a short diary entry that begins: *I am getting fed up with saying goodbye.*

Try This

As you read, put yourself in the place of the main character.

The Visitor

by Christine Pinsent-Johnson

I was getting fed up with saying goodbye. One month five kids disappeared from my shrinking class at Copelin High School. At this rate, there would be a class of one graduating next year, and that one would be me.

I was witnessing the slow death of a town and there was nothing I or anyone else could do about it. All over the world people unite to fight for something they believe in,

like preserving an old-growth forest or protecting the ozone. But no one bothered to fight for Copelin. My dad claimed people had simply accepted their fate; they knew the mines wouldn't last forever and now they realized it was time to move on. *

Last night I overheard my parents talking about moving to St. John's or the mainland. At least my mom was talking; Dad was trying to avoid the discussion.

"The Greenes are leaving next month," Mom said casually while stirring the spaghetti sauce. "Frank got a job in Grand Falls at the mill."

I knew Mom wanted to leave as much as I did. The fridge was cluttered with want ads from the St. John's, Halifax, and Toronto newspapers.

"I guess we'll have to find someone else to play cards with," Dad said. His attempt to avoid the discussion.

"That's not the point. We're losing two more good friends." Mom stopped stirring and started rubbing her neck, which stiffened whenever

* Pause and Think
Who is "I"? What do you know about the person who is telling the story?

Last winter he had to change the locks on two families, forcing them out of their homes.

✳ Pause and Think
Why is William angry with his father?

she was upset. "This is really getting ridiculous," she said quietly. "Why don't you start looking . . ."

"We've already been through this, Joanne. I won't be able to find anything better than what I have."

Dad was sitting across the table from me. I kept staring at my biology textbook, hoping they would keep me out of it.

"I'm committed to stay here at least another couple of years," Dad said as he walked over to Mom. He gently placed her hands at her side and began massaging her neck. "You know I wouldn't be able to find anything better."

Dad was one of the last people to work for the Copelin Mining and Refining Company, which had built the town over sixty years ago. He was the property manager for all the residential buildings, and spent his days running after people for overdue rent and closing up empty houses. About once every couple of months he actually sold a house. Usually it was to one of the retired miners and his wife, determined to stay here until they died.

But most of his days were spent knocking on doors, trying to convince unemployed miners and millworkers to pay months of back rent. Last winter he had to change the locks on two families, forcing them out of their homes. One family quickly left Copelin, but the other ended up living with their relatives in the trailer park near the highway. They still won't talk to my dad. He never changed any more locks after that.

I had to leave. I couldn't stand another non-discussion about leaving Copelin.

"Where are you going?" Mom asked, when she saw me get up from the kitchen table. "Supper will be ready in half an hour."

"I'm going out. I'll be back in a few minutes."

"Do you think it's a good idea to go out just before supper?" Dad asked, clearing his throat nervously.

Why can't he just say "Don't go out" or "Be back before supper," I thought. "I won't be long," I said, closing the textbook.

"Well, William, you said that the other day. Heh hemmm. And you were late for supper." I hated it when he used my full name. It sounded so fake. As if he was trying too hard.

"I'll be back before supper," I snapped, getting even more irritated. I could feel the sweat beading on my forehead in the steamy kitchen. The window beside the stove was dripping with condensation. I had to get out of there. ✳

"Don't use that tone with your father," said Mom sharply.

Why does she have to stick up for him? Why can't he just say I'm being a brat and get it over with? I couldn't even look at him. I kept staring at the moisture droplets racing down the window.

"As long as you say you'll be back, I guess you can go."

"Gee, thanks Dad." I knew I was being a jerk but I couldn't help it.

As I grabbed my coat off the living room chair I heard Mom say, "You know, you really shouldn't let him talk to you like that." Unbelievable.

The night air was overwhelmed by the sharp, almost suffocating smell of pine smoke from people's wood stoves. It had been raining the past few days, and there was a hazy mixture of fog and wood smoke hanging over the town.

Most of the snow had washed away except for some skeletal remains along the edges of the street and in the ditches. Everyone kept saying they were lucky it was such a mild winter because there was no money for snowplowing. But now the potholes needed to be filled, and there was no money for that either.

Out of a dozen homes on the street, five were empty. At the Purdy's house the front door was wide open, leaving the house exposed. I could look straight into the empty living room, where Mrs. Purdy used to sit and wait for her daughter, Michelle, after I walked her home from the dances at the stadium last summer. I ran up the front steps and quickly shut the door.

I turned onto Main Street, walked past the empty lot where the theatre used to be. It had burnt down, along with the bowling alley and company store, ten years ago. The company only rebuilt the store. They'd stopped showing movies at the theatre anyway, and said it was too expensive to rebuild the bowling alley. The only thing left besides the company store was the bank, post office, and Reid's Bakery, which didn't sell sweets anymore, just bread and rolls.

Four streets ran perpendicular to Main. Three of these streets were filled with row houses, three units to a row, three bedrooms in a home. They were neat, orderly army-style homes, low on looks and high on efficiency. No grass in the yards, only rocks and weeds. Almost every home had a clothesline, cutting across the back yard, supported by a cedar rail in the middle. The fourth street, which was ours, was a combination of row homes and small single houses that looked just like row houses, except for the metre gap in between. The bigger single homes were uptown, closer to the mine offices. They were for the geologists, engineers, and office employees. The miners with families lived downtown, and the men from around the bay lived in the bunk houses on the outskirts of town.

I should have been born twenty years ago when the mines were still running and the company took care of everything. There was no other place like Copelin in all of Newfoundland. For a small town, about 3,000 at its peak, Copelin had everything you'd find in a city like St. John's or Corner Brook. There was a movie theatre, restaurant, bowling alley, shooting range, swimming pool, playing fields, and a stadium. For years, Copelin had one of the best hockey teams on the island. The company

would even pay for train tickets so fans could cheer on the team during road games. Now there wasn't even a hockey team. It wasn't fair. *

In early spring Spruce first wandered into town. He was seen ambling silently down Main Street stooping occasionally to munch the dandelions growing beside the road, as if he were doing nothing out of the ordinary. Mrs. Tilley saw him first, although she didn't know what she saw at the time. I heard her in the post office talking to a group of women.

"My dears, you're not going to believe what I saw last night," she said breathlessly. "I was out for my walk and when I rounded the corner of Ore Street I stared straight into the glaring red eyes of the devil itself."

The women in the post office passed knowing glances to each other and smiled politely.

"You must have been frightened," said the postmaster, from behind the counter.

Mrs. Tilley didn't seem to notice his mocking tone. "My dears, I nearly jumped out of me skin. Them eyes was some creepy, and he didn't even move. I just backed up slow so I wouldn't startle him. Then I high-tailed it home." *

Reverend Sharpe saw Spruce a couple of days later. The devil which appeared in front of Mrs. Tilley was actually a young bull moose. This time he was spotted downtown, sniffing around the trash bins behind the company store.

Then later that same morning, Daisy Miller said she saw Spruce in the empty lot beside the bank, where the theatre once stood. He was once again nuzzling through the trash cans.

After the first sightings, people began to see Spruce a couple of times a week. It was Daisy Miller who started calling him Spruce. Ten years ago her Uncle Spruce and a few other men rescued a moose that had fallen through the ice on Beothuk Lake. It was Spruce Miller who crawled across the ice to lasso the semi-conscious moose, which they tied to a bulldozer from one of the mines and hauled out.

I first saw Spruce a few days later. He began to get a little bolder and wandered into town during the late afternoons. He usually came out of the bush at the north end of town around three o'clock, as if he was waiting for a polite time to come calling.

I was struggling with the last question on a math test. Looking out the classroom window for some divine inspiration, I saw Spruce strolling through the school yard. I watched him in silence, hoping no one else would notice him. There were only five other students in my grade ten class. Ever since I was in grade six the school board had been threatening to close the school and bus everyone into the nearest town, an hour's drive up the highway.

* Pause and Think
According to William, what isn't fair? Do you agree with him?

* Pause and Think
What do you think Mrs. Tilley actually saw?

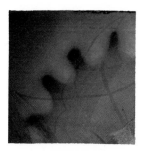

His antlers were just beginning to grow and were covered with a velvety soft fuzz.

* Pause and Think
Why does Albert
Smith think the moose
must be "some
stunned"?

* Pause and Think
Why do you think
William's father is so
anxious to feed Spruce?

Spruce was taking his time, obviously having no destination in mind. He was a picture of contradictions. His long spindly legs looked like they would break under his round bulk of a body. His soft brown eyes were overwhelmed by a massive snout which ended with a flapping upper lip, and his ears looked too small for his long, narrow face. His antlers were just beginning to grow and were covered with a velvety soft fuzz. I was surprised to see how gracefully he moved. I always thought moose were awkward-looking and clumsy, with their long, homely faces and humped backs.

I'd seen a couple of moose before, slung over the hood of a car after being hit on the highway or in the back of a pickup after hunting. My father was probably the only man in Copelin who didn't hunt, so I'd never seen a moose in the wild.

Just that morning, I'd overheard Albert Smith talking to Amanda Higgins, the bank teller, about the moose's lack of intelligence.

"He must be some stunned to come wandering into a town full of hunters," said Mr. Smith on the steps of the company store. "Don't he realize people here live all winter on a freezer full of his distant relatives?" *

Amanda Higgins' double chin shook in agreement. "Maybe he's one of them backward moose. Maybe he's brain-injured."

"He'll be brain-injured if he don't quit eating my flowers. Sure, last week I found all my tulips stripped bare. I woulda' got my shotgun and killed him right then and there if I'd caught him."

Amanda Higgins' chins jiggled with excitement. They looked like the dewlap under Spruce's chin. "Yes bye. I knows I'd be hollerin' after him if I caught him in my garden. The animal's got no sense. No sense at all."

But not everyone thought Spruce was a nuisance. People began to set out treats for him, including my father. Rumour was he ate all the Purity Lemon Creams but left the carrots. Every time a sighting was made, Dad would run into the kitchen, grab a handful of biscuits and a couple of apples and set them on the back porch. One night I heard him walking around the back yard just after 2 A.M. He was calling out to the night, "Come on Spruce my son. I've got your favourites here."

I don't know if Spruce ever came that night. Dad was still out there when I fell asleep, and neither of us said anything the next morning. *

When I walked in the door after playing road hockey in front of Dave Rideout's place, the first thing I heard was the booming voice of Reverend Sharpe. He and Dave's father were having a cup of coffee with Dad in the kitchen. The two of them were on the town council; Mr. Rideout was the mayor and the Reverend was a councillor.

"He's getting to be a nuisance," said Reverend Sharpe. "Last week he dug up three flower gardens, eating up people's hard work and enjoyment."

"I heard he's been dragging people's trash all over their yards," said the mayor. "What happens if he ever gets aggressive and goes after of one of the kids? You know kids. A little harmless teasing and in a second they could have a two-ton moose chasing after them."

"Sure, I heard Fanny Reid nearly ran into him as she rounded the corner of Main Street in her car the other evening. There he was standing in the middle of the road, refusing to budge," said the Reverend.

"It's our responsibility to do something before someone gets hurt," added the mayor. He was looking straight at my father, waiting for his input. The mayor often stopped by to discuss council issues with my dad. I guess my dad had a certain status in the town as one of the last company employees. Dad also gave the mayor an ego boost, since he would never disagree with him.

My father remained silent. I could see him swallowing, his Adam's apple bulging, as he prepared to clear his throat. But he didn't say anything. He didn't always agree with everything the mayor and Reverend did on council, like the decision to stop subsidizing the summer baseball league, but he went along with them anyway. *

Come on, say something, I silently urged from the hall. I knew he disagreed with them. He'd set out at least two bags of apples and three packages of biscuits since Spruce started visiting regularly. I could feel myself turn red when I heard him clear his throat. I slowly backed down the hall and went upstairs to my room.

*Pause and Think
How does William feel about his father "going along" with the mayor and Reverend?*

The mayor called a town meeting to discuss Spruce. Once people found out that the mayor was thinking about getting rid of the moose they began to take sides. It was all they could talk about for a week. Petitions were sent around and signs were posted in front yards and along fences, some saying *Let Him Be* and others saying *He's Got To Go*. I'd never seen people get so worked up over something. No one protested this much when the mines closed.

The council meeting was moved from the municipal office, a small room in the basement of the library, to the union hall so everyone could attend. There was a reporter from the St. John's newspaper, which never before bothered with small town council meetings. The reporter wasn't much older than me. He didn't even try to hide his boredom, just yawned and doodled in his steno book.

The moose issue was shuffled to the bottom of the evening's agenda. I think the mayor hoped people would get bored and leave the meeting before it ended. His nerves were frazzled, speaking in front of so many people, and he kept shuffling the papers in front of him. He'd never seen so many bodies at a council meeting. The only people who usually attended the meetings were a couple of old-timers with nothing better to do and the editor of the town paper.

My father asked me to go to the meeting with him. He said it was an important issue for the town, and it went beyond a simple decision to let Spruce stay or to force him out. I agreed to go partly because I was feeling guilty for the way I had been treating him the past few weeks.

After passing motions to recruit another volunteer firefighter, start collecting a dog tax, and approve a letter requesting the donation of library books, they finally reached the end of the agenda. A group of men, followed by a haze of their own cigarette smoke, stepped into the stifling hall, and everyone else stopped shuffling and whispering.

The discussion about Spruce started off respectfully enough. Representatives from both sides of the issue carefully stated their case as we sat in silence. My father looked over at me once, and started to smile but changed his mind and looked down at a piece of folded up paper he was holding.

The mayor, in an attempt at a compromise, asked the audience, "Why don't we get one of them tranquillizer guns, knock him out, and let him go somewhere one hundred kilometres from here?"

A man in the back stood up. I'd seen him before, standing outside the Legion every afternoon, waiting for it to open. "We're some stunned to be sitting here arguing about this moose. Why don't we just kill it and get a nice bunch of steaks out of him."

Then St. John's reporter jerked his head up and began writing madly.

"Yes, bye, we do that and we'll have them peace freaks and animal rights activists accusing us of cruelty to animals," said a woman from the middle of the crowd.

"What harm is he doing to ye. I say we just let him do his thing and leave him alone. It's the proper thing," said Mrs. Tilley. Her husband sat beside her shaking his head.

Then one of the old-timers jumped up and yelled, "Kill him before he tramples some poor child." Someone else in the back yelled, "Let the poor thing alone."

Then St. John's reporter jerked his head up and began writing madly. Then everyone got into it. People were yelling back and forth at each other. The mayor kept banging his gavel on the table, but everyone ignored him. The reporter stopped his frantic writing for an instant to take a picture of the mayor yelling at everyone to shut up.

In the middle of the yelling and screaming my father stood up slowly. He never said a word in any sort of public meeting. I wanted to slip into the cracks of the floor and disappear. He unfolded his piece of paper and looked at it quickly. Then he folded it back up and held it tightly in his hand. The people around us stopped talking and looked at my father. Like a wave, silence gradually fell over the rest of the hall. He just stood there, waiting, gripping on to that piece of paper as if it gave him the strength to stand.

He quietly cleared his throat. His first words didn't quite make it out. Someone yelled, "Speak up, we can't hear you." He stopped. I thought he'd pack it in right there. But he didn't. He looked over at me. I couldn't help it, but I turned my eyes away and stared at my shoes.

He began again, a little louder this time, "Spruce has done something for this town that no one has seen for years."

"Yeah, he's picked up the garbage regularly," some wise-cracker yelled out.

"Uh, that's not my point," said Dad quietly. He started to unfold his paper and look at his notes. He was totally thrown off.

"Tell them about the treats," I whispered. "Tell them about all the times you and other people set out treats for Spruce, like it was Christmas or something." Dad looked down at me, nodded his head slightly, and smiled. Then he released his grip on the paper and let it fall to the floor. I thought he had dropped it, and when I bent down to pick it up he whispered, "Leave it there."

He began again. This time his voice was loud enough the first time. "How many of us have run into our kitchens to find special treats for Spruce every time he was spotted in town? When is the last time you felt that same excitement about something?"

It was like he was a kid looking for someone to say he did the right thing.

✳ Pause and Think
Why were people talking about William's Dad? What surprised them?

I looked up at him, hoping he would see that I was listening to every word.

"Spruce has given us all a little hope, something almost magical, during a time when we don't have much of anything that's good." A few people in front of us were nodding in agreement. "I think it would be a foolish idea to get rid of him. I think we should just let him be." Dad didn't waste any time sitting down. People were still looking at him but he didn't acknowledge their stares.

I could tell people were stunned. No one said a word for a few seconds. The mayor screwed up his face as if he had a bad taste in his mouth. The reverend shrugged his shoulders and sighed. Once people digested everything an excited buzz spread throughout the union hall. I caught bits and pieces of the conversations around us.

"Maybe he's got a point."

"I can't believe Graham Percy stood up and . . ."

"But what if Spruce . . ."

"I've never heard him say that much at one time."

People were talking as much about my dad as they were about Spruce, but I didn't care. I reached down and picked up the crumpled paper my Dad had dropped and put it in my pocket. ✳

"Thanks for your help, Willy," he said.

"You would have done fine without me. People really listened to what you had to say." I looked straight at him. For the first time I noticed the flecks of gold in his deep brown eyes. I had those same flecks.

"You think so?" He really didn't know. It was like he was a kid looking for someone to say he did the right thing.

"I know so," I said.

A week later council passed a special by-law protecting Spruce, and he was allowed to wander throughout the town freely. The newspaper article from the St. John's reporter ended up being reprinted in the *Globe and Mail*. Then early in June a CBC crew from St. John's did a piece about Spruce and troubled times for Copelin. Our forgotten town ended up being on the national news with the help of Spruce!

That summer my dad and a couple of other people, including the mayor, formed the C.C.C., the Citizens' Coalition for Copelin. They helped people get low-interest loans from the government so they could afford to buy their homes. People began painting their houses again, the sidewalks were fixed, and some of the potholes were repaired. Copelin would never be the same as it once was, but at least it wouldn't become a forgotten ghost town, and maybe I wouldn't be the only one left by the time I graduated from high school.

First Reaction

1. Write down three words or phrases that stand out in your mind when you think about *The Visitor*. Write a sentence or create a visual image (picture, cartoon, or symbol) for each word or phrase that conveys something important about the story.

Look More Closely

2. List the reasons *for* and *against* letting Spruce stay that were given at the town meeting. Which side would you be on? Write a short letter to the editor giving your point of view. Remember to start with a clear statement of opinion, then give specific and convincing reasons and examples to support your view.

3. Create a found poem about one of the following: the father, the town, Spruce, or the narrator.

- Review the story, writing down words and phrases the author uses to describe your chosen character or the town.

- Decide on the theme or main idea you want to convey about the character or the town.

- Arrange the words and phrases you have found to create a poem.

- Ask a partner to review your poem and offer feedback.

- Share your poem with the class.

4. Dialogue is important in many stories. It lets us know what is going on and why. Even more important, dialogue lets us get to know the people in the story. We learn about them by *listening* both to what they say and how they say it. Choose a short passage of dialogue from *The Visitor*. Make a chart like the one on the next page to show what you learned about one of the speakers.

Name of the Character:	
Situation (Who is the conversation with? What's going on?):	
What the character says:	What this tells us about the character:

Develop Your Ideas

5. Choose or invent a situation in which two or three family members or friends are talking about an everyday matter — what they're having for dinner, what they're going to do on the weekend, or what they did at school that day. Visualize the characters and try to *hear* their voices. Decide on one or two qualities for each character. Write a short dialogue that lets your readers get to know the characters by what they say and how they say it.

Think About Your Found Poem

6. Look back at your found poem. How well were you able to:

- Convey your theme or main idea about the character or the town.

- Combine words and phrases in a way that makes sense.

- Include important features of the character or town (physical description, personality, motivation, and relationships with the other characters).

- Add something special, such as language or ideas that might surprise your readers.

Before You Read

In *The Defender*, a young man faces his final competition as a high-school athlete. As you read, you'll find that this sport of the future is very different from the sports played in schools today!

What's the most important sporting event or other competition you've ever watched? What made it important — what was at stake for the competitors? Write the headings, *Before, During,* and *After* at the top of three columns. In each column, list the words and phrases that come to mind when you think of how the competitors in this event looked, felt, and acted *before, during,* and *after* the competition.

Try This

When you read a science fiction story, it's important to take some time to set the scene for yourself at the beginning. Read the opening paragraphs slowly and carefully. Ask yourself questions such as: "When and where is this happening? What is this world like? What's going on here? Who are these people?" As you read on, pause from time to time to think about what's happening, then predict what will happen next.

THE

DEFENDER

The Interscholastic Galactic Defender was licked awake by ice blue energy rays. Coach gently rocked his floating sleep slab. "Perfect day for the match, No. 1. Low humidity, no sunspots."

Coach tipped the slab and the Defender slid to the floor. He stepped out of his paper pajamas and onto the cleansing pedestal. A million beams refreshed his body, scraped his teeth, washed his hair, shaved his chin. The Defender then wrapped himself in a tunic of blue and gold, the school colors.

The Varsity was already at the training table. The Defender felt their admiration and envy as he took the empty seat at the head of the table.

He felt calm. His last high-school match. Across the table, his best friend, No. 2, winked. Good old No. 2, strong and steady. They had worked their way up the rankings ladder together since Basic School, rivals and teammates and buddies. It was almost over and he should have felt sad, but he didn't. One more match and he could be free to —

by Robert Lipsyte

No. 4 caught his eye. He sensed that her feelings were the same. One more match and they wouldn't be numbers anymore, they would be Sophia and José, and they wouldn't have to guard their thoughts, or worse, turn them into darts and bombs. *

Coach lifted a blue and gold competition thought helmet out of its recharging box and eased it down over the Defender's head. He fastened the chin strap, lengthened the antennae, and spun the dial to the lowest reception and projection power, just strong enough for noncompetitive thought in a small room.

For a moment, the Defender's mind was filled with a quivering crosscurrent of thought waves. There was a nasty pinprick from No. 7, only a sophomore but one of the toughest competitors in the galaxy, a star someday if he didn't burn himself out. There was a soothing velvet compress from No. 4, a hearty shoulder-banger from old No. 2.

The Defender cleared his mind for Coach, who was pacing the room. Psych talk time.

"As you know, the competition today, the Unified High School of the Barren Planets, is the first non-Earth team to ever reach the Galactic Finals. It wasn't expected and our scouting reports are incomplete."

No. 7 thought a blue and gold fireball wrecking the barren planets.

"Overconfidence can beat you," snapped Coach. "These guys are tough — kids from the orphan ships, the prison planets, the pioneer systems. They've lived through things you've only screened."

The freshperson substitute, No. 8, thought, "What about their Greenie No. 1?"

"We don't use the word *Greenie*," said Coach. "It's a bias word."

"A Greenie?" sneered No. 7. "A hairy little round Greenie?"

"Don't judge a mind by its body," snapped No. 4, blushing when she saw the Defender's approving blinks.

No. 7 leaned back and flashed an image of himself wearing hairy green bedroom slippers. Only No. 8 laughed. *

Coach said, "We respect the Challenger. It wouldn't be here if it wasn't good."

"'It'?" asked No. 2. "Male or female? Or a mixed gender?"

"We don't know anything about it," said Coach. "Except it's beaten everybody."

In silence, they drank their pregame meal — liquid fish protein and supercomplex carbs.

Back on his slab, the Defender allowed his mind to wander. He usually spent his prematch meditation period reviewing the personality of his opponent — the character flaws, the gaps in understanding that would leave

* Pause and Think
When and where is this story happening?

Why do you think they might have to guard their thoughts?

* Pause and Think
How do these people communicate with each other?

one vulnerable to a lightning thought jab, a volley of powerful images. But he knew nothing about today's opponent and little about Homo Vulgaris, mutant humans who had been treated badly ever since they began to appear after a nuclear accident. They were supposed to be stupid and unstable, one step above space ape. That one of them could actually have become No. 1 on the Power Thought Team of a major galactic high school was truly amazing. Either this one was very special, the Defender thought, or Earthlings hadn't heard the truth about these people.

He closed his eyes. He had thought he would be sentimental on the day of his last match, trying to remember every little detail. But he wished it were already over.

The wall-lights glowed yellow and he rose, dialing his helmet up to the warm-up level. He slipped into his competition robe. He began to flex his mind — logic exercises, picture bursts — as the elevator rose up through the Mental Athletics Department. When he waved to the chess team they stopped the clock to pound their kings on their boards in salute. The cyberspellers hand-signed cheers at him. *

Officials were in the locker room running brain scans. The slightest trace of smart pills would mean instant disqualification.

Everyone passed.

The Defender sat down next to No. 2. "We're almost there, Tombo." He flashed an image of the two of them lying in a meadow, smelling flowers.

Tombo laughed and bounced the image back, adding Sophia and his own girlfriend, Annie, to the meadow scene.

"Think sharp!" shouted Coach, and they lined up behind him in numerical order, keeping their minds blank as they trotted out into the roaring stadium. The Defender tipped his antennae toward his mother and father. He shook the Principal's hand.

"This is the most important moment of your life, No. 1. For the good of humanity, don't let those Unified mongrels outthink you."

The varsity teams from the Physical Athletics Department paraded by, four-hundred-pound football players and eight-foot basketball players and soccer players who moved on all fours. Some fans laughed at youngsters who needed to use their bodies to play. The Defender was always amazed at his grandfather's stories of the old days when the captain of the football team was a school hero.

It was in his father's time that cameras were invented to pick up brain waves and project them onto video screens for hundreds of thousands of fans in the arenas

* Pause and Think
What do you already know about the competition? What questions do you have?

and millions more at home. Suddenly, kids who could think hard became more popular than kids who could hit hard.

"Let's go," roared Coach, and the first doubles team moved down into the Brain Pit.

The first match didn't last long. No. 7 and No. 4, even though they rarely spoke off the field, had been winning partners for three years. No. 7 swaggered to the midline of the court, arrogantly spinning his antennae, while No. 4 pressed her frail shoulders against the back wall. The Unified backcourter was a human female, but the frontcourter was a transspecies, a part-human lab creature ten feet tall and round as a cylinder.

The Defender sensed the steely tension in the Unified backcourter's mind; she was set for a hellfire smash. He was proud of No. 4's first serve, a soft, curling thought of autumn smoke and hushed country lanes, an ancient thought filled with breeze-riffled lily ponds and the smell of fresh-cut hay.

Off-balance, the backcourter sent it back weakly, and No. 7 filled the lovely image with the stench of backpack rockets, war gases, and kill zone wastes and fireballed it back. The Unified brainies were still wrestling with the image when the ref tapped the screamer. Too long. One point for the home team. *

As usual, No. 7 lost points for unnecessary roughness — too much death and destruction without a logical lead-up to it — but as the fans cheered wildly he and No. 4 easily won. Their minds

* Pause and Think
How does the game work? How do the competitors win points?

had hardly been stretched; the Psycho-Chem Docs in the Relaxant Room would need little tranquilspray to calm them down. Good, thought the Defender; No. 4 would be out in time for his match.

Except for thinking about her, the Defender began to lose interest in the day. How many times had he waited to go down into a Pit and attack another mind? It had seemed exciting four years ago when Coach had pulled him out of a freshperson mental gym class and asked him to try out for the team. His tests had shown mental agility, vivid imagery, and, most important, telepathic potential.

It was the first thing he had ever been really good at. After he won a few matches, the popular kids began talking to him in the halls. Teachers asked him about the team. Letters began arriving at home from colleges owned by major corporations. His parents were so proud. He would be set for life.

But now it seemed like such a waste — fighting with thoughts instead of creating with them. Maybe he was just tired at the end of a long, tough season of defending his title. He thought about the meadow, with Sophia and Tombo and Annie. Instead of thoughts, they would throw an ancient toy around. It was called something like frisbill. Frisboo? Frisbee!

Coach tapped his helmet. "Pay attention."

No. 5 and No. 6 were staggering under a vicious barrage. They lost, and the standings at the end of the doubles were even, 1-1.

The crowd fell silent as No. 3 lost her singles match and the scoreboard blinked Visitors 2, Home 1. As No. 2 lumbered down to the Pit, the Defender sent an image of a victory wreath to him.

Good old No. 2, steady and even-tempered and sure of himself. Mentally tough. He might have been No. 1 on any other high-school team, but he never showed resentment. For a moment, the Defender almost wished that No. 2 would lose; then the score would be 3-1 and nothing No. 1 could do would be able to salvage the team match. No pressure — he could play the game just for himself. If he won, great, he'd be the first player in history to win the championship twice. If he lost he would only disappoint himself; he wouldn't be letting his team and his school — and humanity, according to the Principal — down.

But No. 2 won and the score was tied and it was up to him.

The No. 1 player for the Unified High School of the Barren Planets, the Interscholastic Galactic Challenger, was waiting for him in the Pit.

He (she? it?) looked like a green teddy bear. The Defender had never seen one in the flesh. He forced his mind to think of the creature only as an opponent.

The Defender served first, a probing serve to test the quickness of the Challenger. He used an image, from a poet who had written in the dying language called English, of a youth gliding over a hilltop at night to catch a star falling from a shower of milk-white light.

The Challenger slapped it right back; the star was nothing but a burnt-out children's sparkler made from fuel wastes. The youth on the hilltop was left with a sticky purple mess.

The Defender was surprised at how long he struggled with the sadness of the thought. A Judge hit the screamer. Unified led, 1-0.

Coach called time-out.

The falling-star image had been one of his best serves, a frequent ace. No one had ever handled it so well, turning the beautiful vision of humanity's quest for immortality into an ugly image of self-destruction.

They decided to switch tactics — to serve a fireball, No. 7 style. The Defender hurled a blazing tornado of searing gases and immeasurable heat. The Challenger's mind scooped it up like a hockey puck and plopped it into an ocean filled with icebergs.

Off-balance, the Defender tried to give himself time by thinking steaming vapors from the ocean, but the Challenger turned the vapors into great fleecy clouds that shaped themselves into mocking caricatures of famous Earthlings.

Desperately, the Defender answered with another fireball, and a Judge hit the screamer, calling it a Non Sequitur — the thought had not logically followed the Challenger's thought.

Unified led, 2-0.

The Defender served a complex image of universal peace: white-robed choruses in sweet harmony, endless vials of nutrient liquids flowing through galaxies aglow with life-giving stars, and hands — white, brown, green, orange, blue, black, red, and yellow — clasped.

The Challenger slashed back with mineral dredges that drowned out the singing, lasers that poisoned the vials, and a dark night created by monster Earth shields that were purposely blocking the sunlight of a small planet. The clasping hands tightened until they crushed each other to bloody pulp.

The Defender was gasping at the bitter overload when he heard the screamer. He was down, 3-0. He had never lost his serve before.

The Challenger's first serve was vividly simple: black Earthling trooper boots stomping on thousands of green forms like itself.

Screamer.

The Judge called "Foul" and explained that the thought was too political — the Galactic League was still debating whether Earth colonists had trampled the rights of the hairy green offspring of the accident victims.

The Challenger's second serve was an image of black-gloved Earthling hands pulling apart Greenie families and shoving parents and children into separate cages.

Foul screamer. *

The third serve was an image of Earth rocket exhausts aimed to burn down Greenie houses.

Foul screamer.

Tie score, 3-3. The Judge called an official time-out.

Coach's strong thumbs were working under the Defender's helmet. "Register a protest, right now. Don't let that little fur ball make a farce of the game."

"He's allowed to think freely," said the Defender. He wondered if the Challenger was a "he." Did it matter?

"He's using the game just to further his cause."

"Maybe he has a just cause."

"Doesn't matter," said Coach. "This is a game."

"I'll get him next period," said the Defender, trying to sound more confident than he was.

The second period was a repeat of the first. The Defender's best serves were deflected, twisted, sent back in bewildering patterns while the Challenger fouled on three more images of Earthling inhumanity. As the scoreboard glowed 6-6, the crowd buzzed angrily.

Coach said, "I order you to register a protest or you will never play for this high school again."

"It's my last game here."

"I'll see you don't get a college scholarship."

"I'm not sure I ever want to play this game again."

"Look, José" — Coach's voice became soft, wheedling — "you

* Pause and Think
What does "foul screamer" mean? What are some of the things competitors can lose points for doing?

are the best high-school player who ever —"

"Not anymore," said the Defender.

His helmet had never felt so tight — it was crushing his mind numb — as he trudged out for the last regulation period.

His three serves were weak, random flashes of thought that barely registered on the video screens. The Challenger easily re-created them into bursting thoughts that made the Defender's head spin. The Challenger's three serves were cluster bombs of cruelty and greed, horrible images of his people trapped in starvation and hopelessness because of Earth. They were all called foul.

It was 9-9 going into sudden-death overtime.

✳ Pause and Think
Why does the Principal want the Defender to protest? Why doesn't the Defender want to register a protest?

The Principal was waiting for No. 1 at the edge of the Pit. With him was the Chief Judge, the Superintendent of Earth High Schools, the Commissioner of the Mental Athletics Association, the Secretary-General of the Galactic League, and other important-looking faces he recognized from telepathé-news.

They all nodded as the Principal said, "You are the Defender. You have a responsibility to your school, your people, the planet. I order you to register a protest. We cannot be beaten by a foul little malcontent Greenie."

"It's only a game," said the Defender. ✳

"Maybe to you," snapped the Superintendent.

He strode back into the Pit.

The Challenger had never left; the Defender suddenly realized the little creature had no coach or friends. He had come up alone to stand and fight for himself and his people.

The warning buzzer sounded. Seconds to serve. Sudden death. The Defender would go first. He thought of his all-time best serves, the ones he saved for desperate situations, because coming up with them was so exhausting, so mind-bending that if they failed he was lost. He thought of the end of the world, of sucking black holes, of nightmares beyond hope.

Suddenly he knew what to do.

He served an image of a dry and dusty field on a lonely colony planet. The land was scarred and barren, filled with thousands of round green creatures standing hopelessly beyond barbed wire as a harsh wind ruffled their dry fur.

For the first time, the Challenger took the full five seconds to return serve. He was obviously puzzled. His return was his weakest so far, merely widening the image to include a ring of Earthlings, healthy and happy, pointing and laughing at the Greenies. It was just what the Defender had expected.

He took his full five, then sent a soft, slow image of two Earthlings leaving the circle to walk among the Greenies until they picked one whose hands they held.

They led it skipping into a golden meadow under a sunny blue sky. The Earthlings were José

✳ Pause and Think
Why couldn't the Challenger return the Defender's final serve?

and Sophia, and the Greenie who danced and sang with them was the Challenger.

In the shocked silence of the arena, the Challenger took the thought as if it were a knockout punch, his mind wobbling.

He was unable to deal with the thought, the kindness in it, the fellowship.

He can't handle love, thought the Defender. What a way to win.

The Challenger was still struggling to answer when the screamer sounded. ✳

The match was over, 10-9. The crowd was roaring, the Principal was dancing on his chair, the video screens were filled with the face of José Nunez, the first ever to win the galactic championship twice.

They swarmed around him now, the important faces, calling his name, slapping at his helmet, but he pushed through, shutting out their congratulations, the screams of the crowd, the exploding scoreboard.

He made his way through to the Challenger, alone and quivering in the middle of the Pit. I don't even know its name, thought the Defender. "It"? Sophia and Tombo were running toward them. They knew what José was thinking.
It was only a game.
But it might be a start.

First Reaction

1. What image stands out in your mind when you think of *The Defender*? Sketch it or describe it in your own words.

2. Write down a quotation from the story that you think is particularly meaningful or powerful. What do you think it means? Why does it have a powerful impact?

Look More Closely

3. Briefly explain how the Defender's attitude to the Challenger changes during the story. Provide examples to support your ideas.

4. Represent the events of the competition (the serves, the returns, the screamers) in a visual form, such as a series of cartoons, a diagram, or a chart. You might want to use labels.

5. Make a chart to compare life in the Defender's time with life today.

Category	Today	In the Defender's Time
heroes	physical athletes	mental athletes
sports events	test for steroids	test for *smart* drugs
big crowds		

6. In this story, the author shares his ideas about several topics. Choose one of the topics below. What do you are think are the author's opinions about this topic? Find two or three pieces of evidence from the story to support your answer.

   • Violence.

   • Accepting people who are different.

   • Courage.

   • The most important qualities for a person to have.

   • Competition and winning.

   • Love.

Develop Your Ideas

7. The final sentence in the story is, "But it might be a start." A start of what? Create a sequel to the story. You might choose to write your sequel, or to tell it through a series of storyboards, cartoons, illustrations, or a list of events.

Think About Your Responses

8. How well did you show that you had read and understood the story by:

- Writing clear and complete answers.

- Providing specific evidence — words, phrases, and examples from the story — to support your ideas.

- Using your own words to explain your ideas and opinions.

- Focusing on exactly what the activity asked you to do.

Before You Read

The White Umbrella is set in a small town at a time when some people were ashamed if the mother had to work outside of the home to help support the family.

Think about a time when you wished for something that belonged to someone else. Write down some words and phrases that describe how you felt.

Try This

The narrator in this story wants a white umbrella that belongs to someone else. It becomes a symbol of the life she wants to live. As you read the story, try to put yourself in her place and imagine how she is feeling.

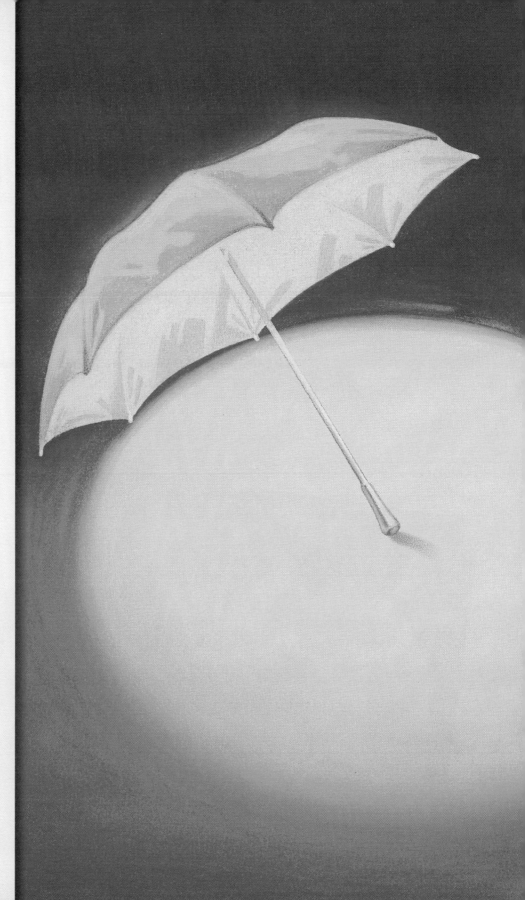

The White Umbrella

by Gish Jen

When I was twelve, my mother went to work without telling me or my little sister.

"Not that we need the second income." The lilt of her accent drifted from the kitchen up to the top of the stairs, where Mona and I were listening.

"No," said my father, in a barely audible voice. "Not like the Lee family."

The Lees were the only other Chinese family in town. I remembered how sorry my parents had felt for Mrs. Lee when she started waitressing downtown the year before; and so when my mother began coming home late, I didn't say anything, and tried to keep Mona from saying anything either. ✷

"But why shouldn't I?" she argued. "Lots of people's mothers work."

"Those are American people," I said.

Nevertheless, she tried to be discreet; and if my mother wasn't home by 5:30, we would start cooking by ourselves, to make sure dinner would be on time. Mona would wash the vegetables and put on the rice; I would chop.

✷ Pause and Think
Who is "I" in this story? What do you know about her?

For weeks we wondered what kind of work she was doing. I imagined that she was selling perfume, testing dessert recipes for the local newspaper. Or maybe she was working for the florist. Now that she had learned to drive, she might be delivering boxes of roses to people. *

"I don't think so," said Mona as we walked to our piano lesson after school. "She would've hit something by now."

A gust of wind littered the street with leaves.

"Maybe we better hurry up," she went on, looking at the sky. "It's going to pour."

"But we're too early." Her lesson didn't begin until 4:00, mine until 4:30, so we usually tried to walk as slowly as we could. "And anyway, those aren't the kind of clouds that rain. Those are cumulus clouds."

We arrived out of breath and wet.

"Oh, you poor, poor dears," said old Miss Crosman. "Why don't you call me the next time it's like this out? If your mother won't drive you, I can come pick you up."

"No, that's okay," I answered. Mona wrung her hair out on Miss Crosman's rug. "We just couldn't get the roof of our car to close, is all. We took it to the beach last summer and got sand in the mechanism." I pronounced this last word carefully, as if the credibility of my lie depended on its middle syllable. "It's never been the same." I thought for a second. "It's a convertible." *

"Well then make yourselves at home." She exchanged looks with Eugenie Roberts, whose lesson we were interrupting. Eugenie smiled good-naturedly. "The towels are in the closet across from the bathroom."

Huddling at the end of Miss Crosman's nine-foot leatherette couch, Mona and I watched Eugenie play. She was a grade ahead of me and, according to school rumor, had a boyfriend in high school. I believed it. She had auburn hair, blue eyes, and, I noted with a particular pang, a pure white, folding umbrella.

"I can't see," whispered Mona.

"So clean your glasses."

"My glasses *are* clean. You're in the way."

I looked at her. "They look dirty to me."

"That's because *your* glasses are dirty."

Eugenie came bouncing to the end of her piece.

"Oh! Just stupendous!" Miss Crosman hugged her, then looked up as Eugenie's mother walked in. "Stupendous!" she said again. "Oh! Mrs. Roberts! Your daughter has a gift, a real gift. It's an honor to teach her."

Mrs. Roberts, radiant with pride, swept her daughter out of the room as if she were royalty, born to the piano bench. Watching the way Eugenie carried herself, I sat up and concentrated so hard on sucking in

* Pause and Think
Why do you think the girls didn't just ask their mother what kind of work she was doing?

* Pause and Think
Why does the main character lie about having a convertible?

my stomach that I did not realize until the Robertses were gone that Eugenie had left her umbrella. As Mona began to play, I jumped up and ran to the window, meaning to call to them — only to see their brake lights flash then fade at the stop sign at the corner. As if to allow them passage, the rain had let up; a quivering sun lit their way.

The umbrella glowed like a scepter on the blue carpet while Mona, slumping over the keyboard, managed to eke out a fair rendition of a catfight. At the end of the piece, Miss Crosman asked her to stand up.

"Stay right there," she said, then came back a minute later with a towel to cover the bench. "You must be cold," she continued. "Shall I call your mother and have her bring over some dry clothes?"

"No," answered Mona. "She won't come because she . . ."

"She's too busy," I broke in from the back of the room.

"I see," Miss Crosman sighed and shook her head a little. "Your glasses are filthy, honey," she said to Mona. "Shall I clean them for you?"

Sisterly embarrassment seized me. Why hadn't Mona wiped her lenses when I told her to? As she resumed abuse of the piano, I stared at the umbrella. I wanted to open it, twirl it around by its slender silver handle; I wanted to dangle it from my wrist on the way to school the way the other girls did. I wondered what Miss Crosman would say if I offered to bring it to Eugenie at school tomorrow. She would be impressed with my consideration for others; Eugenie would be pleased to have it back; and I would have possession of the umbrella for an entire night. I looked at it again, toying with the idea of asking for one for Christmas. I knew, however, how my mother would react. ✳

"Things," she would say. "What's the matter with a raincoat? All you want is things, just like an American."

Sitting down for my lesson, I was careful to keep the towel under me and sit up straight.

"I'll bet you can't see a thing either," said Miss Crosman, reaching for my glasses. "And you can relax, you poor dear. This isn't a boot camp."

When Miss Crosman finally allowed me to start playing I played extra well, as well as I possibly could. See, I told her with my fingers. You don't have to feel sorry for me.

"That was wonderful," said Miss Crosman. "Oh! Just wonderful."

An entire constellation rose in my heart.

"And guess what," I announced proudly. "I have a surprise for you."

Then I played a second piece for her, a much more difficult one that she had not assigned.

"Oh! That was stupendous," she said without hugging me. ✳ "Stupendous! You are a genius, young lady. If your mother had started you younger, you'd be playing like Eugenie Roberts by now!"

✳ Pause and Think
Why do you think the umbrella is so important to the girl who is telling the story?

✳ Pause and Think
Why does the girl mention that Miss Crosman did not hug her?

I looked at the keyboard, wishing that I had still a third, even more difficult piece to play for her. I wanted to tell her that I was the school spelling bee champion, that I wasn't ticklish, that I could do karate.

"My mother is a concert pianist," I said.

She looked at me for a long moment, then finally, without saying anything, hugged me. I didn't say anything about bringing the umbrella to Eugenie at school.

The steps were dry when Mona and I sat down to wait for my mother.

"Do you want to wait inside?" Miss Crosman looked anxiously at the sky.

"No," I said. "Our mother will be here any minute."

"In a while," said Mona.

"Any minute," I said again, even though my mother had been at least twenty minutes late every week since she started working.

According to the church clock across the street we had been waiting twenty-five minutes when Miss Crosman came out again.

"Shall I give you ladies a ride home?"

"No," I said. "Our mother is coming any minute."

"Shall I at least give her a call and remind her you're here? Maybe she forgot about you."

"I don't think she *forgot*," said Mona.

"Shall I give her a call anyway? Just to be safe?"

"I bet she already left," I said. "How could she forget about us?"

Miss Crosman went in to call.

"There's no answer," she said, coming back out.

"See, she's on her way," I said.

"Are you sure you wouldn't like to come in?"

"No," said Mona.

"Yes," I said. I pointed at my sister. "She meant yes, too. She meant no, she wouldn't like to go in."

Miss Crosman looked at her watch. "It's 5:30 now, ladies. My pot roast will be coming out in fifteen minutes. Maybe you'd like to come in and have some then?"

"My mother's almost here," I said. "She's on her way."

We watched and watched the street. I tried to imagine what my mother was doing; I tried to imagine her writing messages in the sky, even though I knew she was afraid of planes. I watched as the branches of Miss Crosman's big willow tree started to sway; they had all been trimmed to exactly the same height off the ground, so that they looked beautiful, like hair in the wind.

It started to rain.

"Miss Crosman is coming out again," said Mona.

"Don't let her talk you into going inside," I whispered.

"Why not?"

"Because that would mean Mom isn't really coming any minute."

"But she isn't," said Mona. "She's *working*."

"Shh! Miss Crosman is going to hear you."

"She's working! She's working! She's working!"

I put my hand over her mouth, but she licked it, and so I was wiping my hand on my wet dress when the front door opened.

"We're getting even *wetter*," said Mona right away. "Wetter and wetter."

"Shall we all go in?" Miss Crosman pulled Mona to her feet. "Before you young ladies catch pneumonia? You've been out here an hour already."

"We're *freezing*." Mona looked up at Miss Crosman. "Do you have any hot chocolate? We're going to catch *pneumonia*."

＊ Pause and Think
Why does the older
sister refuse to go
inside?

"I'm not going in," I said. "My mother's coming any minute." ＊

"Come on," said Mona. "Use your *noggin*."

"Any minute."

"Come on, Mona," Miss Crosman opened the door. "Shall we get you inside first?"

"See you in the hospital," said Mona as she went in. "See you in the hospital with *pneumonia*."

I stared out into the empty street. The rain was pricking me all over; I was cold; I wanted to go inside. I wanted to be able to let myself go inside. If Miss Crosman came out again, I decided, I would go in.

She came out with a blanket and the white umbrella.

I could not believe that I was actually holding the umbrella, opening it. It sprang up by itself as if it were alive, as if that were what it wanted to do — as if it belonged in my hands, above my head. I stared up at the network of silver spokes, then spun the umbrella around and around and around. It was so clean and white that it seemed to glow, to illuminate everything around it.

"It's beautiful," I said.

Miss Crosman sat down next to me, on one end of the blanket. I moved the umbrella over so that it covered that too. I could feel the rain on my left shoulder and shivered. She put her arm around me.

"You poor, poor dear."

I knew that I was in store for another bolt of sympathy, and braced myself by staring up into the umbrella.

"You know, I very much wanted to have children when I was younger," she continued.

"You did?"

She stared at me a minute. Her face looked dry and crusty, like day-old frosting.

"I did. But then I never got married."

I twirled the umbrella around again.

"This is the most beautiful umbrella I have ever seen," I said. "Ever, in my whole life."

"Do you have an umbrella?"

"No. But my mother's going to get me one just like this for Christmas."

"Is she? I tell you what. You don't have to wait until Christmas. You can have this one."

"But this one belongs to Eugenie Roberts," I protested. "I have to give it back to her tomorrow in school."

"Who told you it belongs to Eugenie? It's not Eugenie's. It's mine. And now I'm giving it to you, so it's yours."

＊ Pause and Think
Why does she feel
this way?

"It is?"

She hugged me tighter. "That's right. It's all yours."

"It's mine?" I didn't know what to say. "Mine?" Suddenly I was jumping up and down in the rain. "It's beautiful! Oh! It's beautiful!" I laughed.

Miss Crosman laughed too, even though she was getting all wet.

"Thank you, Miss Crosman. Thank you very much. Thanks a zillion. It's beautiful. It's *stupendous*!"

"You're quite welcome," she said.

"Thank you," I said again, but that didn't seem like enough. Suddenly I knew just what she wanted to hear. "I wish you were my mother."

Right away I felt bad. ＊

"You shouldn't say that," she said, but her face was opening into a huge smile as the lights of my mother's car cautiously turned the corner. I quickly collapsed the umbrella and put it up my skirt, holding onto it from the outside, through the material.

"Mona!" I shouted into the house. "Mona! Hurry up! Mom's here! I told you she was coming!"

Then I ran away from Miss Crosman, down to the curb. Mona came tearing up to my side as my mother neared the house. We bothed backed up a few feet, so that in case she went onto the curb, she wouldn't run us over.

"But why didn't you go inside with Mona?" my mother asked on the way home. She had taken off her own coat to put over me, and had the heat on high.

"She wasn't using her noggin," said Mona, next to me in the back seat.

"I should call next time," said my mother. "I just don't like to say where I am."

That was when she finally told us that she was working as a check-out clerk in the A&P. She was supposed to be on the day shift, but the other employees were unreliable, and her boss had promised her a promotion if she would stay until the evening shift filled in.

For a moment no one said anything. Even Mona seemed to find the revelation disappointing.

"A promotion already!" she said, finally.

I listened to the windshield wipers.

"You're so quiet." My mother looked at me in the rear-view mirror. "What's the matter?"

"I wish you would quit," I said after a moment.

She sighed. "The Chinese have a saying: one beam cannot hold the roof up."

"But Eugenie Roberts's father supports his family."

She sighed once more. "Eugenie Roberts's father is Eugenie Roberts's father," she said.

As we entered the downtown area, Mona started leaning hard against me every time the car turned right, trying to push me over. Remembering what I had said to Miss Crosman, I tried to maneuver the umbrella under my leg so she wouldn't feel it.

"What's under your skirt?" Mona wanted to know as we came to a traffic light. My mother, watching us in the rearview mirror again, rolled slowly to a stop.

"What's the matter?" she asked.

"There's something under her skirt," said Mona, pulling at me.

"Under her skirt?"

Meanwhile, a man crossing the street started to yell at us. "Who do you think you are, lady?" he said. "You're blocking the whole crosswalk."

We all froze. Other people walking by stopped to watch.

"Didn't you hear me?" he went on, starting to thump on the hood with his fist. "Don't you speak English?"

My mother began to back up, but the car behind us honked. Luckily, the light turned green right after that. She sighed in relief.

"What were you saying, Mona?" she asked.

We wouldn't have hit the car behind us that hard if he hadn't been moving, too, but as it was our car bucked violently, throwing us all first back and then forward.

"Uh oh," said Mona when we stopped. "*Another* accident."

I was relieved to have attention diverted from the umbrella. Then I noticed my mother's head, tilted back onto the seat. Her eyes were closed.

"Mom!" I screamed. "Mom! Wake up!"

She opened her eyes. "Please don't yell," she said. "Enough people are going to yell already."

"I thought you were dead," I said, starting to cry. "I thought you were dead."

She turned around, looked at me intently, then put her hand to my forehead.

"Sick," she confirmed. "Some kind of sick is giving you crazy ideas."

As the man from the car behind us started tapping on the window, I moved the umbrella away from my leg. Then Mona and my mother were getting out of the car. I got out after them; and while everyone else was inspecting the damage we'd done, I threw the umbrella down a sewer. *

* Pause and Think
Why does she throw the umbrella down the sewer?

The White Umbrella

First Reaction

1. Divide a page of your notebook into four parts: *Important Ideas in the Story, Questions I Have About the Story, Connections to Things I Have Read or Heard About,* and *Interesting Words and Phrases.* Use words and sketches to record some of your ideas in each box.

Look More Closely

2. Make and complete a chart like the one below.

Event	What the Protagonist Says and Does	What That Tells Us About Her
Mother starts to work.	Tries to keep it a secret. Makes dinner when mother is late.	Ashamed that family doesn't have more money.
	Wonders what kind of work she's doing.	Curious, but afraid to ask.
Gets wet on way to music lesson.		

3. How do you think the author wants you to feel about the main character? Find evidence in the story to support your opinion.

4. Why is the white umbrella important in this story? What does it symbolize for the main character?

Develop Your Ideas

5. The story is told from the older sister's point of view. Retell one or more of the events from the music teacher's, the mother's, or Mona's (the sister) point of view. Write about the event as a conversation with someone who is not in the story, or as a letter to a friend in another place.

Think About Your Reading Strategies

6. As you read the story, how well were you able to:

- Set the scene — read carefully to figure out what was going on in the beginning of the story.

- Put yourself in the main character's place to understand how she was feeling.

- Understand the conflict the characters faced and make predictions about how it would turn out.

- Pause to think about what was going on.

- Use your word skills to understand words you didn't know.

Make Connections

Now you can demonstrate what you've learned in *Actions and Reactions*. Read and think about the questions below.

Ask Yourself . . .

 GOAL 1 Have you learned how stories develop from the actions and reactions of characters as they encounter a variety of challenges?

GOAL 2 Have you learned a variety of strategies that effective readers use to understand, respond to, and interpet stories?

GOAL 3 Have you learned about some of the strategies and techniques that writers use to create interesting stories and did you use these techniques to create your own works?

GOAL 4 Did you use a variety of ways to share your ideas about the stories you read?

The following activities can help you think about your work in this unit and plan how to use what you've learned in the future. Each activity is keyed to the questions in *Ask Yourself . . .*

Look Back . . .

1. Create a poster or collage that illustrates how some of the story characters you met in this unit acted and reacted when they met challenges. Focus your work around one or two key ideas or themes. **❶❹**

2. Review the writing and representing that you did during this unit. Choose one or two pieces of work that are particularly satisfying to you. For each, explain: **❸❹**

   • What you were trying to accomplish. What your purpose was and who your intended audience was.

   • Some of the specific strategies and techniques you used.

   • What the work shows about your writing or representing skills.

   • How you can use what you learned in future works.

3. Look back at *Tips On: Reading Short Stories*, page 75, and *Focus On: Interpreting Fiction*, page 86. Rate your current skills at using the strategies described in both as: **❷**

   0 - I've never tried it.
   1 - I don't really understand how to use it.
   2 - I've started practising and improving.
   3 - I'm able to use this effectively in some of my reading.
   4 - This is a powerful strategy for me. It helps me a lot.

4. Make a list of the writing techniques that you identified and practised, including: point of view and dialogue. Use the rating scale on page 122 to rate your skill at using each technique on your list. ➌

Show What You've Learned . . .

5. What makes a good story? Brainstorm a list of the qualities that appeal to you when you are selecting or reading a story. Compare your list with a partner or others in a small group. Select four or five criteria you can use to judge your own stories and those of other writers. ➊ ➍

6. With your teacher's help, choose a novel or short story for independent reading.
➊➋➌➍

   • Before you read, review *Tips On: Reading Short Stories*, page 75. After you have read the story, list one or two strategies you found particularly useful. Explain how these strategies helped you read and respond to the selection.

   • Write a brief journal entry giving your first impression of the story. How did you like it? What stands out in your mind? How does it connect to your own experiences or to other things you've read?

   • Create a chart, diagram, or series of illustrations that show how the main character acts and reacts to the challenge he or she faces. Before you begin your representation, review *Focus On: Interpreting Fiction*, page 86.

   • Choose a character or setting in the story and create a found poem to share your ideas. Before you begin, review the instructions and criteria on page 86.

   • Use the criteria you developed in Activity 5 to evaluate the story. Be prepared to justify your decisions.

7. Several of the activities in this unit asked you to plan or write part of a story. Choose the one that is most interesting to you, and develop a short story. Remember to plan your story around a challenge or problem, and to show how your character(s) act and react. Use the criteria you developed in Activity 5 to evaluate your short story.
➊➌➍

Reconstructing Past Lives

You might have heard the expression "Dead men tell no tales." What do you think it means?

There are scientists who do not agree that dead men and women tell no tales. These scientists study the bodies of dead people and the items found with them. These clues help scientists to answer questions such as: How did this person die? When did this person die? What was life like for this person?

The selections in this unit are about these scientists and their work. You will learn how they are able to reconstruct past lives from small amounts of evidence.

SETTING GOALS

In this unit you can:

■ Learn techniques that authors, designers, and editors use to help you understand and remember information.

■ Practise strategies to help you become a better reader of information.

■ Demonstrate ways to summarize and organize information so you can share your ideas effectively.

Warrior's remains found *126*
A newspaper article about scientists finding the grave of an ancient warrior.

Bodies and Bones: The Tales They Tell *128*
by Larry Verstraete
An excerpt from a book that explains the work of physical anthropologists.

How to Make a Mummy Talk? *134*
by James M. Deem
Two chapters from a book on Egyptian mummies that explain how Egyptians mummified their dead and how modern scientists study mummies.

I Am the Mummy Heb-Nefert *142*
by Eve Bunting
A poem that explains mummification from the point of view of a mummy.

Discovering the Iceman *145*
by Shelley Tanaka
An excerpt from a book about the discovery of the Iceman, an ancient man frozen in a glacier.

Frozen Man *152*
by David Getz
An excerpt from a book about the Iceman explaining how long ago the Iceman lived.

Convicted by a Cat *162*
from Maclean's *magazine,* May 5, 1997
A magazine article describing how police used cat hair to convict a killer.

Skeletal Sculptures *156*
by Donna M. Jackson
An excerpt from a book on forensic anthropology in which a forensic sculptor reconstructs a face from a skull.

Before You Read

Warrior's remains found is about the discovery of an ancient grave. A discovery like this is exciting to scientists because it gives them information about how people might have lived long ago.

What other stories have you heard about people finding old graves or tombs?

Try This

Read the selection twice — once fairly quickly to get the gist of it, then again more slowly to pick up the detailed information.

---

aristocratic Having qualities of the highest class in society.

The Vancouver Sun   Thursday, April 24, 1997, page A7

Warrior's remains found

NORTHAMPTON, England—Scientists say they have discovered the remains of an aristocratic Anglo-Saxon warrior, buried more than 1,200 years ago with his helmet, sword, and ornamental bronze bowl.

"This is probably the most exciting thing you can imagine. It's the find of a lifetime," Ian Meadows, the site director, told the British Broadcasting Corp. Tuesday. A metal detector helped the team find the shallow grave, located metres from the route of an old Roman road 110 kilometres north of London.

Associated Press

First Reaction

1. How do you think you would react if you found an ancient grave site? What would you do? Why?

Look More Closely

2. Journalists write articles for newspapers and magazines. In their articles, they often answer the questions: Who? What? Where? Why? and When? Reread *Warrior's remains found* and answer each of the five Ws.

   - *Who* made the discovery?

   - *What* did they find?

   - *Where* did they find it?

   - *Why* is it exciting?

   - *When* did they find it?

3. What did the scientists find in the grave to make them think the man was a warrior and an aristocrat?

Develop Your Ideas

4. Scientists will be studying the remains of this warrior for a long time to learn as much about his life as they can. Make a list of questions you have about the warrior and his life. Put an asterisk (*) beside the ones you think scientists might be able to answer.

5. We often know more about ancient people from what was buried with them than from their bones. Anthropologists call these items *captured context*. Another way to capture the context of your life is to put items into a time capsule and bury it for many years. Make a list of items that you would put in a time capsule. When you make your selections, choose items that would help someone who found them to understand your life.

Before You Read

The excerpt you are about to read describes the work of physical anthropologists. Physical anthropologists are scientists who study human bodies and bones like the ones found in the warrior's grave.

Imagine a human skeleton. What could you tell about a person just by looking at the bones?

Write *skeleton* in the middle of your page. Brainstorm and list all the things you think you could learn about someone by looking at his or her skeleton. You might be able to add to this list after you read the selection.

Try This

As you read, look for main ideas and record them by taking brief notes.

BODIES + BONES

THE TALES THEY TELL

BY LARRY VERSTRAETE

(Above) Grid marking area of human skeletons found in cave unearthed at the Roman town of Herculaneum, covered with mud and ash during the volcanic eruption of Mount Vesuvius in 79 A.D.

(Left) A photograph of a site in Herculaneum.

You've likely heard the phrase "Dead men tell no tales." It's a popular expression. But in the world of modern science it is not true. The dead can tell a lot about the past.

When human remains are uncovered at a dig site a physical anthropologist may be called to investigate them. A physical anthropologist is a scientist who examines, measures, and interprets human bodies and bones. From this information the scientist learns about the appearance, habits, health, hardships, and triumphs of an individual or a group.

Even a single bone can be revealing. The femur, or thigh bone, is the longest and strongest bone in the human body. From measurements of this bone alone, the probable height and size of an individual can be calculated.

The study of a skull can reveal an individual's age. When a baby is born its skull is made of several separate bones. As a person ages these bones begin to grow together and eventually become smooth and continuous. By studying how advanced this skull growth is, a person's age at the time of death can be estimated.

Teeth can also help to determine age. Because they grow in over many years and at a set rate — baby teeth, then permanent teeth, then wisdom teeth — an examination of what teeth are present in a skull can be a good indicator of age at death.

An expert in ancient bones excavates a skeleton at Herculaneum.

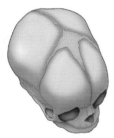

Infant's Skull

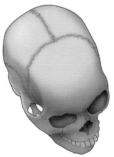

Adult Skull

Bones can also tell whether an individual is male or female. The skull of a female is normally thinner and lighter than that of a male, while the femur and other bones are shorter. The pelvis or hip bone of a female is wider and shaped differently too.

Bones can tell other stories of the past as well. Worn teeth may indicate great age, but they may also tell about the foods and eating habits of early people. Cracks and fractures may indicate accidents or injuries. Unusual bumps or growth may be signs of illness and disease. Even signs of ancient operations can be detected.

Sometimes a whole population of skeletons can tell a more complete story of the past than a single skeleton. Such is the case in Herculaneum, one of the Italian cities destroyed by the eruption of Vesuvius in A.D. 79.

In 1982 archeologists discovered a large number of skeletons in rooms near what had once been the beach. Apparently many Herculaneans had taken shelter there when the disaster struck. Dr. Sarah Bisel, a physical anthropologist, was asked to study this population of skeletons.

Dr. Bisel was able to read the lives of many individual Herculaneans from their bones. One skeleton has been called Pretty Lady because the shape of her skull shows she had a beautiful face. She also had well-developed arm bones, so Bisel suspects she worked as a weaver. Another skeleton is known as the Soldier. Several missing

---

archeologists People who study history and prehistory through the analysis of physical remains.

front teeth and evidence of a serious leg wound suggest that he lived a very rough life. A third skeleton is of a 14-year-old girl who died clutching an infant. Her teeth show that she was starved or very ill as a baby, and her leg and arm bones show that she did a lot of heavy work. She was probably a slave who died trying to protect her owner's baby.

But the group of skeletons as a whole tells a larger story of the Herculanean people of that time. Their average height was shorter than today's, they were generally well nourished, they had good teeth because of their diet, and the slaves among them led very difficult lives. All of this Bisel was able to deduce just from their bones.

Sometimes a well-preserved body, one that includes more than just bones, is unearthed at a site.

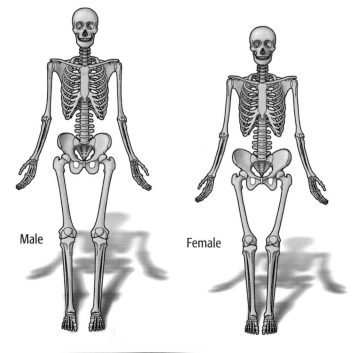

Male   Female

Because such bodies enable scientists to examine skin, hair, and tissue, they provide unique opportunities to understand the past.

Laboratory tests provide many clues. They can reveal information about the age, sex, and racial background of an individual. They can also determine the chemical make-up of a body, giving scientists valuable information about diet and diseases of long ago.

An autopsy may also be performed on a body, just as when a person dies today. Autopsies are revealing and can divulge much about the life of an individual. An autopsy on a 2,100-year-old mummy of a Chinese lady, for example, showed that she had gallstones, tuberculosis, and a painful back. But none of these caused her death. The arteries leading to her heart were blocked with a build-up of hard material known as plaque. Inside her stomach were 138 melon seeds. Shortly after eating a meal of melon, apparently, she suffered a sudden heart attack and died.

Such autopsies are interesting, but they have drawbacks too. In an autopsy the body is altered and any wrappings may be damaged.

Another way to study a body is to X-ray it. X-rays enable scientists to examine the bone structure and condition of a body without damage. They can be used to establish the age at death and to show diseases, fractures, and other phenomena.

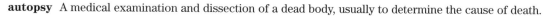

autopsy A medical examination and dissection of a dead body, usually to determine the cause of death.

First Reaction

1. How would you feel about being a scientist who studies human bodies and bones?

Look More Closely

2. *Bodies and Bones* explains many things scientists can learn from bones. Some or all of the information in this selection may have been new to you. Organizing the information for yourself will help you remember what you learned. Make a chart like the following.

Bone	What it tells scientists:	How scientists know that:
femur (thigh bone)	height of person	The femur (thigh bone) is the longest bone in the body. The longer it is, the taller the person was.

3. Writers use techniques that help you understand the information they are giving you. One technique is to give examples. Look back over the selection. Notice the writer gives you all the information in the first third of the article. In the rest of the article, the writer gives you examples of how physical anthropologists use this information in their work.

   Reread the examples. Choose the one you found most helpful. Retell it to a partner in your own words. Have your partner tell you which example she or he found most helpful. Was it the same one? Why do you think writers use more than one example?

Develop Your Ideas

4. If you wanted to find out more about the bones of the human body, where could you look? Make a list of all the places you could look. Pick one and research information about human bones. Write down one new piece of information you found and where you found it.

Tips On Reading for Information

Authors, designers and editors use a number of techniques and text features to help you understand and remember information. Here are some tips to help you recognize and use these techniques when you read for information.

Set a Purpose

You can read informational material for pleasure or to find specific information. The strategies you use as you read will depend on your purpose. Think about what information you are looking for and how you plan to use that information.

Preview the Selection

Check to see how the selection is organized. The author may have used techniques or text features such as chapter headings or subtitles to help you find the main ideas. Look for charts, maps, or illustrations that can help you understand the text.

Monitor Your Pace

If you are reading for information, you might want to read more slowly than if you are reading for pleasure. You might want to read the selection twice — once fairly quickly to get the gist of it, then again more slowly to pick up the detailed information.

Clarify Meaning

When reading for information, you might encounter specialized vocabulary. Sometimes you can tell what a new word means from the words around it. You might need to look some words up in a dictionary. As you read, look for main ideas. You might want to record the main ideas by taking notes. If you find part of the selection confusing, pause and think about what you have read so far before you continue to the end of the selection. You might find it helps to look back and reread parts of the selection.

Summarize Information

Use notes, webs, or charts to summarize what you learned. You might need to reread or skim parts of the selection to check details. Summarizing and organizing the information makes it easier to use in the future.

How to Make a Mummy Talk

by James M. Deem

1. THE ART OF ARTIFICIAL MUMMYMAKING

ACCIDENTAL MUMMIES.

Despite what many people think, ancient Egyptians did not at first make mummies artificially. Rather, they observed the natural process that took place after they buried their dead.

Before 3000 B.C., Egyptians buried their dead in shallow graves in the desert. The body was put in a flexed position, usually face down and wrapped

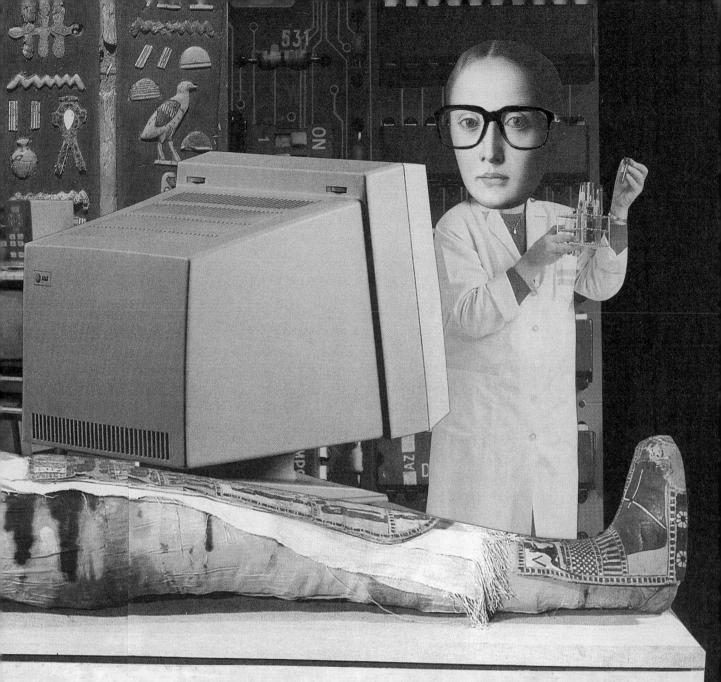

in linen or animal skins, and accompanied with small objects. Poorer people were buried with knives or pots of food and water, while wealthier people were buried with jewelry, combs, or other adornments. The grave was lined with reed mats, boards, or bricks.

Then an amazing — and quite natural — thing happened. The hot sand that pressed up against the body quickly soaked the fluids from

it and dried out the body's tissues before they could decay. When animal scavengers like the jackal (who might dig up a body in search of food) and human scavengers (who might rob graves of jewelry or other goods) uncovered the bodies, the Egyptians realized that the dead had been preserved.

Mummification was an important part of ancient Egyptians' religion. Here's why:

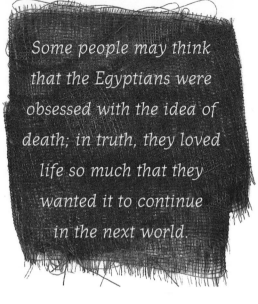

Some people may think that the Egyptians were obsessed with the idea of death; in truth, they loved life so much that they wanted it to continue in the next world.

The ancient Egyptians believed that inside the heart of every person was a spirit called *ka*. The ka resembled the living person in every way, but it was not released from the body until death. Egyptians would say, for example, that a woman "went to her ka," meaning that she had died. The ka lived an afterlife. But it could also die, they believed, unless a likeness of the person was placed in the burial chamber to become the ka's home. It was crucial, therefore, that the ka recognize the likeness, since no other shelter could keep it alive. Sometimes a small statue of the person was used; more often a mummy of the person was created. In order to stay alive, the ka also needed sustenance, which explains why food and water were placed in the chamber.

Some people may think that the Egyptians were obsessed with the idea of death; in truth, they loved life so much that they wanted it to continue in the next world. The fact that the dead were well preserved in the shallow graves was definitely comforting: the ka would be able to live.

Eventually, the idea of a sand burial did not appeal to members of the royal family and wealthy persons — they wanted something fancier. Between the years 3100 and 2686 B.C., some bodies were buried in coffins that were placed in underground tombs. However, the coffins and the large empty chambers eliminated the ingredients necessary for accidental mummification. Since hot sand no longer surrounded the body, it could not soak up the body's fluids. And in the damp burial chambers, the bodies began to rot.

That led to the need to make mummies artificially. In trying to copy the work done by the sand and sun, ancient Egyptians employed a number of mummymaking methods.

MOLDED MUMMIES.

From 2686-2181 B.C., Egyptian mummymakers experimented with "stucco mummies." They draped bodies with linen, covered them with plaster, and attempted to mold the body and facial features to keep them as natural-looking as possible, like a statue.

A stucco mummy — discovered at Saqqâra, Egypt, in 1966 — is so well preserved that an observer can easily spot a callus on the bottom of one foot. No matter how real stucco mummies appeared, however, their insides usually decayed, leaving only a skeleton.

THE BEST MUMMIES.

By the Twenty-first Dynasty (from about 1090 to 945 B.C.), mummymakers in Egypt had hit upon two important components of successful preservation - the removal of the internal organs, and the drying out of the body with a saltlike substance called *natron*.

Depending on how much money a person could pay, the mummymaking process differed dramatically. The Greek historian Herodotus described the most expensive technique, the medium-priced technique, and the least expensive technique.

Of the most expensive technique, he wrote:

First they draw out the brains through the nostrils with an iron hook, taking part of it out in this manner, the rest by infusion of drugs. Then with a sharp Ethiopian stone they make an incision in the side, and take out all the [internal organs]; and having cleansed the abdomen and rinsed it with palm wine, they next sprinkle it with pounded perfumes. Then having filled the belly with pure myrrh . . . and cassia, and other perfumes . . . they sew it up again; and when they have done this, they steep it in [natron], leaving it under for 70 days. . . . At the end of the 70 days they wash the corpse and wrap the whole body in bandages of flaxen cloth, smearing it with gum, which the Egyptians commonly use instead of glue.

Afterward, they placed the body in a coffin shaped like a man or woman and set it, upright, in a burial tomb.

How We Got the Word mummy

When the word *mummy* was first used in the English language in the early 1400s, it did not mean a body, as it does now. Instead, it was the name of a medicine. Mummy comes from *mumiyah*, an Arabic word for bitumen, a sticky oil now used to make roads.

In the Middle Ages, people in Europe thought bitumen could cure diseases. They also thought ancient Egyptians had used bitumen in mummy wrappings. This, people felt, gave bitumen extra healing power. Around 600 or 700 years ago, Europeans began grinding up mummy wrappings and selling the powder as medicine. People put mummy powder on wounds to help them heal and even ate it in hopes of curing stomach troubles!

At first, only the wrappings were made into medicine. Later, whole bodies — thousands of them — were ground into powder. As old mummies became harder to find, Egyptians started making fake mummies from bodies of people who had recently died. They stuffed the bodies with bitumen, wrapped them in linen, and dried them in the sun. When they were dry enough to look like real mummies, the bodies were sold to be ground into powder.

We now know that Egyptians used resin, not bitumen, in mummy wrappings. So the powder made from real mummies had no bitumen in it at all. Still, doctors all over Europe told patients to use mummy powder.

In the late 1500s, a doctor from France visited a factory that made fake mummies. When he learned that the Egyptians did not bother to find out how the people died, he was afraid. Fake mummies could carry diseases that could spread to people taking mummy powder as medicine. The Frenchman urged doctors to stop using mummy powder. Soon it was against the law to make fake mummies or to take mummies out of Egypt. This put the mummymakers out of business. People stopped using mummies for medicine, and by the 1600s the word came to mean what it does today — a preserved body.

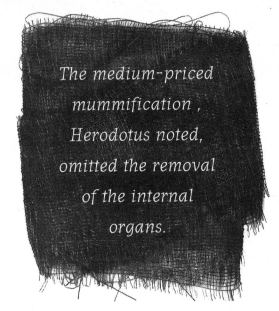

> *The medium-priced mummification, Herodotus noted, omitted the removal of the internal organs.*

Natron is a natural salt found around desert lakes near Cairo.

The medium-priced mummification, Herodotus noted, omitted the removal of the internal organs. Instead, the body was filled with a natron solution, which helped dissolve the internal organs. After a time, they flushed the natron from the body.

As for the least expensive method, the body was merely soaked in salt and hot bitumen (a tarlike substance) or salt alone. Most Egyptologists agree that bodies treated with salt and bitumen were the first to be called mummies, since the word *mummy*, it is thought, comes from the word for bitumen in Arabic.

During this period, embalmers sometimes added one other important technique to make the mummy look more lifelike: they padded the face and body with various materials, such as sawdust, mud, cloth, or even butter. Because the eyeballs quickly deteriorated, artificial eyes made of stone or cloth were also used.

By 600 B.C., these excellent techniques had been gradually abandoned, and more emphasis was placed on the outward appearance of the mummy rather than the preservation of the body. After Egypt was conquered by the Greeks in 305 B.C., the appearance of the coffin became as important as that of the mummy. The coffin sometimes bore a portrait of the person, painted on wood during his or her life. Inside, the mummy would be decoratively wrapped in linen, often in a geometric pattern. Underneath the wrappings, however, the body was poorly preserved.

2. How to Make a Mummy Talk

In order to study a mummy, scientists perform a number of procedures, similar in some ways to those used by a medical examiner who conducts an autopsy. Of course, it wasn't always like this. During the 1800s and early 1900s, when studying Egyptian mummies was a popular pastime, a mummy would be unrolled and destroyed in front of a number of invited guests. After the unwrapping was over, the mummy and its wrappings were simply thrown away. Today, scientists try to preserve the mummy under analysis. Most mummies studied with nondestructive methods not only survive such examination in good shape, they reveal much more information than in the past.

What exactly do scientists do, then? Here's a list of the steps a team will take to coax a mummy to talk and yet keep it safe.

Document its appearance with photographs.

Before work on a mummy — especially an accidental one that was just discovered — is begun, a series of photographs will be taken to record every aspect of its appearance. In this way, scientists will be able to see if the mummy's condition starts to deteriorate or otherwise change.

X-RAY THE BODY COMPLETELY.

X-rays will reveal what is inside a wrapped mummy and the condition of the body.

Sometimes more than one body has been found inside a wrapped mummy; other times an extra head or leg or even a baby has been discovered. X-rays may also reveal certain diseases or afflictions that the person suffered. By using X-rays, a scientist does not have to unwrap or undress the mummy.

EXAMINE THE MATERIAL IN WHICH THE MUMMY IS WRAPPED.

Before any type of internal study can be undertaken, textile or basketry experts are called in to examine the material encasing the mummy. The textile expert may take a microscopic snippet of material to analyze. If the material is very rare, scientists may be unable to examine the body further.

CONDUCT A DENTAL EXAMINATION.

A thorough check of a mummy's teeth will reveal a great deal about the type of food a person ate and his health. A scientist will want to know if and how the teeth were worn down, which teeth are decayed or missing, and whether the mouth contains any signs of injury. All of this can reveal the person's diet and perhaps even show how he died. But scientists will only conduct this type of exam if the mummy's mouth is open.

STUDY SAMPLES OF THE MUMMY'S TISSUES UNDER A MICROSCOPE.

Called a histological exam, this allows scientists to get a close-up look at the soft tissues taken from muscles and organs. It is particularly valuable to show any diseases that the person had at the time of death. But such an examination is not always possible; it depends on the condition of the mummy and

EXAMINE THE MUMMY'S ESOPHAGUS, STOMACH, AND INTESTINES.

An endoscope, a medical tool which normally allows doctors to examine the stomach and intestines for ulcers or cancer, has most recently been used by some mummy scientists. With an endoscope, a scientist can look for signs of disease and even discover the last meal that the person ate. This examination avoids the problems associated with the older methods; it does not damage the mummy since the scientist uses the mouth or rectum (the body's normal openings) as the route for the endoscope.

RECONSTRUCT THE MUMMY'S FACE.

Some scientists might ask an artist to sculpt the face of the mummy to get a better sense of what the person looked like. No matter how lifelike the mummy seems, it probably does not really resemble the living person. A good artist will bring the mummy back to life with a careful and accurate reproduction of the face.

how much of it remains. Often, a mummy will be quite brittle and dry. In this case, tissues must be rehydrated (that is, mixed with a solution of water and other chemicals) to bring them back to the original condition. But scientists are unwilling to damage a mummy to retrieve any tissue samples.

Microscopic skin samples, for example, may be snipped from the areas of the body that will not be on display (from its underpart, for example). Organ samples (from the lungs or liver, for example) cannot be taken if the scientist must make an incision and thereby mutilate the mummy. However, scientists are often helped by the mummymakers themselves. Sometimes they made incisions that provide today's scientists access to internal organs. Other times, they removed a person's internal organs and preserved them separately in jars or wrapped packages; samples can be taken without disturbing the mummy.

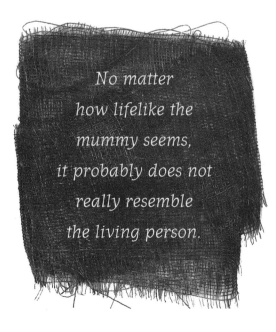

No matter how lifelike the mummy seems, it probably does not really resemble the living person.

First Reaction

1. What was one thing you learned from the chapter of *How to Make a Mummy Talk* you just read that you did not know before?

Look More Closely

2. Sometimes when you read for information, you need to take notes to remember what you read. The notes do not always have to be in words. You can also make notes by drawing illustrations.

   Draw a mummy in the middle of your page. Add illustrations around the edge of the page to show all the ways scientists study mummies. Your illustrations can be in a cartoon style if you wish. With an arrow, connect each drawing to the mummy. Reread the selection to make sure you include all the information.

3. What advantages did the best mummies, the ones made during the Twenty-First Dynasty, have over accidental mummies and moulded mummies?

Develop Your Ideas

4. Use your library to learn more about a famous mummy such as Ramses II, Tutankhamen, Queen Nodjmet, or another of your choice. As you gather information, make notes in your own words.

Think About Your Note-Taking

5. As you take notes, keep the following questions in mind.
   - Am I identifying the main ideas?
   - Am I recording enough detail?
   - Am I recording my sources of information?
   - Are there gaps in the information? Do I need to go to other sources to fill the gaps?

I Am the Mummy

by Eve Bunting

Before You Read

This poem is about Heb-Nefert, a fictional Egyptian woman, who dies and is embalmed. The author writes from the point of view of the mummy. We hear the mummy describe her own embalming, burial, and eventual display in a museum. Although the poem is a work of imagination, it is based on factual information.

> Imagine how the ancient warrior, the slave girl from Herculaneum, or the Chinese lady who died after eating melons might have felt if they had known that some day their remains would be discovered and studied.

Try This

This poem could be read for pleasure or for information. Try reading it once just for pleasure. Then reread it, perhaps more slowly, paying attention to the information.

---

nomarch Nomarch ('nä-märk) is the chief magistrate of a province of ancient Egypt.

I am the mummy Heb-Nefert,
black as night,
stretched as tight
as leather on a drum.
My arms are folded
on my hollow chest
where once my live heart beat.
My ears are holes
that hear no sound.
Once I was the daughter of a nomarch,
favored, beautiful.
But all things change.

I was a cherished wife.
The palace was my home.
I lived for him and he for me.

My golden cat, Nebut, I loved.
She loved me, too,
and came with me
into the silent twilight of the afterlife
when day changed to eternity.

I rose above myself
and watched.

I watched as they
anointed me with oils and spices,
took away the parts of me
that were inside,
and filled me up
with natron, cinnamon, and herbs.
My eyes were closed and plugged.

Heb-Nefert

Beeswax filled my nose.
They capped my nails with gold
studded with precious stones,
bejeweled me from head to toe,
and bound me up in linen,
layer on layer.
I was to be
for all eternity
well kept for him.
They made a mask
painted to look like me,
bound up my cat and masked her, too,
my faithful cat, Nebut.
Placed me in my sarcophagus
pictured around with likenesses
of gods who would receive me.

The sled that took me to my tomb
was pulled by oxen.

Behind, the lines of weepers wept
and sprinkled dust about their heads
to show their grief.
Porters carried things that I would
need,
the food that I would eat,
my jewels, amulets, my offerings to the
gods.

They placed me gently in the tomb,
juniper berries at my head and feet,
my gilded cat, Nebut, to stay with me.

My Noble One grew old
and also left that life
to lie at last beside me
in the night that followed night.
Time passed and time,
dark time and years,
till we were found,
our bodies moved,
placed in glass coffins
under lights
in quiet rooms.

I rose above myself and watched
as people came.
They peered into the cases where we
lay.
They spoke,
the words unknown to me
but understood as they were said.
"This was a person? This . . . and this?"

How foolish that they do not see
how all things change
and so will they.
Three thousand years from now
they will be dust and bones.
I am the mummy Heb-Nefert,
black as night,
stretched as tight
as leather on a drum.
Once I was beautiful.

First Reaction

1. *I Am the Mummy Heb-Nefert* contains some of the same factual information as you found in *How to Make a Mummy Talk*. Which selection did you prefer? Why?

Look More Closely

2. Why do you think the writer chose to tell the story from the mummy's point of view?

3. How do you think Heb-Nefert feels about having her remains on display in a museum? How would you feel?

4. The poem contains factual information but also some imagined content. When reading for information, it is important to be able to separate fact from imagination. Make a two-column chart. List three or four facts in the first column and three or four imaginative ideas in the second.

Facts	Imaginative Ideas

Develop Your Ideas

5. Using the factual information in the poem and in *How to Make a Mummy Talk*, develop an oral presentation called *How to Make a Mummy*. Give step-by-step directions accompanied by drawings and diagrams as necessary. Choose the point of view you will write from. For example, you could write from the point of view of an embalmer from ancient times, a modern scientist who studies mummies, or the mummy itself (as in the poem).

Think About Your Presentation

6. After you have made notes for your oral presentation and completed your illustrations, give your draft work to a classmate and ask him or her to assess it by answering the following questions.

   - Are the steps clear and in the right order?
   - Is there enough detail to follow the directions?
   - Are the illustrations clear and understandable?
   - What could be changed or added to make the presentation clearer?

Discovering the

ICEMAN

by Shelley Tanaka

Before You Read

You have learned that not all mummies are made for the purpose of embalming. Some are made accidentally by nature. This is the story of a mummy that was made naturally by freezing.

It was discovered in September 1991 by Erika and Helmut Simon, two tourists who were hiking on a glacier in the Alps, a mountain range in Switzerland. Finding a body on their vacation was a big surprise to them. Dr. Spindler, a scientist who studies bodies and bones, got an even bigger surprise when he realized how old it was.

> Think back to your vacations. What is the most unusual thing that has ever happened to you on a vacation?

Try This

As you read, use the map, illustrations, and boxed information that the writer has included to help you understand information about the Iceman.

Early in the morning of September 24, 1991, the phone rang in Spindler's office. It was the university's forensic department.

Spindler learned that air rescue operators and mountaineers had been hacking at the body for several days. Finally they were able to pull it out of the ice. It had been wrapped in a plastic bag, stuffed into a coffin, and taken to the nearest medical lab. At that very moment, it lay on a stainless-steel table — in a building that was only minutes away from Spindler's office. Would he like to see it?

It was very quiet and cool in the laboratory. The room smelled like a hospital. The forensic experts led Spindler to a dissecting table covered with a sheet. A clock ticked softly.

Where was the Iceman found? The Iceman was discovered in the Ötztal Alps, a mountain range that lies between Austria and Italy. His body was found just inside the Italian border.

GERMANY

AUSTRIA

SWITZERLAND Otzal Alps

Boizano

Venice

ITALY

ITALY Adriatic Sea

Spindler would remember this precise moment for the rest of his life. It was exactly 8:05 A.M.

The sheet was pulled away. And there lay the shriveled, naked body of a man.

His nose was squashed. His mouth was gaping. His eyelids were open, and sunken eyeballs gazed out of their sockets. His left hip had been torn open by a jackhammer that had been used to try to free him from the ice.

But what interested Spindler the most were the things that lay beside the body — the objects that had been found with the man. There was a long piece of wood that had been broken off at one end. There was a smooth, flat white bead attached to a fringe of tassels. There were odd-looking pieces of wood, rope, and leather. There was a pouch with a stone knife sticking out of it.

And there was an ax. It was small but well made. The handle had been carefully carved and shaped. The blade had been bound into the wood with leather straps.

Spindler's mind raced. He had seen axes like this before. He knew that such tools had been made only a very, very long time ago.

This was not the body of a mountain climber who had been dead for several decades — or even a warrior from the Middle Ages, as some people had guessed.

In fact, Konrad Spindler knew immediately that this man had died at least four thousand years ago . . .

Experts identified the metal in the man's ax. They X-rayed his equipment. They tested his skin and bones and the grass found with him by a method known as carbon-14 dating.

Then all the tests were performed again, and the results were compared with those done by other scientists.

Finally there was no doubt. The body was even older than Konrad Spindler had guessed. The Iceman was 5,300 years old — his was the oldest human body that had ever been found so well preserved.

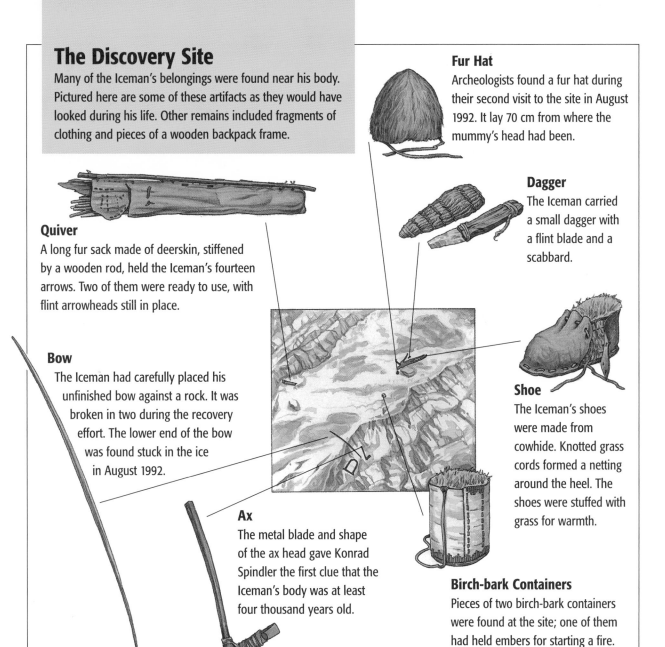

The Discovery Site

Many of the Iceman's belongings were found near his body. Pictured here are some of these artifacts as they would have looked during his life. Other remains included fragments of clothing and pieces of a wooden backpack frame.

Fur Hat

Archeologists found a fur hat during their second visit to the site in August 1992. It lay 70 cm from where the mummy's head had been.

Dagger

The Iceman carried a small dagger with a flint blade and a scabbard.

Quiver

A long fur sack made of deerskin, stiffened by a wooden rod, held the Iceman's fourteen arrows. Two of them were ready to use, with flint arrowheads still in place.

Bow

The Iceman had carefully placed his unfinished bow against a rock. It was broken in two during the recovery effort. The lower end of the bow was found stuck in the ice in August 1992.

Shoe

The Iceman's shoes were made from cowhide. Knotted grass cords formed a netting around the heel. The shoes were stuffed with grass for warmth.

Ax

The metal blade and shape of the ax head gave Konrad Spindler the first clue that the Iceman's body was at least four thousand years old.

Birch-bark Containers

Pieces of two birch-bark containers were found at the site; one of them had held embers for starting a fire.

WHAT IS CARBON-14 DATING?

Archeologists use carbon-14 dating to find out how old the remains of a plant, animal, or human are. Living things are made up of millions of tiny particles called atoms, and some of these are of a special kind called carbon 14. When a living thing dies, most of the atoms remain, but the carbon-14 atoms slowly begin to break down. By counting how many carbon-14 atoms were left in small pieces of the Iceman's bone and tissue, and in grass blades from his cape, scientists could tell that he died about 5,300 years ago.

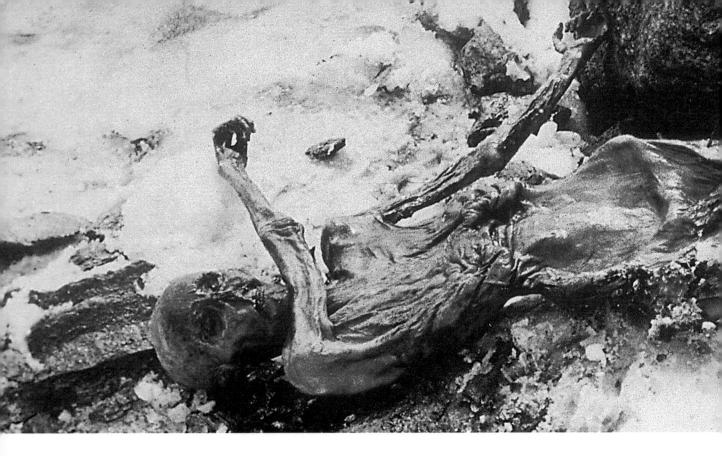

The Iceman lived during the late Stone Age. He died five hundred years before the Egyptians built the first pyramids. He was already dead more than three thousand years before Jesus Christ was born.

For the archeologists, the real work was just beginning. There were hundreds of questions that needed to be answered.

What were all of the Iceman's belongings, and how had they been used? Could the long piece of wood really belong to a bow that had measured more than 1.8 metres? Why did it have no bowstring, and why were the arrows that the Iceman carried unfinished? What was the meaning of the flat white bead, and what could it have been used for? Why were a sour berry and pieces of animal bone found near the body? And why had he carried fresh maple leaves in a birch-bark container?

Who *was* the Iceman? What was he doing so high up on the mountain, and how did he die?. . .

The Iceman and Us

Nobody knows for certain where the Iceman came from, or exactly how he died. He could have been a shepherd who was caught in a sudden snowstorm while bringing his herd down the mountain. He could have been hunting animals or looking for precious metals on the rocky mountain slopes. He could have been fleeing an enemy attack on his village. Maybe he was a religious leader who had gone up to the mountains to pray. Or perhaps he was just on his way to visit friends in a hilltop village.

The Iceman may not even have died alone. He could have been with other people. His friends may have survived and returned to their homes, or their bodies may have been ground up by the glacier. Or they may still lie under the ice, waiting to be discovered.

Already more than one hundred scientists from seven countries have studied the Iceman, probably considered cooked dog a pretty good meal. Cheese was also a new invention. They used deer antler and chipped stone for tools. They buried their dead in rows in huge stone tombs. Men were placed on their right side, females on their left side. People were buried with what they would need in the afterlife: axes, knives, and beads.

Since the Iceman died on his way to work, he wasn't buried in a tomb. Even so, the Iceman is the oldest, best-preserved body ever discovered.

A number of chance events made the Iceman's trip to the present possible.

Most creatures disappear shortly after they die, especially if they die and are left out in the open, as the Iceman was. Blood stops flowing in their veins, and the body starts to decay. Scavengers, such as vultures, rodents, and insects, dine on the decaying body. Flies lay eggs in its eyes. Microscopic organisms finish off what the bigger animals started. The weather, wind, and rain scatter what's left.

The Iceman avoided disappearing by chance. He died at the bottom of a gap between two large rock formations in the mountains. This shelter probably hid him from most large scavengers, such as vultures. By luck, it probably began to snow right as he died.

---

contemporaries People alive at the same time.

First Reaction

1. Which explanation of the age of the Iceman did you prefer — the one using words only, or the timeline? Why?

Look More Closely

2. Using the timeline, answer these questions.

   • How long before the first pyramid was built did the Iceman live?

   • Could the Iceman have seen or used a wheeled vehicle?

   • If the Iceman had been discovered 50 years earlier, would scientists have known how old he was? Why or why not?

Develop Your Ideas

3. Make a timeline about your life or your family. Indicate the dates of important events.

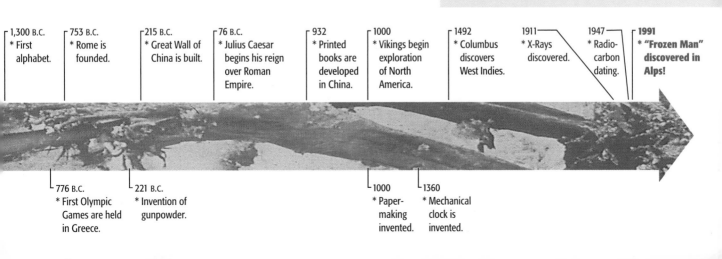

1,300 B.C.
* First alphabet.

753 B.C.
* Rome is founded.

215 B.C.
* Great Wall of China is built.

76 B.C.
* Julius Caesar begins his reign over Roman Empire.

932
* Printed books are developed in China.

1000
* Vikings begin exploration of North America.

1492
* Columbus discovers West Indies.

1911
* X-Rays discovered.

1947
* Radio-carbon dating.

1991
* "Frozen Man" discovered in Alps!

776 B.C.
* First Olympic Games are held in Greece.

221 B.C.
* Invention of gunpowder.

1000
* Paper-making invented.

1360
* Mechanical clock is invented.

Writing Historical Fiction

We can never know exactly what happened in the past, but it is interesting to try to imagine the lives of people who lived long ago.

Writers of historical fiction use the facts they know as the basis for their work. They then use their imaginations to dress up the facts and create interesting stories. The idea for a story often comes from something a writer has read, seen, or heard about a particular historical figure.

In this unit, you have read about several people who lived long ago. Here are some strategies you could use to write a story about one of them.

Getting Started

Choose a person who interests you. This person will become the main character in your story.

Prepare for your writing by drawing a circle map on a large piece of paper. In the centre circle, write all the thing things that scientists know for sure about your chosen character. This information should include whether the person is male or female and any objects found with the person. In the next circle, list all the things that are good guesses based

on those facts. For example, if you were writing about the girl from Herculaneum, you'd want to note that she was probably a slave. Complete the the outer circle by using your imagination to add details such as a setting and events.

Before you start writing your first draft, decide on a form for your story. This might be a play, a short story, or a script for a movie.

The First Draft

As you write your first draft, include both factual information and the imaginative details that will make those facts come to life for your readers.

Revising

Ask other students to read your draft and make suggestions about revisions. Ask your readers to suggest questions they have about your character that you could answer in your story.

When you revise, here are some things to check for.

- ☑ The factual parts are accurate.
- ☑ The imaginative parts are believable for the time and place.
- ☑ The main character seems like a real person.

Publishing and Sharing

Share your finished work with your friends and parents. If possible, read it aloud to younger children. A fictional story is a good way to interest young children in history.

Before You Read

Physical anthropologists don't just study ancient bones; sometimes they study more recent ones to try to solve crimes. This excerpt is about Dr. Michael Charney, a forensic anthropologist, or *bone detective*, who tried to solve a recent crime.

A skull was found in Missouri, U.S.A. in 1987. Police searched the area but found only a few other bones, a few strands of hair, a pair of tattered blue jeans, and a metal button that had been manufactured in Hong Kong. From those items, Dr. Charney managed to determine the height, weight, age, sex, and race of the person, but it was not enough to solve the crime. So he asked a forensic sculptor, Angela Nelson, to reconstruct the woman's face from her skull. Together they identified the victim and solved the crime.

Try This

In *Skeletal Sculptures*, Nita Bitner, another forensic sculptor, shows how Angela reconstructed the dead woman's face. Use the photographs to help you understand the steps in Bitner's work.

SKELETAL

by Donna M. Jackson

❶

Up till now, Dr. Charney's expertise in forensic anthropology has enabled him to take a few pieces of a skeleton and compile a portrait of a five-foot, 120-pound Asian woman in her mid-twenties. Still, that isn't enough to identify her. The dead woman's "face" needs to be brought back to life.

Reconstructing the likeness of a person in clay, using the skull as a guide, is a last resort at identification, Dr. Charney says. It gives police a new lead to follow, a visual clue that can be photographed and displayed in the media so that others can help solve the mystery.

Facial reconstruction in itself is not an identifying tool, he warns. The goal is to trigger

SCULPTURES

Plaster and clay bring a murder victim back to "life."

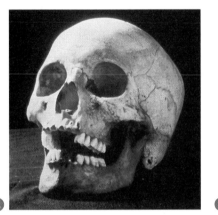

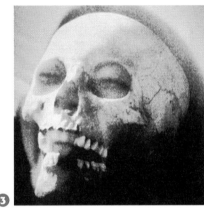

❶ A photograph sent to Dr. Charney by police for superimposition.

❷ A projected photograph of the victim's skull.

❸ The two images fit together, indicating a match.

someone to recognize the clay model and to then identify the person through scientific means.

"All that's needed is a general recognition that it looks like so-and-so," he says. "After that, you can go to the family, see if someone's missing, and proceed from there."

Before re-creating a face, Dr. Charney and forensic sculptor Nita Bitner search the skull for signs of disease, injury, and structural defects.

"We look for things that shouldn't be there," Bitner says. "Sometimes we find broken noses, cuts, or dentures." These affect the face's appearance and aid in the identification process. If the nose bone is curved to one side, for example, it's important to show it in the face because it's a distinguishing feature.

"We have to be careful, however, not to include anything that happened at the time of death," Bitner notes, "because it wouldn't be recognizable to others."

Age also influences how a face is built. Wrinkled skin, which might help illustrate an older person, is often incorporated into a sculpture for accuracy.

---

superimposition When one image is put on top of another.

After studying the Missouri woman's skull, Bitner makes a latex mold and pours a plaster cast. Now she's ready to sculpt the face.

First, she cuts thirty round rubber pegs into various lengths and glues them to the skull. Each peg, called a landmark, represents the thickness of the soft tissue (composed of muscle, fat, and skin) at different points on the face and helps her sculpt along the blueprint of the bone. These tissue depths, which differ for men and women of varying ages, were first calculated from corpses by nineteenth-century scientists and later updated.

Next Bitner connects the dotlike pegs with modeling clay. Starting at the forehead, she carefully works her way to the cheekbones, nasal area, chin, and mouth.

"I follow the face and do what it tells me to do," she says.

Once the "dots" are connected, Bitner fills in the spaces between the crisscrossing strips of clay and fleshes out the face. Now the prominent cheekbones of the Missouri woman become strikingly clear. Suddenly her broad face and delicate nose emerge.

As Bitner smooths the clay with her thumbs, the face develops like a photograph. When she sets the plastic brown eyes in their sockets and bends the lids around them, the sculpture springs to life.

After the front profile is complete, Bitner molds the ears and pats the face with a damp sponge. This lends a natural, textured look to the sculpture's "skin."

Because the Missouri woman is presumed to be Asian, Bitner adorns the model with a black wig and adds a scarf for a finishing touch.

The model is now ready to be photographed and publicized in the media so that millions of amateur detectives can help solve the riddle of her identity.

> "I follow the face and do what it tells me to do," she says.

The Face Is Familiar

. . . The State Highway Patrol releases photos of the Missouri woman's facial restoration to television and newspaper reporters. "The victim was buried in a shallow grave at a Boy Scout camp," reads the attached notice. "Anyone who can identify the woman . . . should call Sergeant Bizelli or Sergeant Conway at the Highway Patrol."

Three days later, the phone rings.

"The photo in the newspaper looks like a friend my wife and I haven't seen in several years," a man tells Sergeant Conway. "Her name is Bun Chee Nyhuis, and she's a native of Thailand."

The caller continues. He says Mrs. Nyhuis's husband told him that Bun Chee had left him and returned to Thailand. But the caller and his wife had found it hard to believe that Mrs. Nyhuis would leave without telling them.

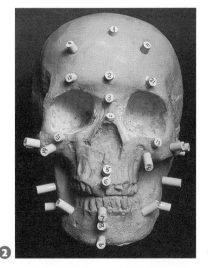

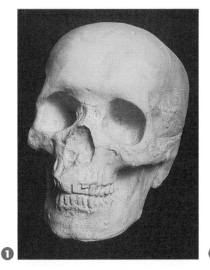

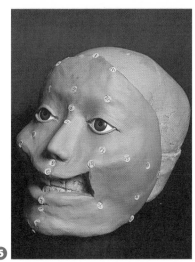

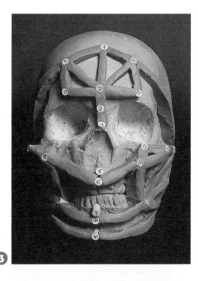

1. Plaster cast of the skull.

2. The landmarks in place.

3. Clay connecting the landmarks.

4. The first layer of clay.

5. Filling in the shape.

6. The finished face.

7. Hair and clothing make the model appear more lifelike.

Now, after seeing the photo, they are really worried about their friend. . . .

"Send me a photo of her," Dr. Charney said. "I'll superimpose it over the skull and see if it matches."

Police sent Dr. Charney two photos of Mrs. Nyhuis. One was rejected because she was looking down and the view of her face was limited. The other pictured her clowning around, playfully sticking out her tongue. This unusual pose made the superimposition more difficult for the bone detective, but not impossible.

Using 35-millimeter slides of the skull and the photograph, Dr. Charney projected the slide of the skull over the picture of the woman.

Unlike previous photos that had been sent to Dr. Charney's office for study, the photo of Mrs. Nyhuis fit perfectly with the image of the skull. The forehead, cheeks, chin, and nasal bone all snapped into place.

Mrs. Nyhuis also fit the profile Dr. Charney had developed by reading her bones: She was a petite thirty-three-year-old Asian mother of three who was about five feet tall.

"That's her," Dr. Charney told police. "This skull belongs to the woman in the photograph."

Witness From the Grave

With Dr. Charney's identification of Bun Chee Nyhuis, Missouri police began searching for evidence linking Richard Nyhuis to the murder of his wife. . . .

On July 17, 1989, police confronted Mr. Nyhuis near the area where his wife's remains were found. At first, Mr. Nyhuis stuck to the original story about his wife's disappearance. But after police pointed out several discrepancies, he broke down and confessed to killing her. . . .

The case went to trial, and Dr. Charney took the stand as an expert witness. Using slides, photos, and bone displays, the forensic anthropologist explained his findings to the court for more than three hours.

As events of the trial unfolded, the clay model of Bun Chee Nyhuis — now exhibited as evidence — eerily stood watch. "It was the only murder case I've tried where the victim came face-to-face with the accused in the courtroom," says prosecuting attorney Tim Braun.

Thanks to the testimony of the bone detective and other experts, it took a jury only two hours to find Richard Nyhuis guilty of first-degree murder. Today he's serving a life sentence without parole in a Missouri state prison.

> "It was the only murder case I've tried where the victim came face-to-face with the accused in the courtroom."

First Reaction

1. What in *Skeletal Sculptures* surprised you? Why?

Look More Closely

2. Forensic sculptors are both artists and scientists. In what parts of Nita's work was science most important? In what parts of her work was art most important?

Develop Your Ideas

3. The writer knows you have probably never watched a forensic sculptor at work. He helps you to understand the sculptor's work by including photographs. How do the photographs help you understand the stages of work done by a forensic scientist? Practise using this strategy in your own writing. Write an explanation of how to do something such as tying your shoe, or how to make something such as building a model. Draw a sequence of illustrations to help your readers understand the information.

   Have a friend read your draft copy and look at your illustrations. Ask your friend to give you some ideas to make your illustrations even more complete and clear.

4. Work with a partner to produce an audiotape or videotape interview explaining the work of a physical anthropologist, a forensic anthropologist, or a forensic sculptor. One of you can play the role of the interviewer, and the other the role of the scientist.

Before You Read

Have you heard of DNA testing? DNA is a substance in our cells that contains the genetic blueprint which determines our eye colour, hair colour, and other characteristics. Unless you have an identical twin, your DNA is different from everyone else, in the same way your fingerprints are different. If criminals leave tiny traces of body tissues like skin or hair, or body fluids like saliva or blood at crime scenes, police can use DNA testing to identify the criminal.

Animals have DNA, too. In *Convicted by a Cat*, animal DNA was used to catch a human criminal.

Try This

The journalist who wrote this magazine article answers the Five Ws — who, what, when, where, and why. As you read the selection, notice the answer to each question.

Convicted by a cat

Maclean's *May 5, 1997*

It is a murder case without precedent in Canada. And instead of the usual legal journals, it has attracted the attention of the British scientific journal Nature. That is because the evidence against a Summerside, P.E.I. man convicted of the second-degree murder of his former girlfriend included some unusual forensic science — analysis of DNA taken from the murderer's cat, Snowball. While analysis of human DNA is now common, scientists say the trial last year of Douglas Beamish is the first in which animal DNA was admitted in court. In part, that is why Beamish's lawyer, John MacDougall, has lodged an appeal. Testing cat DNA, says MacDougall is highly suspect. And, as he told jurors last July, "without the cat, the case falls flat."

It all started when Shirley Duguay disappeared in October, 1994. About three weeks later, the RCMP found a leather jacket covered with blood, which tests later showed was Duguay's. (Her body was discovered in May, 1995.) The jacket lining also contained several strands of white cat hair. A DNA test matched the hair to Snowball — and helped to link the jacket to Beamish. One of the scientists who tested Snowball, Marilyn Menotti-Raymond of the National Cancer Institute in Frederick, Md., said the methods used are accurate and were "acceptable for publication in two highly respected journals." True, but the appeal, which might be heard as early as November, could help determine whether the science is, in fact, legally sound.

First Reaction

1. What were your initial thoughts when you read *Convicted by a Cat?*

Look More Closely

2. To make sure you understand how the cat hair got from the cat to the DNA testing lab, briefly summarize the steps in your own words. Reread parts of the selection if necessary.

Develop Your Ideas

3. The convicted man's lawyer thinks the court should not allow animal DNA evidence. Why? What do you think?

Make Connections

Now you can demonstrate what you've learned in *Reconstructing Past Lives*. Read and think about the questions below.

Ask Yourself . . .

GOAL 1 Did you learn about the techniques authors, editors, and designers use to help you understand and remember information?

GOAL 2 Did you learn about strategies to use when reading information?

GOAL 3 Did you demonstrate a variety of ways to summarize and organize information to share your ideas effectively?

The following activities can help you think about your work in this unit and plan how to use what you've learned in the future. Each activity is keyed to the questions in *Ask Yourself . . .*

Look Back . . .

1. Review the selections in this unit. What information did you find most difficult to understand? What technique or text features helped you to understand the information?

2. Review *Tips On: Reading for Information*, page 133. Think back to the strategies you have learned in this unit. As well, think about the strategies you use to read for information in your other classes. Beside each of the following strategies, give an example of when you used the strategy. ➋

Strategy	When I Used It
Before You Read • Set a purpose for reading. • Preview the selection.	
As You Read • Monitored your pace. • Clarified meaning.	
After You Read • Summarized the information.	

3. Look back over the written, oral, and visual work you did in this unit. Which presentation do you think helped you most to learn new skills? Which form of presentation have you used in another subject area? Which form do you think you will use in future presentations? ➌

Show What You've Learned . . .

4. The selections in this unit use several techniques and various text features to help readers understand the information. Here is a chart listing these techniques and features.

Techniques & Text Features	Example
The Five Ws.	
Chapter Headings.	
Maps.	
Illustrations.	
Boxes of Additional Information.	
Timelines.	
Photographs or illustrations of steps in a process.	

Look through your textbooks in other subjects and identify one example of each technique or text feature. ❶

5. Choose a selection of informational material for independent reading. Pay particular attention to the strategies you use as you read it. What strategies do you find most effective? What strategies do you think you need to improve? ❷

6. Identify one personal goal for improving your reading of informational material. How can you work on this goal as you read for information in other subject areas? ❷

7. Imagine that the remains of you and your classmates, along with some of your possessions, are found and studied by scientists thousands of years from now. In a small group, develop a written piece, play, poster, or videotape that describes what the scientists find and what conclusions they reach about you and your classmates. ❶ ❸

It's Showtime!

An evil scientist. A secret formula. Can the two detectives solve the case?

This unit is about drama, and drama is about entertainment. A television show, a movie, and a play on a stage are all different types of drama. *The Mystery of the Stone Statues* — the play you'll read in this unit — is pure fun. As the curtain goes up, prepare to enjoy yourself!

SETTING GOALS

In this unit you can:

- Learn about the parts of a play and the people involved in a theatrical production.

- Learn techniques playwrights use to make plots and characters interesting.

- Find out how actors use speech, gestures, and movement to bring characters to life.

- Work in a group to plan and present an episode of *The Mystery of the Stone Statues.*

It Takes Many People *168*
by Sharon Sterling

A photo essay that shows who's involved in putting on a play.

The Mystery of the Stone Statues *174*
by Sue Alexander

A mystery spoof about an interesting collection of statues.

The Back Flip *192*
by Kathy Vanderlinden

In this article, an actor tells you how he gets *in character.*

Before You Read

Every play begins with a written *script*. The script is the author's idea of what the play is all about.

Many people work together to turn a script into a live production. The *cast* consists of the actors in the play. The *crew* are the people who handle everything else, such as lighting, wardrobe (costumes), and stage sets.

A production can be as simple as a few people using masks to represent different characters, or as elaborate as a full-scale musical with several stages and many special effects. In all plays, the cast and crew do their best to help the people in the audience imagine that they are watching people in another place or time.

Have you ever been part of a play or other performance? Imagine yourself on a stage now. Draw a cartoon of yourself that includes a thought bubble describing how you are feeling and why.

Try This

It Takes Many People is a photo essay. When you read a photo essay, pay equal attention to the pictures and the *captions* — the words with the pictures. Look for interesting details in the photos that aren't mentioned in the captions.

It Takes Many People

"Where's my wig?" "I want to hear the *fear* in your voice." "Bring up the amber." Here's a look behind the scenes at what it takes to put on a play.

by Sharon Sterling

1 The director is the team leader. The director decides many things, such as who is the best actor for each part and the mood of the play. It's the director's job to keep "the big picture" in mind — what is this play all about?

2 Actors get some of their information from the script, some from the director, and some from their own ideas about the character. An actor has to bring his or her character to life in a way that fits with the other characters and with the plot of the play.

3 The actors have to memorize their lines and practise their movements while they are on the stage. Each actor thinks about how his or her character would naturally move, the right facial expressions for each line, and the tone of voice and volume for each line.

It Takes Many People

Monty Greenshields, Banff Centre for the Arts

Don Lee, Banff Centre for the Arts

4 The costume designer decides what each character will wear. Even before the actor speaks, the costume tells the audience a lot about the character. Costumes must also be designed to allow the actor to move as required by the part. The set designer and costume designer must work together so that the set and costumes suit each other.

Don Lee, Banff Centre for the Arts

5 The set consists of all the physical features on the stage. The set designer works with the director to make sure the colours and shapes on the stage suit the mood of the play. Some parts of the set are for show, such as the background. Other parts, such as doors and stairs, must actually work and be safe for actors to use.

Monty Greenshields, Banff Centre for the Arts

Don Lee, Banff Centre for the Arts

6 There are also people who create the sound effects, operate the lights, make sure the props — the objects the actors handle — are in the right place, make the curtains open and close, help the actors change costumes, and so on. There's plenty to do.

7 *The result . . .* a polished performance!

First Reaction

1. Would you rather be cast or crew in a theatrical production? Which job interests you the most? Why?

Look More Closely

2. Make a *Putting on a Play* chart. Reread the descriptions of the different jobs involved in putting on a production. For each of the four main jobs described — director, actor, set designer, and costume designer — summarize the person's main contribution to the production.

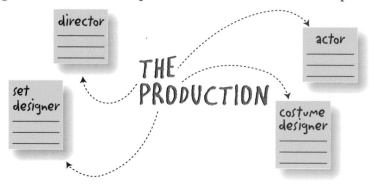

3. *It Takes Many People* explains that actors must think about nonverbal communication in order to bring their characters to life. Much of nonverbal communication involves the way things look. Briefly explain how the costume designer helps the actor interpret the character.

Develop Your Ideas

4. *It Takes Many People* gives you some information about producing a play. Research to find one or two more points to add to each box in your *Putting on a Play* chart. You can find information about producing plays at the library, on the Internet, or by talking to people who work in theatre. Before you start, look at the information you have already and decide what you'd like to know more about or what's missing. If you are doing library or Internet research, list some key words to help you in your search.

   During your research, you might find out about a job in theatre that isn't mentioned in *It Takes Many People*. If you want, you can add more boxes to your chart.

Tips On Nonverbal Communication

Verbal communication refers to your choice of words. *Nonverbal* communication is everything else that you do to get your message across, such as tone of voice, facial expressions, and *body language* — gestures, the way you stand, and how you move.

When you see a play, you are watching actors interpret characters. The playwright has written the lines for the actor to say — that's the verbal communication part. It's up to the actors, however, to make the characters believable as real people. The techniques used by actors to interpret characters are polished versions of nonverbal communication skills that you can use to make yourself understood in many different situations.

Here are some tips to keep in mind the next time you make a formal presentation or are asked to star in the class production of *Grease!*

Using Your Voice

- Speak clearly. Say the final consonants in all words.

- Speak loudly or softly, depending on the mood you want to create. Vary the volume of your voice to keep the listener interested.

- Use tone of voice to give feeling to your words. Emotions such as sadness, happiness, and anger are expressed more by tone of voice than actual words.

Facial Expressions

- Use facial expressions to support the meaning of your words, or to give another meaning. If you frown and say *yes*, the message is *no*.

- Use facial expressions to show feelings. Facial expressions, with no words at all, can clearly communicate emotions.

- When you use facial expressions, think about whether you want to be subtle or *ham it up* a bit. Exaggerated facial expressions usually create a humorous effect.

Body Language

- Think about how other people might interpret your posture or gestures. Some postures, such as hands on hips, give a clear message.

- Be aware of the mood you create by the way you move. For example, sudden, rough movements have a different meaning than slow, graceful movements.

The Mystery of the Stone Statues

Before You Read

A production of a play is based on a script. The elements of a script are similar to the elements of fiction.

- There is a *conflict* that an individual or group of *characters* must face.

- The *plot* is the series of events that happens as the characters try to resolve the conflict.

- The *setting* is where the action takes place.

A good script, like good fiction, usually has a believable setting and a conflict that starts you wondering what will happen. As the conflict builds, the plot moves forward and the play reaches a *climax*. After that, the conflict is usually *resolved*.

Many plays start with an *exposition*. In the exposition, the characters give the audience background information to help them understand the plot.

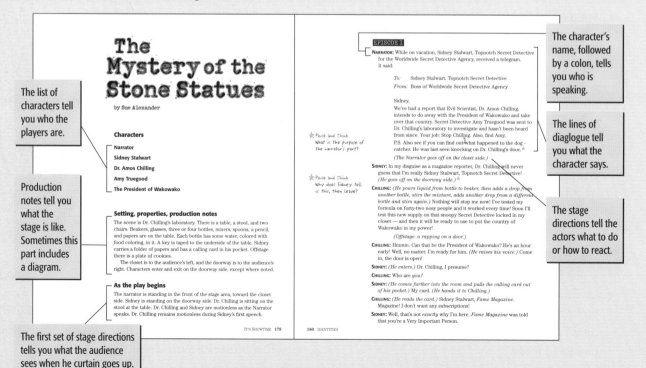

The list of characters tell you who the players are.

Production notes tell you what the stage is like. Sometimes this part includes a diagram.

The first set of stage directions tells you what the audience sees when he curtain goes up.

The Mystery of the Stone Statues

by Sue Alexander

Characters

Narrator
Sidney Stalwart
Dr. Amos Chilling
Amy Truegood
The President of Wakowako

Setting, properties, production notes

The scene is Dr. Chilling's laboratory. There is a table, a stool, and two chairs. Beakers, glasses, three or four bottles, mixers, spoons, a pencil, and papers are on the table. Each bottle has some water, colored with food coloring, in it. A key is taped to the underside of the table. Sidney carries a folder of papers and has a calling card in his pocket. Offstage there is a plate of cookies.

The closet is to the audience's left, and the doorway is to the audience's right. Characters enter and exit on the doorway side, except where noted.

As the play begins

The narrator is standing in the front of the stage area, toward the closet side. Sidney is standing on the doorway side. Dr. Chilling is sitting on the stool at the table. Dr. Chilling and Sidney are motionless as the Narrator speaks. Dr. Chilling remains motionless during Sidney's first speech.

IT'S SHOWTIME 179

★ *Pause and Think*
What is the purpose of the narrator's part?

★ *Pause and Think*
Why does Sidney tell us this, then leave?

The character's name, followed by a colon, tells you who is speaking.

The lines of diaglogue tell you what the character says.

The stage directions tell the actors what to do or how to react.

EPISODE 1

NARRATOR: While on vacation, Sidney Stalwart, Topnotch Secret Detective for the Worldwide Secret Detective Agency, received a telegram. It said:

To: Sidney Stalwart, Topnotch Secret Detective
From: Boss of Worldwide Secret Detective Agency

Sidney,
We've had a report that Evil Scientist, Dr. Amos Chilling, intends to do away with the President of Wakowako and take over that country. Secret Detective Amy Truegood was sent to Dr. Chilling's laboratory to investigate and hasn't been heard from since. Your job: Stop Chilling. Also, find Amy.
P.S. Also see if you can find out what happened to the dog - catcher. He was last seen knocking on Dr. Chilling's door.

(The Narrator goes off on the closet side.)

SIDNEY: In my disguise as a magazine reporter, Dr. Chilling will never guess that I'm really Sidney Stalwart, Topnotch Secret Detective! *(He goes off on the doorway side.)* ★

CHILLING: *(He pours liquid from bottle to beaker, then adds a drop from another bottle, stirs the mixture, adds another drop from a different bottle and stirs again.)* Nothing will stop me now! I've tested my formula on forty-two nosy people and it worked every time! Soon I'll test this new supply on that snoopy Secret Detective locked in my closet — and then it will be ready to use to put the country of Wakowako in my power!

(Offstage: a rapping on a door.)

CHILLING: Hmmm. Can that be the President of Wakowako? He's an hour early! Well, no matter. I'm ready for him. *(He raises his voice.)* Come in, the door is open!

SIDNEY: *(He enters.)* Dr. Chilling, I presume?

CHILLING: Who are *you?*

SIDNEY: *(He comes further into the room and pulls the calling card out of his pocket.)* My card. *(He hands it to Chilling.)*

CHILLING: *(He reads the card.)* Sidney Stalwart, *Fame Magazine.* Magazine! I don't want any subscriptions!

SIDNEY: Well, that's not *exactly* why I'm here. *Fame Magazine* was told that you're a Very Important Person.

180 IDENTITIES

The Mystery of the Stone Statues is a *mystery spoof*. This means that the play has the elements of a mystery, but the elements are used in a humorous and exaggerated way.

What do you think are the elements of a good plot for a mystery? What about the characters, setting, or conflict? Make a *Mystery Web* that shows your ideas. Meet with a partner and discuss your webs. You might want to revise your web after your discussion.

Try This

Here are some strategies to help you enjoy reading *The Mystery of the Stone Statues*.

- *Use your imagination.* Read the stage directions and think about what things might look and sound like. Try to hear the characters speak inside your head.

- *Spot the conflict.* As you read, ask yourself, "What is the problem the characters have to solve? When does the problem reach a crisis? How is the problem resolved?"

- *Look for clues.* The clues can be about the characters or the mystery. If a character does something odd, ask yourself, "Why? What does this tell me about the character?" Answering these questions will help you understand why characters do what they do.

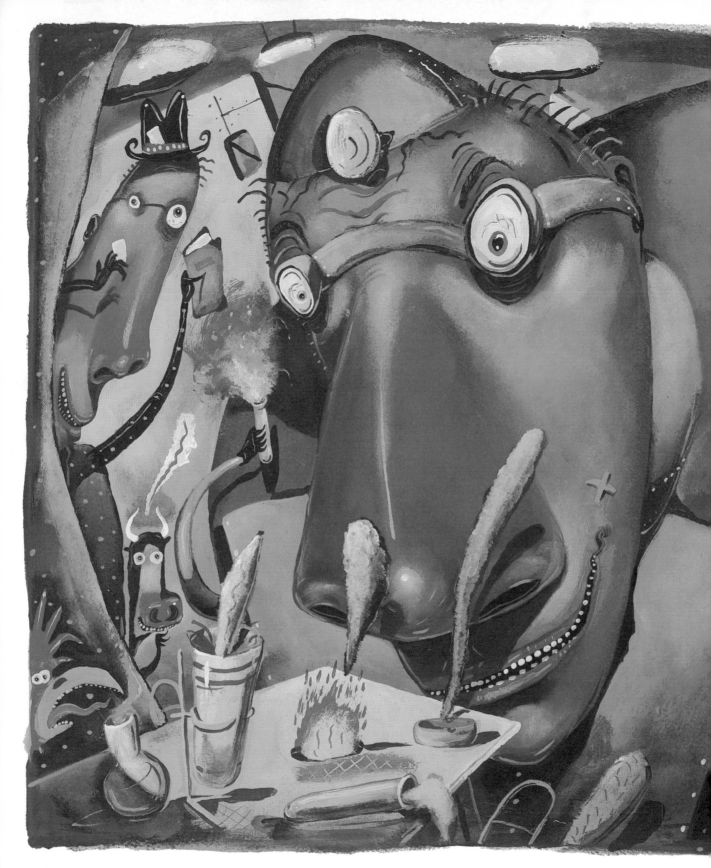

by Sue Alexander

Characters

Narrator **Sidney Stalwart** **The President of Wakowako**

Amy Truegood **Dr. Amos Chilling**

Setting, properties, production notes

The scene is Dr. Chilling's laboratory. There is a table, a stool, and two chairs. Beakers, glasses, three or four bottles, mixers, spoons, a pencil, and papers are on the table. Each bottle has some water, colored with food coloring, in it. A key is taped to the underside of the table. Sidney carries a folder of papers and has a calling card in his pocket. Offstage there is a plate of cookies.

The closet is to the audience's left, and the doorway is to the audience's right. Characters enter and exit on the doorway side, except where noted.

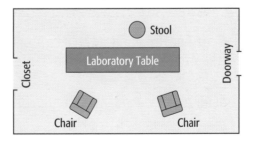

As the play begins

The narrator is standing in the front of the stage area, toward the closet side. Sidney is standing on the doorway side. Dr. Chilling is sitting on the stool at the table. Dr. Chilling and Sidney are motionless as the Narrator speaks. Dr. Chilling remains motionless during Sidney's first speech.

NARRATOR: While on vacation, Sidney Stalwart, Topnotch Secret Detective for the Worldwide Secret Detective Agency, received a telegram. It said:

> *To:* Sidney Stalwart, Topnotch Secret Detective
>
> *From:* Boss of Worldwide Secret Detective Agency
>
> Sidney,
>
> We've had a report that Evil Scientist, Dr. Amos Chilling, intends to do away with the President of Wakowako and take over that country. Secret Detective Amy Truegood was sent to Dr. Chilling's laboratory to investigate and hasn't been heard from since. Your job: Stop Chilling. Also, find Amy.
>
> P.S. Also see if you can find out what happened to the dog-catcher. He was last seen knocking on Dr. Chilling's door. ✶

(The Narrator goes off on the closet side.)

SIDNEY: In my disguise as a magazine reporter, Dr. Chilling will never guess that I'm really Sidney Stalwart, Topnotch Secret Detective! *(He goes off on the doorway side.)* ✶

CHILLING: *(He pours liquid from bottle to beaker, then adds a drop from another bottle, stirs the mixture, adds another drop from a different bottle and stirs again.)* Nothing will stop me now! I've tested my formula on forty-two nosy people and it worked every time! Soon I'll test this new supply on that snoopy Secret Detective locked in my closet — and then it will be ready to use to put the country of Wakowako in my power!

(Offstage: a rapping on a door.)

CHILLING: Hmmm. Can that be the President of Wakowako? He's an hour early! Well, no matter. I'm ready for him. *(He raises his voice.)* Come in, the door is open!

SIDNEY: *(He enters.)* Dr. Chilling, I presume?

CHILLING: Who are *you?*

SIDNEY: *(He comes further into the room and pulls the calling card out of his pocket.)* My card. *(He hands it to Chilling.)*

CHILLING: *(He reads the card.)* Sidney Stalwart, *Fame Magazine.* Magazine! I don't want any subscriptions!

SIDNEY: Well, that's not *exactly* why I'm here. *Fame Magazine* was told that you're a Very Important Person.

✶ Pause and Think
What is the purpose of the narrator's part?

✶ Pause and Think
Why does Sidney tell us this, then leave?

★ Pause and Think
How do Chilling's
actions help show the
meaning of his words?

★ Pause and Think
What does this tell
you about Sidney?

CHILLING: That's true. Very true. I AM very important. And after today I might just become the most important person in the world. *(He rubs his hands together gleefully.)* ★

SIDNEY: Is that so? In that case, I'm sure you won't mind answering some questions. After all, an interview in *Fame Magazine* will make you famous as well as important.

CHILLING: Hmmm. I've always wanted to be famous. *Fame Magazine*, you say? Come in, come in, Mr. Stalwart! Sit down! You understand that I'm a busy man. And I'm expecting a guest to arrive soon. But I can't deny the world the pleasure of knowing about me — so I'll answer your questions.

EPISODE 2

SIDNEY: I had a feeling you would. *(He sits down on a chair, opens his folder, and shuffles the papers. One paper drops to the floor, but he doesn't notice it.)* Let's see, that list of questions is here somewhere. *(He shuffles the papers some more and then pulls out a single sheet of paper.)* All right, first question. Are you ready?

CHILLING: Yes, yes. Get on with it. *(He coughs.)*

SIDNEY: *(He reads from the paper.)* Will you go to the movies with me on Saturday?

CHILLING: WILL I WHAT? *(He coughs again.)*

SIDNEY: I said, will you . . . Oh! Sorry, wrong paper. *(He looks carefully at it.)* Hmmm. Amy never did answer me. Now I know why. I forgot to give her the question. Hmmm. ★

CHILLING: Mr. Stalwart! Will you please get on with the interview! I'm a very busy man, you know. *(He coughs several times.)*

SIDNEY: That's a bad cough you have. Did you ever try molasses and honey? It's good for your throat.

CHILLING: *(He coughs once more.)* Never mind my throat. Just ask your questions.

SIDNEY: *(He shuffles the papers in the folder again.)* That list of questions is here somewhere. *(He pulls out another sheet of paper.)* Here it is. First question: Do you live by yourself?

CHILLING: Yes. I'm all alone here.

SIDNEY: *(He looks in his pockets and in the folder.)* Hmmm. What did I do with that pencil? *(He looks up.)* You wouldn't happen to have an extra pencil, would you?

CHILLING: For a reporter, you're not very well prepared. *(He takes the pencil from his table and gives it to Sidney.)*

SIDNEY: Thank you. Now where were we? Uh . . . you were saying that you were alone here.

CHILLING: That's right.

SIDNEY: Actually, that's wrong. I'm here.

CHILLING: But you're interviewing me!

SIDNEY: I know that. But I'm *here*. Now, did you leave out anyone else?

CHILLING: *(He shakes his head in confusion.)* No. *(He coughs.)*

SIDNEY: You really ought to do something about that cough. How about molasses and lemon?

CHILLING: Mr. Stalwart! Please! Just ask your questions!

SIDNEY: If you insist. *(He looks at the paper again.)* Next question. How many rooms are there in your house?

CHILLING: Forty-two.

SIDNEY: Are you sure about that?

CHILLING: Of course! I live here don't I?

SIDNEY: Yes. But since you didn't know how many people were here, you may be wrong about the number of rooms, too. And you want the readers of *Fame Magazine* to have the right answers, don't you?

CHILLING: With you asking the questions, I don't think that's possible. *(He sighs and shakes his head.)* Do you want to count the rooms yourself?

SIDNEY: Now that's an idea!

CHILLING: *(He sighs again.)* Very well, go ahead.

> *(Sidney gets up and goes out.)*

EPISODE 3

CHILLING: *(He comes out from behind the table and walks back and forth.)* There's something strange about that reporter. *(He looks down and sees the piece of paper that Sidney dropped.)* What's this? *(He bends down and picks it up.)* It's a telegram. *(He reads it to himself.)* Reporter, indeed! Another one of those snoopy Secret Detectives! Well, this new supply of my formula will take care of both of them! *(He goes back behind the table and mixes the water some more and then pours it into a glass.)*

SIDNEY: *(He enters.)* You were right. There *are* forty-two rooms. This is a very interesting house. Did you know that there are stone statues in every room?

CHILLING: Yes, of course I know! I — ah — *collect* them.

* Pause and Think
Do you think Sidney
has figured out what
these statues are?
Have you?

SIDNEY: All the statues have drinking glasses in their hands. And one of them has a dog-catcher's cap on. It's a special kind of collection, isn't it? *

CHILLING: Yes. A VERY special collection.

SIDNEY: The readers of *Fame Magazine* will want to know that. *(He opens his folder and pulls out a sheet of paper and pencil. Then he sits down and begins to write.)* Dr. Chilling collects stone statues.

CHILLING: You look a bit warm, Mr. Stalwart. Would you like a glass of iced tea? *(He holds out the glass he has filled.)*

SIDNEY: That's very nice of you. It *is* a bit warm in here. *(He takes the glass, but does not drink.)*

CHILLING: That should cool you off — for a long time.

SIDNEY: Er — I hate to be a bother, Dr. Chilling. But you wouldn't happen to have any cookies, would you? Iced tea tastes better when I have something sweet with it — like cookies.

CHILLING: Cookies! *(He sighs.)* Very well. I think there are some in the kitchen. I'll get them. *(He goes out, shaking his head.)*

EPISODE 4

SIDNEY: There must be a place where Dr. Chilling keeps all of his secrets. All I have to do is find it. *(He gets up and goes over to the laboratory table. He puts the glass down and begins to pick up the other things on the table and look at them and then put them down. He glances around the room.)* Hmmm. I didn't see that closet before. Maybe his secrets are in there. *(He goes to the closet side and pantomimes*

---

pantomime Acting without words or props. There is no door on the imaginary closet.

trying to open the door.) It's locked! Hmmm. If I were the key to the closet, where would I be? Of course! Under the table! *(He reaches under the table and gets the key.)* I'm not called Sidney Stalwart, Topnotch Secret Detective for nothing! *(He goes to the closet side and pantomimes opening the door. He backs up as Amy Truegood comes out of the closet.)*

AMY: Oh, Sidney! Thank goodness! I thought I'd never get out of there!

SIDNEY: I'm surprised at you, Amy Truegood. Hiding in that closet. You know this is no time to be playing hide and seek. Especially since the Boss is worried about you.

AMY: Sidney, I wasn't — oh dear. Sidney, there's no time to lose. The President of Wakowako will be here soon. We have to stop Dr. Chilling!

SIDNEY: I think you and the Boss are imagining things, Amy. Dr. Chilling seems to be a very nice man. He even noticed that I was warm and fixed me a glass of iced tea. And now he's gone to get me some cookies to have with it.

AMY: Sidney, Dr. Chilling is *not* nice! He's invented something that turns people into STONE STATUES!

SIDNEY: So *that's* where he got his collection.

AMY: And that's how he's planning to take over the country of Wakowako. Dr. Chilling is going to get the President to sign some papers giving him the right to rule the country. Then the President will be turned into stone, too!

SIDNEY: And Dr. Chilling will have another statue for his collection. Hmmm. I wonder what room he'll put it in?

AMY: Sidney!

SIDNEY: You're right, Amy. We're going to have to stop Dr. Chilling. *(He walks back and forth, picks up the glass as if to drink, then he thinks of something that he wants to say, and he lowers the glass.)* You know, all those stone statues have drinking glasses in their hands. What Dr. Chilling has invented must be in something you drink.

AMY: Like that iced tea.

SIDNEY: Yes. Like this iced . . . *(He looks at the glass in his hand and then quickly puts it down.)* I don't think I'm thirsty anymore.

AMY: Sidney, those papers must be in this room. Dr. Chilling had them in his hand when he shoved me in that closet. *(She goes over to the table and looks for them.)* Here they are! *(She picks them up and brings them over to Sidney.)* ✷

✷ Pause and Think
What does this tell you about Amy's abilities as a detective?

SIDNEY: *(He reads the papers to himself and then looks up.)* Very clever. What the President of Wakowako *thinks* he's signing is an agreement with Dr. Chilling to start a zoo in his country. But in the fine print . . .

AMY: Sidney! I hear footsteps! Dr. Chilling must be coming back!

SIDNEY: I'll think of something, Amy. In the meantime, you get back in the closet! And take these with you! *(He shoves the papers into her hand.)* Hurry! *(Amy runs off the closet side.)*

EPISODE 5

CHILLING: *(He enters, carrying a plate of cookies.)* Here are the cookies you asked for, Stalwart. *(He hands the plate to Sidney. Then he begins to cough.)*

SIDNEY: Molasses and buttermilk might help that cough. You really ought to try it. *(Offstage: a rapping on a door.)*

CHILLING: Ah! That must be my guest. Don't go away, Stalwart. Just — ENJOY — your tea. *(He goes out.)*

SIDNEY: That must be the President of Wakowako! I've got to get him out of here as quickly as I can!

CHILLING: *(He enters, followed by the President of Wakowako.)* Yes, indeed, Mr. President, you're right on time. Do come in. We can take care of our business right away.

PRESIDENT: But you have another guest! I do not wish to intrude.

CHILLING: He's no guest! He's a — um — ah — a magazine reporter, name of Stalwart.

PRESIDENT: *(He bows to Sidney who bows back.)* Mr. Stalwart.

CHILLING: Do sit down, Mr. President. *(He goes behind his table.)* Those papers are right here . . . *(He shuffles through the papers on the table.)* somewhere.

PRESIDENT: *(He sits down.)* Do not hurry yourself, Dr. Chilling. My journey has been a long one. I should welcome a few moments of rest.

SIDNEY: Er . . . would you like a cookie, Mr. President? They look very good. *(He offers the plate to the President.)*

PRESIDENT: Thank you. *(He takes a cookie.)* But really, I am thirsty. You will not mind if I drink this? *(He picks up the glass and begins to lift it to his mouth.)*

SIDNEY: Mr. President!

PRESIDENT: *(He lowers the glass and looks at Sidney.)* Yes?

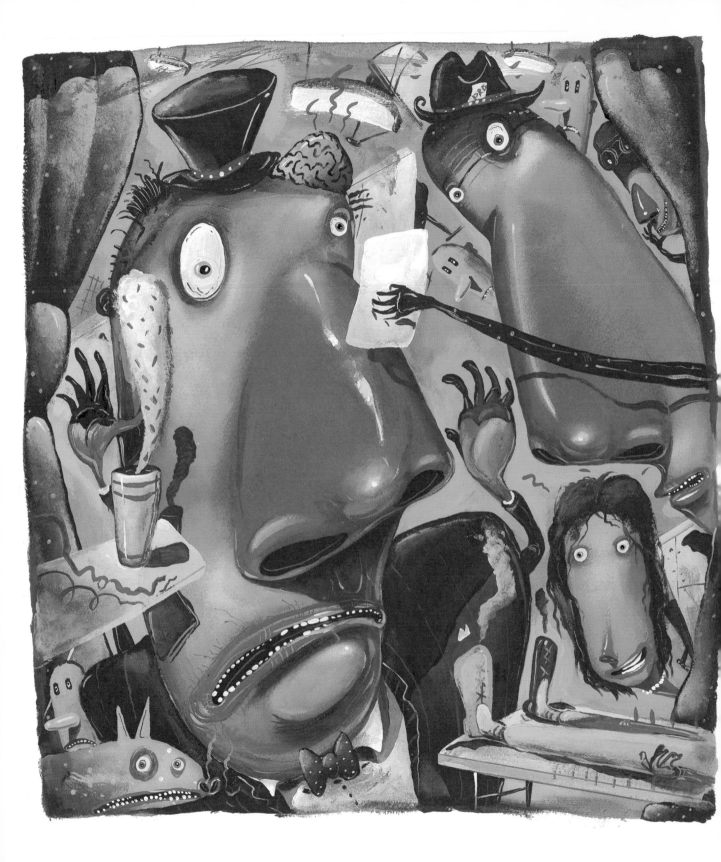

SIDNEY: Ah — Mr. President, you don't want to drink that.

PRESIDENT: I beg your pardon?

SIDNEY: There's a fly in it.

PRESIDENT: A fly? *(He looks into the glass.)* I don't see any fly.

SIDNEY: No? Well, it's one of those very small ones. You know, the kind that bite when you're not looking. I wouldn't want you to get a bite on your tongue. I had one once, right here . . . *(He sticks out his tongue at the President and points to a spot on it.)*

CHILLING: *(He coughs.)* Mr. President! I think that before you drink anything we ought to sign the papers.

PRESIDENT: Perhaps you are right, Dr. Chilling. *(He puts the glass down on the table.)* After all, that is why I am here.

CHILLING: *(He shuffles through the papers some more.)* I was *sure* those papers were here! *(He coughs again.)*

SIDNEY: Your cough is getting worse, Dr. Chilling. If I were you . . .

CHILLING: *(He coughs several times.)* That's one thing I can be thankful for, Stalwart. You are NOT me! Excuse me, Mr. President. I must have taken the papers into the other room. I'll go get them. *(He goes out, coughing.)*

EPISODE 6

SIDNEY: Mr. President, I would advise you to leave here — right now!

PRESIDENT: Leave? Right now? Mr. Stalwart, you overstep yourself!

SIDNEY: Perhaps I should introduce myself.

PRESIDENT: But we've already met!

SIDNEY: Not really. You met my *disguise*. Actually, I'm Sidney Stalwart, Topnotch Secret Detective!

PRESIDENT: Secret Detective?

SIDNEY: Yes. From the Worldwide Secret Detective Agency. *(He bows.)*

> *(Sidney goes to the closet side and pantomimes opening the door, and Amy enters.)*

SIDNEY: And this is Amy Truegood. She's a Secret Detective, too. Dr. Chilling had her locked in the closet.

PRESIDENT: *(He shakes his head in confusion.)* I don't understand any of this!

AMY: If you read the fine print on this contract that Dr. Chilling wants you to sign, you'll understand. *(She hands the papers to the President.)*

PRESIDENT: Let me see . . . *(He finds the place on the paper and reads aloud.)* "I hereby agree that the signing of this document shall make Dr. Amos Chilling the President of Wakowako and all the money in the treasury shall then belong to him." Why — why — this is terrible! Dr. Chilling must have stones in his head!

SIDNEY: Actually, stones in his bedrooms would be more accurate. Stones that once were PEOPLE.

AMY: Yes. That's what he was planning for me. And that's exactly what he is planning for you — as soon as you sign these papers.

PRESIDENT: *(He jumps up.)* Oh, no!

SIDNEY: Unfortunately, it's "oh, yes." Unless you leave right away, that is.

PRESIDENT: You are right, Mr. Stalwart. Good-bye, then, and thank you. *(He bows to Sidney who bows back.)*

AMY: I'll see you safely out, Mr. President. *(They go out.)*

EPISODE 7

CHILLING: *(He enters.)* That's strange. I can't seem to find . . . *(He looks around.)* Why, where's the President?

SIDNEY: Er . . . he couldn't wait. He had somewhere to go.

AMY: *(She enters.)* You have somewhere to go too, Dr. Chilling. To the POLICE!

CHILLING: *(He whirls around and sees Amy.)* You! How did you get out of the closet? *(He starts to cough.)* I'll fix you! *(He coughs several times.)* I'll fix you both! Snoopy Secret Detectives! *(He coughs very hard and several times at once.)* My throat! *(He grabs the glass and begins to drink.)*

SIDNEY: Dr. Chilling, don't drink that! It's your . . .

> *(Chilling drinks. As he does so, he slowly turns to "stone," becoming rigid. Both of his arms are bent at the elbows. From this moment on, he does not move.)*

AMY: It's too late, Sidney! He's become one of his own statues!

SIDNEY: So I see. Hmmm. *(He walks all around Chilling, looking at him.)* Amy, don't we owe the Boss a birthday present?

AMY: You mean? . . .

SIDNEY: Yes. A Secret Detective should never leave a stone unturned. Help me carry him out, Amy.

> *(They each lift Chilling by an elbow and carry him out.)*

First Reaction

1. What do you think of *The Mystery of the Stone Statues?* Is it mysterious? Funny? Just plain silly?

Look More Closely

2. What elements of a mystery are exaggerated for humorous effect in *The Mystery of the Stone Statues?* Start with your *Mystery Web* and make point-form notes of examples of humour and exaggeration for as many elements as you can.

3. One plot technique that playwrights use to keep the audience interested is to let the audience know something that the characters don't know. Reread *The Mystery of the Stone Statues*, looking for two examples of this technique. For each example, explain:

- What the information is.

- Which character reveals the information and to whom.

- Which character doesn't know the information.

- Why this information gets or keeps the audience's interest.

4. A script has three ways to tell you about a character:

- What the playwright says about the character.

- What the character says and does.

- What other characters say about the character.

Juliet, from Romeo and Juliet

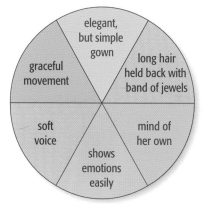

graceful movement · elegant, but simple gown · long hair held back with band of jewels · soft voice · shows emotions easily · mind of her own

Select two characters from *The Mystery of the Stones Statues* and make a pie chart of words to describe each character. Base your ideas on how the character is presented in the play, but use your imagination to add details. For example, any of the male characters could be female. Include information on gender, physical build, clothing, voice, ways of moving, and personality characteristics.

5. Write a mini-review of *The Mystery of the Stone Statues*. Your mini-review should briefly summarize the highlights of the plot and express your opinion of the script. Give the script a one- to four-star rating, one being the lowest, four the highest. Here's a sample to get you thinking.

Romeo and Juliet ☆ ☆ ☆

This sizzling love story gets off to a good start. The attempts of the two families to keep the lovers apart is charged with tension and excitement, but the plot twist at the end is a little hard to believe.

Develop Your Ideas

6. The author of *The Mystery of the Stone Statues* was having fun when she named her characters. *Dr. Chilling*, *Amy Truegood*, and *Sidney Stalwart* — all these names actually have other meanings. You can probably figure out the reasons for *Chilling* and *Truegood*, but you might need to look up *Stalwart* in the dictionary.

Invent three characters for an imaginary play. Name the play, then briefly describe each character and give her or him a name that describes the character's role or personality. Here's an example.

CAST OF CHARACTERS FOR

The Music Hall Mystery

Merry Twinkletoes

Merry is a twenty-two-year-old tap dancer. She dresses in short skirts and large bows. She giggles whenever she speaks and tends to fidget.

Solomon Sorrowful

Solomon is a tuba player, approximately thirty years old. He dresses in baggy corduroys and turtleneck sweaters. He is round-shouldered and shuffles when he walks.

---

7. In the *Mystery of the Stone Statues*, all the action takes place at one location and during one period of time. In your text, the script has been divided into episodes to make it easier to see the plot development — this is something a director commonly does when beginning to work on a play.

Longer plays are often divided into *acts* and *scenes*. Research a play that has acts and scenes and write a complete definition for *act* and for *scene*, using examples from the play you have found. You might find it helps to look up *act* and *scene* in a dictionary, or in a dictionary of literary terms.

Think About Your Mini-Review

8. Your mini-review consists of one or two sentences. Use this checklist to decide if there is anything you need to revise. Each sentence:

- ☑ Begins with a capital letter and ends with a period, question mark, or exclamation mark.

- ☑ Expresses a single complete thought, or two closely related thoughts in a compound structure.

- ☑ Is free of spelling errors.

If you'd like to find out more about sentences, see page 286 of *Help Yourself*. If you're not sure about the spelling of a word in your sentences, use your dictionary to check. If you're still having trouble, ask a classmate for advice.

Making Decisions in a Group

When you make decisions on your own, you have to collect information, consider your options, and decide what to do.

Groups follow the same general process. The big difference is that group decision-making involves discussing each aspect with others. This means your decisions benefit from the ideas of many people. The challenge is finding a way to get everyone to agree on the decisions.

Here's what every group member needs to know in order to meet the challenge and work effectively in groups.

Three General Stages

No matter what the group project, there are three things you need to do, in this order.

1. Agree on the task. What do you want to get done?

2. Agree on the process. How are you going to get the job done?

3. Actually get the job done.

Contributing to the Group

During discussions, do your best to:

- Stay focused on the topic.
- Contribute your ideas to the discussion.
- Express your ideas in the form of suggestions.
- Listen to the ideas of others.
- Contribute by adding to the good ideas of others.
- Express your disagreements politely.
- Encourage other people in the group to contribute.
- Do the jobs assigned to you on time and as agreed.

Follow the Leader

Most groups work better if there is a leader. You can make choosing a leader one of the things you do when you agree on the process. The leader's job is to help the members of the group stick to the points listed in *Contributing to the Group*. When discussing the process, the group should decide what role the leader will take if the group cannot come to a decision. Will there be a vote? Or will the leader decide the best thing to do?

Group Work

Use this scale to rate your group work.

0 - Didn't do this.
1 - Need some work in this area.
2 - Did a pretty good job of this.
3 - Yes!

- We began by agreeing on our goals.
- We worked out a process and then followed it.
- Each member of the group had an opportunity to contribute.
- We resolved disagreements without too much trouble.
- We got the job done.

Before You Read

In *The Back Flip*, the actor Colin Heath tells you what it's like for him when he does a *read-through*. A read-through is one of the first things the members of the cast do when they begin work on a new play. Everyone sits together, and each person reads out her or his part. The actors don't actually act out all the movements, but they do practise gestures and facial expressions and get to know how the other people in the group see the play. In rehearsals, the actors work on one small part of the play at a time. The read-through is important for giving the cast a sense of the play as a whole.

> Have you had any acting experience? How about role-playing?

> Make a list of five to ten things you think you'd need to decide about a character in order to play the part well. Consider nonverbal communication when you make your list. Under a separate heading, note ideas that occur to you, but you're not sure about.

Try This

The Back Flip is Colin Heath's description of his experiences as an actor. Before you read it, think about what information you'd expect to get from this type of article. How could Colin Heath's experiences help you revise your list of what you'd need to know to play a character?

The Back Flip

by Kathy Vanderlinden

*C*olin Heath is an actor, acrobat, director, and playwright with twenty years experience in Canadian theatre, including a two-year tour of the U.S. and Europe with the Cirque du Soleil. He has acted in a variety of plays, from Shakespeare productions to the musical Crazy for You.

He has written two plays, For Art's Sake (which has toured elementary schools in British Columbia) and Oliver Sudden's Instant Circus — a participatory circus for kids. Here's what he has to say about doing a read-through.

WHEN YOU START THE READ-THROUGH, YOU'VE already read the play to yourself silently. Then you read it together. At the first read-through, you're looking for the overall picture — it's hard to get specific about characters at that stage. You follow the main characters, look for the laugh points. It's the beginning of a huge adventure — you're getting acquainted with the other people in the production. People experiment with the meanings of their lines at first. The interpretation of the lines in the final production might be totally different than in the first read-through.

When you read silently, you often don't notice the little characters with few lines, but at the read-through, suddenly they're living and breathing. Sometimes the finest parts of a production come out of these little roles. Once, when I played in *The Merchant of Venice*, the actor playing the Prince of Aragon stole the show. You make the most of whatever you've got.

At the read-through you see the journey of the play — the overall structure. Once you start rehearsal, the next step after the read-through, you don't see that. You rehearse the play in bits — scenes from the end, beginning, middle. The read-through gives you the overall picture, even if it's fuzzy.

Also, the designer will show costume sketches and models of the set — that's exciting — to see what space you're going to fill. For me, it's impossible to create living characters until I have the costume — the mask.

A script is just a blueprint. Just as you can't see a building from the architect's drawings, you can't see a play from the script. Plays can go in so many directions from the script.

Personally, when I read a script, I'm looking for where I can fit in a back flip, how I can make the role more physical. The bottom line is that the play must be engaging — not necessarily make you laugh, but draw you in. You take something ordinary and make it extraordinary — that's what theatre is all about.

First Reaction

1. What parts of a read-through might you enjoy? Explain your reasons.

Look More Closely

2. In this article, Colin Heath tells you how he gets in character for a role. Think about these questions:

- Why is the article called *The Back Flip?*

- What is it about Colin Heath's skills and background that make him want to make a role more physical?

    Now review your list of things you think you'd need to decide about a character in order to play the part well. Reread *The Back Flip* to see if there is anything you'd like to add to your list.

3. An *analogy* is when a writer or speaker makes the meaning of something clear by comparing it to something else. Sometimes an analogy uses the words *like* or *as*. Then it is called a *simile*.

    Colin Heath uses an analogy to explain what a script is. He says: "Just as you can't see a building from an architect's blueprint, you can't see a play from a script."

    Write an analogy that explains why reading a play out loud helps you understand it.

Develop Your Ideas

4. Form a group to do a read-through of an episode of *The Mystery of the Stone Statues*. Use the information in *Focus On: Making Decisions in a Group*, page 190, to help you organize and carry out your group work.

Think About Your Read-Through

5. No play sounds perfect on the first read-through. That's why actors need rehearsals.

    As a group, discuss the following rating scale and rate your read-through. You might want to set a goal for improvement and try it again.

The Read-Through

Use this scale to rate your read-through.

0 - Not much sign of this.
1 - Lots of rehearsing still needed.
2 - Almost have it.
3 - This is starting to go very well.

- The characters sound as though they are actually speaking, not reading.

- It's easy to hear what each person is saying.

- Each character has a unique voice.

- The actors use facial expressions to interpret the meaning of their lines.

- The actors use body movement to interpret the meaning of their lines.

- The actors work together to create a whole episode.

- The mood (serious or humorous) is the same throughout the whole episode.

Make Connections

Now you can demonstrate what you've learned in *It's Showtime!* Read and think about the questions below.

Ask Yourself . . .

 GOAL 1 Have you learned about the parts of a play and the people involved in a theatrical production?

 GOAL 2 Have you learned about techniques playwrights use to make plots and characters interesting?

GOAL 3 Did you learn how actors use speech, gestures, and movement to bring characters to life?

GOAL 4 Did you improve your group skills while planning and presenting an episode of *The Mystery of the Stone Statues?*

The following activities can help you think about your work in this unit and plan how to use what you've learned in the future. Each activity is keyed to the questions in *Ask Yourself . . .*

Look Back . . .

1. When you read *The Mystery of the Stone Statues* to yourself, which of the reading strategies did you find the most helpful? The rating scale at the bottom of this page might help you think about it. ❶ ❷

Strategy	Very Helpful	Somewhat Helpful	Didn t Do It
• Used my imagination to help me understand what was happening.			
• Looked for conflict to help understand the plot.			
• Looked for clues to help understand why characters did what they did.			

2. Review *Tips On: Nonverbal Communication*, page 173. Write down three specific pieces of advice on interpreting characters you would pass on to a group about to do a read-through. ❸ ❹

Show What You've Learned . . .

3. You have just been asked to direct your school's upcoming production of *The Mystery of the Oak Island Treasure* by Canadian playwright Jim Betts. What are the three most important things you need to know about the play to do your job? Explain why each is important. ❶ ❷ ❸

4. Find a scene in one of your favourite mystery books and write it as a scene in a play. You'll probably have to write more dialogue. Make sure you follow the model for a script shown on page 174. ❶ ❷ ❸

5. Form a group and do a read-through of the scene you have written, or an episode from another play that you or your teacher select. ❹

Young People in History

What would you do to find out about an important event that happened before you were born? Read an old newspaper? Look in a history book? Ask someone who lived at the time?

In this unit, you will find out about the sinking of the *Titanic* and the relocation of Japanese Canadians during World War II. You will view and read different forms of information, such as photographs, drawings, newspaper clippings, and maps. You will also read the stories of Jack and Shichan, two young people who lived through the events. Linking the visual information with the personal points of view of Jack and Shichan, can help you increase your understanding of these events in history.

SETTING GOALS

In this unit you can:

- Use strategies to view and interpret materials such as photos, diagrams, pictures, and maps.

- Use the characters' points of view to help you understand the meaning of the stories and the times in history.

- Extend your own background knowledge and link this to new information to help you understand what you read.

- Organize and represent information and ideas in a variety of ways.

On Board the *Titanic* *200*
by Shelley Tanaka

This is a fictionalized account of the true story of seventeen-year-old Jack Thayer, a passenger on the *Titanic*.

A Child in Prison Camp *214*
by Shizuye Takashima

This is a personal narrative by Shichan, a Japanese Canadian who was forced to leave her home and move to a relocation camp in New Denver.

Tips On Viewing

Readers who simply glance at or skip over the visuals such as maps, photos, and charts may overlook important ideas. Here are some tips for viewing so you won't miss key information.

- **Know your purpose for viewing**
  Decide why you are viewing the materials. To learn new information? To answer a specific question? Adjust the speed and the way you view to suit your purpose.

- **Start with headings, titles, and captions**
  Pay attention to the headings, titles, and captions. Reading these first can provide you with an overall impression of the types of information you will find on the page.

- **Question the source**
  Based on what you already know, does what you see make sense?

- **Skim**
  When you need to find certain facts and details, don't reread every word or look again at every piece on the page. Instead, view the material selectively, the way you would look up a friend's number in the telephone book.

- **Draw conclusions**
  Consider the information. What's been left out? Could it be shown differently? What's your opinion?

- **Link the information**
  Remember what you have learned from viewing the materials and link this knowledge to new information you read or view on the same topic.

ON BOARD THE
TITANIC

(Above) The elegant Grand Staircase was the showpiece of the ship.

Before You Read

In 1912, the *Titanic* was the most luxurious oceanliner ever built. Jack Thayer was a seventeen-year-old passenger on board the *Titanic's* first voyage from England to the United States. Imagine some of his thoughts and feelings as he first wandered around the ship.

Have you ever heard of the *Titanic*? Draw and complete a KWL chart. Under the first heading, list everything you think you know about the *Titanic*. Under the second heading, record any questions you have. You can complete the third column later.

K	W	L
What I Know	What I Want To Know	What I Learned

If placed on her end, the *Titanic* would have been taller than any of the buildings of her day (right). The ship's gymnasium (below) had rowing machines, stationary bicycles and even a mechanical horse (left).

☆ WHITE STAR LINE R.M.S "OLYMPIC" ☆
COMPARED WITH VARIOUS FAMOUS BUILDINGS.

Try This

As you view and read *The Unsinkable Titanic*, pages 200 to 203, look for answers to the questions in your chart.

UNSINKABLE TITANIC

(Above) The *Titanic* was well named, for she was indeed a titan or giant among ships. Her enormous black hull weighed more than 50,000 tons. Her nine decks made her as high as an eleven-story building, and she had four huge funnels on top of that. It was claimed that the water-tight compartments in the hull made her almost unsinkable.

(Right) Jack Thayer.

(Left) A room for relaxation after a Turkish steam bath.

(Right) A luxurious first-class stateroom.

TITANIC

by Shelley Tanaka

Try This

Read pages 202 to 203 to understand what it was like for Jack Thayer, a passenger on the ship when it hit the iceberg.

Sunday April 14, 1912, 11:30 P.M.

Inside his stateroom, Jack pulled on his pajamas. Through the closed door he could hear his mother still talking excitedly about her dinner with the captain.

He opened his window a bit and looked out. The black sky hung over the ship like a magician's cape studded with diamonds. Jack had never seen so many stars.

There was a frosty chill in the air. All around him he could feel the soft, steady sound of the *Titanic's* engines churning from below.

Jack wound his watch. It was 11:40 P.M. He pulled down the crisp white sheets of his bed and turned out the light.

Just as he began to climb into bed, the ship swayed slightly, as if it had been nudged gently on the shoulder. The movement was so small that Jack almost thought he had imagined it.

Then the engines stopped. After feeling their gentle hum under his feet for four days, the silence seemed very peculiar. It was like being on a slow-moving train that had suddenly come to a quiet stop. For several seconds Jack could hear nothing but the faint whistle of the breeze coming through his porthole.

Then he heard running footsteps and muffled voices out in the hallway. The ship's engines started up again in a slow, tired way. A moment later, they stopped for good.

Something was definitely going on. Jack pulled a heavy coat over his pajamas and shoved his feet into slippers.

"I'm going out on deck to see the fun," he called to his parents.

"I'm putting on my clothes now, son," Mr. Thayer replied. "I'll be right up to join you."

Outside on the promenade deck, it was very cold — so cold that Jack could see the puffs of his breath. On a lower deck were a few boys from third class, kicking something around on the deck. It almost looked like a piece of ice.

"Is that you, Jack?" Mr. Thayer hurried out on deck. "One of the crewmen says we've hit an iceberg. Can you believe it?"

Jack squinted out into the black night. Iceberg? He couldn't see anything.

He and his father walked upstairs to the first-class lounge. Several passengers stood around looking puzzled.

Up ahead, Jack saw Mr. Andrews.

"Let's ask him," Jack said. "He'll know what's going on."

Mr. Andrews spoke in a low voice. "We have struck an iceberg. I'm afraid that the ship has not much more than an hour to live."

Jack and his father looked at each other in disbelief. Then, without a word, they returned to their rooms. Mrs. Thayer and her maid were already dressed. Jack put on two vests, a suit, and a coat. Then he tied on his bulky life jacket. He put his overcoat on top.

Back outside, other passengers were gathering. Some people had put on several layers of clothes and life jackets, like the Thayers. Others wore their pajamas or bathrobes. A few women were still wearing evening dresses.

Somewhere on deck, the band began to play lively dance music. Above the ship, distress rockets shot up into the sky and burst into colored balls like fireworks. It was almost like being at a party, except nobody talked much.

"Jack!" It was Milton Long. He rushed up to the Thayers like an old friend.

"You haven't organized another shipwreck for our amusement, have you?" Jack said.

Milton shook his head, but he wasn't smiling. He glanced at Mrs. Thayer. "They're loading the women and children into lifeboats. You'd better come."

ON BOARD THE
TITANIC

Before You Read

Jack and his friend have been watching the women and children being loaded into the lifeboats. He was unaware the *Titanic* had only sixteen lifeboats — room for half of the people on the ship. Jack was also unaware of the crisis in the boiler rooms that had been damaged by the impact of the iceberg.

On your KWL chart, record any new information you've learned or questions you have.

Try This

Look at the map, diagrams, and photographs on pages 204 to 205, *The Disaster*, to understand details about the sinking of the *Titanic*.

Deep inside the *Titanic*, in the boiler room nearest the bow, stokers were shovelling coal into the giant boilers. Suddenly water began to pour in from the side of the ship, nearly knocking them off their feet.

The stokers ran through the closing water-tight door, which was operated by a switch on the bridge. But they found water pouring into the next boiler room as well and headed for higher decks.

The mail room was also filling with water. Clerks tried to move sacks of mail up to the post office, but soon it, too, was flooded, with stray parcels and letters floating about.

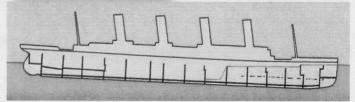

The iceberg scraped against six of the *Titanic's* "water-tight" compartments. They filled with water and, since they were not sealed at the top, water easily spilled from one to the next, ensuring that the *Titanic* would eventually sink.

A • —	J • — — —	R • — •	1 • — — — —
B — • • •	K — • —	S • • •	2 • • — — —
C — • — •	L • — • •	T —	3 • • • — —
D — • •	M — —	U • • —	4 • • • • —
E •	N — •	V • • • —	5 • • • • •
F • • — •	O — — —	W • — —	6 — • • • •
G — — •	P • — — •	X — • • —	7 — — • • •
H • • • •	Q — — • —	Y — • — —	8 — — — • •
I • •		Z — — • •	9 — — — — •
			0 — — — — —

In the radio room of the *Titanic*, Morse code was used to send and receive messages over the radio. Morse code is a system of dots and dashes which represent the letters of the alphabet as well as each number. When the ship was sinking, the SOS signal was sent out — three dots followed by three dashes, then three dots again.

THE DISASTER

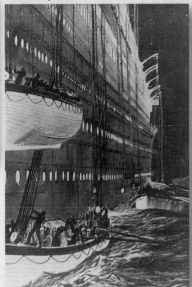

(Right) Captain Arthur Rostron, captain of the Carpathia.

(Above) The overturned lifeboat is the one that provided refuge for 28 people, including Jack Thayer.

(Right) Lifeboats are launched from the *Titanic*.

(Far right) A lifeboat from the *Titanic* is brought alongside the rescue ship *Carpathia*.

The route of the *Titanic* from Southampton to where she collided with the iceberg approximately 400 miles off the coast of Newfoundland. She sank near the edge of the undersea Continental Shelf, indicated below. The ice field that the *Titanic* encountered (inset) was 78 miles long.

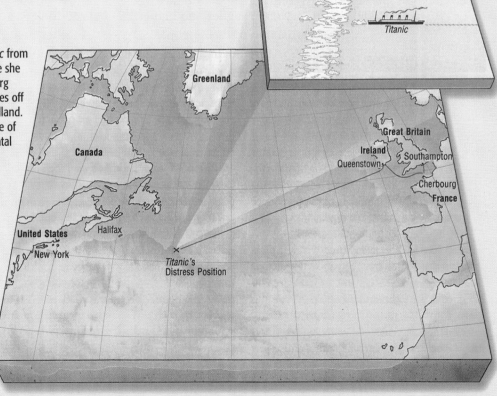

Try This

Read pages 206 to 207 of Jack's story to find out what Jack does as the ship sinks. Does he get in a lifeboat?

Monday April 15, 1912, 2:00 A.M.

Jack Thayer and Milton Long stood together on the *Titanic's* deck. The stern of the ship was tilted up out of the sea. The bow was covered with water, and inch by inch it crept higher and higher.

Nearby, hundreds of people watched the lifeboats being loaded. Most were men, who stood talking or smoking quietly. But there were some women, too, who refused to leave the *Titanic* without their husbands.

There was not much noise. Jack watched a father say goodbye to his two young sons. He kissed the older boy before thrusting him into the arms of a sailor who was waiting in a lifeboat. Thick ropes began to lower the boat to the sea. First one end lurched down, then the other. Then the father picked up the smaller boy. He was so bundled up that he could hardly

move. The man hugged his son and dropped him into the arms of a passenger in the boat. When he stepped back into the crowd, his face was so sad that Jack couldn't bear to look at it.

Another boat close by was already loaded with women and children. But the boat was too full. An officer said that one of the passengers would have to get out. A young woman stepped quickly out of the boat before anyone could stop her. Jack heard her voice clearly. "You are married and have families," she said firmly. "I'm not. It doesn't matter about me." Then she walked calmly away.

Several boats already sat in the water a short distance from the ship. Jack tried to see whether his mother and father were in one of them, but it was too dark. In the crush of the crowd, he had lost

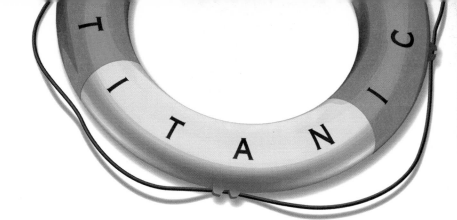

sight of them as they led Mrs. Thayer to the boats.

"Should we try to get in a boat?" he asked Milton. He knew they were supposed to wait until all the women and children were safely off the ship. But Jack had seen that a number of men had managed to get away.

Milton pointed to a group of white-coated bellboys and elevator boys standing quietly together. "If those fellows are waiting, then we should too."

Jack nodded. Some of the boys looked very young.

"What on earth is going on there?" he said.

Farther down the deck were a man in an evening suit and an elderly steward. They seemed to be tangled up in a pile of deck chairs and rope.

"They're tying chairs together."

As Milton said this, the old steward picked up a couple of chairs and heaved them overboard. The chairs floated gently on the glassy water.

Jack felt the back of his neck prickle with fear. What he had known in his heart for the past hour was suddenly very clear.

They would never get in a lifeboat. There simply weren't enough. The floating chairs were makeshift rafts. They would be something to grab on to when the time came to jump.

And that time was now. The ship lurched beneath them. The bow slowly began to slide into the water. From inside the ship came a rumbling sound, like the roar of an express train passing over a steel bridge.

Jack threw off his overcoat. He and Milton climbed up on the railing. In the background, the ship's orchestra was still playing.

"This is it, Jack," Milton said, holding out his hand.

"I'll be right with you," Jack said. He didn't want to say goodbye. "Good luck."

Milton let go. Then Jack, with a push of his arms, jumped into the sea.

The icy cold of the water went through his skin like a knife. The ocean pulled him down and down. Jack used every ounce of his strength to struggle back to the surface.

Then he swam as hard as he could away from the ship.

ON BOARD THE TITANIC

(Left) Mr. Ismay, president of the company that owned the Titanic, confirmed the Titanic's fate in this telegram.

The New York Times.

"All the News That's Fit to Print."

TITANIC SINKS FOUR HOURS AFTER HITTING ICEBERG; 866 RESCUED BY CARPATHIA, PROBABLY 1250 PERISH; ISMAY SAFE, MRS. ASTOR MAYBE, NOTED NAMES MISSING

The Lost Titanic Being Towed Out of Belfast Harbor.

CAPT. E. J. SMITH, Commander of the Titanic.

PARTIAL LIST OF THE SAVED.

Before You Read

Jack hung on to an overturned boat and watched as the *Titanic* went down. He and other survivors were rescued by another ship that had heard their distress call. More than 1500 people died in the disaster.

Meet with a partner. Read your questions to each other and discuss possible answers. Record any new information or questions in your KWL chart.

Try This

Examine the telegram, diagram, newspaper article, and current photo of the *Titanic* to learn about some of the results of the disaster. Who died? Who was saved? How did people around the world find out about the disaster?

Who died and who was saved?

First-class passengers

Second-class passengers

Third-class passengers

Crew

The diagram shows the many lives lost on the Titanic (figures in black) compared to the few who were saved (figures in red).

- *Do I have the materials I need to complete the representation?* Often the materials that are available will determine how you choose to represent your thinking. For example, you may want to make a papier mâché mask, but the only materials you have are clay and paper. Be realistic.

- *What visual forms of representing work well for me?* There may be some visual forms of representing that you've used. There may be ones that you haven't tried. Explore a variety of forms so you can find out what works for you.

Self-Assessing Your Representation

When you complete a visual, you have something you can look at, think about, and self-assess. This is an opportunity to ask yourself questions such as:

- What did I want to communicate?

- Was I able to communicate clearly?

- Did I choose an appropriate form? If not, what might have been a better choice?

- What part of the representing was the easiest to do? What part was the hardest?

- What could have improved my visual representation?

- What suggestions would I give to a friend who is going to try this form of representing?

Keeping a Record

You may want to keep a record of the different visual forms you have used to show what you know.

A Child in Prison Camp

Before You Read

This story is about Shichan, a young Japanese Canadian who lived in Vancouver during World War II. Her family was forced to leave their home and relocate in a camp in the interior of British Columbia.

Think about being forced to leave your home without ever knowing if you could return. What would you worry about leaving behind? What questions would you be asking? Who would you turn to for help? Write the word *relocation* in a circle and record your thoughts, feelings, and questions.

won't go!   I'd hate to move

RELOCATION

what about our dog?   sad   miss my friends

Try This

Skim pages 214 to 219, *Relocation*, to find out what happened to thousands of Japanese Canadians. When and where did the relocation take place? Why did this happen?

Japanese people were taken to relocation camps in trucks and buses.

Women and children lived in buildings at the Exhibition Grounds in Vancouver.

LOCATION

(Right) Little "Shichan" with playmates in Vancouver on the eve of World War II.

The Bearer, whose photograph and specimen of signature appear hereon, has been duly registered in compliance with the provisions of Order-in-Council P. C. 117.

Vancouver
(Date) March 12 1941.

JAPANESE NATIONAL

Issuing
Officer _____

INSPECTOR J.C.M.P.

(Above) Special identification card for a Japanese Canadian.

(Below) Japanese men in trains, on route to the interior.

Japanese to be moved off west coast

Feb. 26, 1942

OTTAWA – All Japanese will be moved from the west coast, the government announced today, to quell fears of Canadian Japanese assisting an invasion.

Previously, the government ordered all Japanese men between 18 and 45 moved more than 160 kilometres inland and their fishing fleet impounded. Today, the government expanded that action to include all people of Japanese origin.

Some government members opposed the mass evacuation. It's also believed the army and the RCMP see no reason to impose it. But the government has been under tremendous pressure from the public and politicians in B.C.

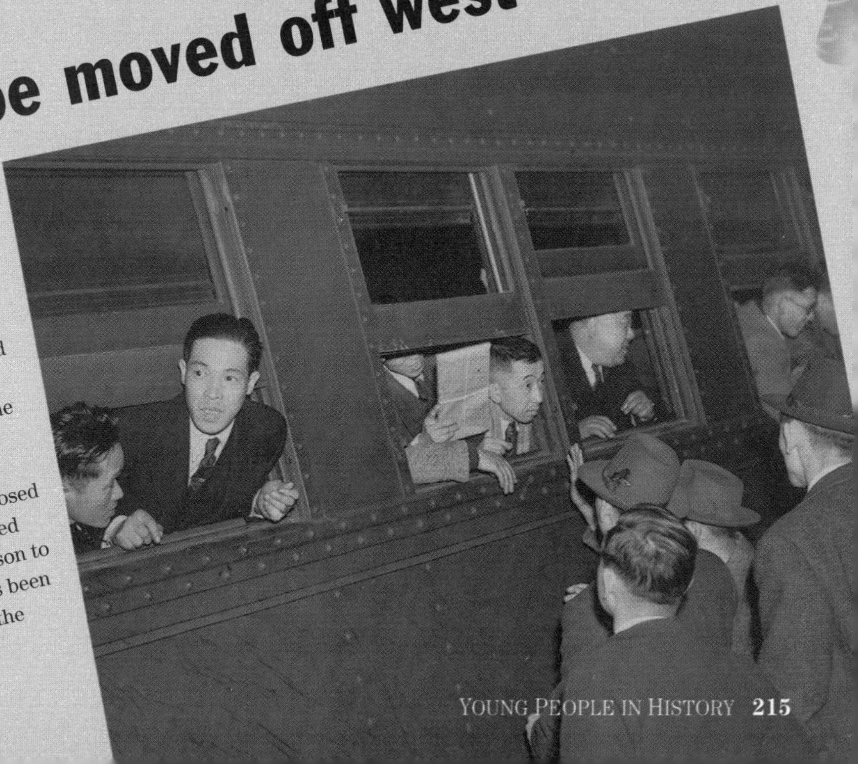

Try This

Read Shichan's story to learn about the relocation from her personal point of view.

Find out why:

- Shichan's dad and brother were taken away.

- The government took their home.

- Many of their friends were living at the exhibition grounds.

A Child in Prison Camp

by Shizuye Takashima

Vancouver, British Columbia
March, 1942

Japan is at war with the United States, Great Britain, and all the Allied Countries, including Canada, the country of my birth. My parents are Japanese, born in Japan, but they have been Canadian citizens for many, many years, and have become part of this young country. Now, overnight our rights as Canadians are taken away. Mass evacuation for the Japanese!

"All the Japanese," it is carefully explained to me, "whether we were born in Tokyo or in Vancouver, are to be moved to distant places. Away from the west coast of British Columbia — for security reasons."

We must all leave, my sister Yuki, my older brother David, my parents, our relatives — all.

The older men are the first to go. The government feels that my father, or his friends, might sabotage the police and their buildings. Imagine! I couldn't believe such stories, but there is my father packing just his clothes in a small suitcase.

Summer 1942

From March to September, 1942, my mother, my sister Yuki, and I are alone in Vancouver. David, our brother, is taken away, for he is over eighteen and in good health. It's hard for me to understand.

Now our house is empty. What we can sell we do, for very little money. Our radio, the police came and took away. Our cousins who have acres of berry farm had to leave everything. Trucks, tractors, land, it was all taken from them. They were moved with only a few days notice to Vancouver.

Strange rumors are flying. We are not supposed to own anything! The government takes our home.

Mother does not know what to do now that father is not here and David too is taken. She does not speak very much; she is too worried how we are to eat with all her men gone. So finally, Yuki goes to work. She is sixteen; she becomes help for an elderly lady. She comes home once a week to be with us and seems so grown up.

Many Japanese families who were moved from the country towns, such as Port Hammond and Steveston on the west coast of B.C., are now housed in the Exhibition grounds in Vancouver, waiting to be evacuated.

One very hot summer day mother and I visit a friend of hers who has been moved there.

A Visit to the Exhibition Grounds

The strong, summer July sun is over our heads
as we near the familiar Exhibition grounds.
But the scene is now quite different from the last time I saw it.
The music, the rollercoasters, the hawkers
with their bright balloons and sugar candy are not there.
Instead, tension and crying children greet us
as we approach the grounds. A strong odor hits us
as we enter: the unmistakable foul smell of cattle,
a mixture from their waste and sweat.
The animals were removed, but their stink remains.
It is very strong in the heat. I look at mother.
She exclaims, "We are treated like animals!"
I ask mother, "How can they sleep in such a stink?"

She looks at me. "Thank our Lord, we don't have to
live like them. So this is where they are.
They used to house the domestic animals here.
Such a karma!"

As we draw close to the concrete buildings, the stench
becomes so powerful in the hot, humid heat,
I want to turn and run.

September 1942

An End to Waiting

We have been waiting for months now. The Provincial
Government keeps changing the dates of our evacuation, first
from April, then from June, for different reasons: lack of
trains, the camps are not ready. We are given another final notice.
We dare not believe this is the one.

Mother is so anxious. She has just received a letter from father
that he is leaving his camp with others; the families will be
back together. I feel so happy.

We rise early, very early, the morning we are to leave.
The city still sleeps. The fresh autumn air feels nice.
We have orders to be at the Exhibition grounds.
The train will leave from there, not from the station
where we said good-bye to father and to David.
We wait for the train in small groups scattered
alongside the track. There is no platform.
It is September 16. School has started. I think
of my school friends and wonder if I shall ever see
them again.

We haven't eaten since six in the morning.
Names are being called over the loudspeaker.
One by one, families gather their belongings and
move towards the train. Finally, ours is called.
Yuki shouts, "That's us!" I shout, "Hooray!"
I take a small bag; Yuki and mother, the larger
ones and the suitcases. People stare as we walk
towards the train. It is some distance away.
I see the black, dull colored train. It looks
quite old. Somehow I had expected a shiny new one.

Yuki remarks, "I hope it moves. You never know
with the government." Mother looks, smiles,
"Never mind, as long as we get there. We aren't
going on a vacation; we are being evacuated."

Bang . . . bang . . . psst . . . the old train gurgles,
makes funny noises. I, seated by the window,
feel the wheels move, stop, move, stop.
Finally, I hear them begin to move in an
even rhythm slowly.

I look out the dusty window.
A number of people still wait their turn.
We wave. Children run after the train.
Gradually, it picks up speed. We pass the gray
granaries, tall and thin against the blue Vancouver sky.
The far mountains, tall pines, follow us
for a long time, until finally they are gone.

Mother sits opposite; she has her eyes closed,
her hands are on her lap. Yuki stares out the window.
A woman across the aisle quietly dabs her
tears with a white cloth. No one speaks.

A Child in Prison Camp

Before You Read

On September 16, 1942, Shichan and her family left Vancouver for New Denver. She had no idea what to expect at the camp they were being sent to. Where would they stay? What would they eat? Would she go to school? How long would they have to stay there? Would they ever go home to Vancouver again?

Try This

Life in the Camp provides a glimpse into the daily lives of people in different relocation camps. View and read the photos and paintings with a partner. Talk about what life might have been like in these camps.

(Top) Community kitchen in an internment camp.

(Right) "I go to the lake for the last time with mother to rinse our clothes. She is singing, she looks so happy."

THE CAMP

(Top) Class photo from a school in an internment camp at Limon Creek.

(Left) "In the distance I see the Red Cross people with another man. They stop to watch us with our buckets of water."

A Child in Prison Camp

Try This

Read pages 222 to 225 to discover what life was like for Shichan in the camp in New Denver.

New Denver, British Columbia
September, 1942

We are in a small village called New Denver, 700 miles
from Vancouver, high in the Rocky Mountains.
Father is waiting with Mr. Fujiwara, our cousin,
at the small gas station. They both are brown from the sun and
seem to look different. I wonder if I too have changed in six
months. I feel suddenly shy as I peer at my father from the bus.

Before me is our little new home.
It looks like a summer bungalow with shingle roof,
one square chimney in the middle, a door in the
center, two windows on either side of the
door. It still smells sharp from the wood.
I wrinkle my nose every time I go inside.

Everything is so new. All in a row, the same
houses are built; some are larger than others but all have the
same number of rooms, three; two bedrooms and
a kitchen in the center. The larger houses are for
families with many children. We, being only
four, have only one small bedroom and a kitchen
which we share with another family,
Mr. and Mrs. Kono. They have one child.

Our Home at Night

It is night. We light our two candles.
There is no electricity.
The frail, rationed candles burst into life and
the darkness slinks away. The smell of fresh-cut trees
burning fills the room. The pine pitch cracks and pops
in the fire. I sit, watch my mother.
She places the rice pot on the black, heavy stove.
The wet, shiny pot begins to sputter.

"Rice tastes better cooked like this," she says,
smiles. Her dark eyes look even darker in this semi-light
and I feel love for her. "Why?" I ask. "Because natural
fire is best for cooking. Food tastes pure."
I stare at the now boiling rice and wonder why all people
do not use such stoves and fuel.

School
October 1942

During the last week of October, school starts for the children, but
just from grades one to eight. "The Japanese people do not need,
nor do they deserve, higher education." Father says that's what they
told him and Mr. Sumi, our other spokesman. So Yuki cannot finish
high school and she has only one more year to go. Mother is very
upset. Yuki remains quiet.

We are taught by older girls. They have completed high school,
but they are not "teachers," so everything is noisy and very
un-school-like at first. We are given correspondence sheets
which we must follow. I don't like this at all. We have books, too,
but nothing else. I miss the familiar desks and my school friends.

Each class or grade has one house.
I hear the wind outside. Our black, pot-fat
stove is in the far corner of the room. I cannot
feel the heat. I bend forward and put my hands in
my overcoat. I wish I were home. I sigh.

Winter 1942

We must walk over a mile into the village for our drinking water.
The water from the lake is not pure, and we are told not to drink
it, even if it is boiled. There is an old mine up in the mountains, not
far from New Denver. It is closed now, but during the time it

was open, the miners threw all their waste into the stream which gushes down the mountains into Lake Slocan. It's the same small river we cross going into the village. So even if this lake looks lovely and pure, the water is not to be drunk. We may use it only to do our dishes and wash our clothes. Almost every day, we go to fetch drinking water. Yuki goes most of the time now that I am at school.

Today is Saturday. We hear that the Red Cross people are touring the camps because of so many complaints by our parents. Everybody is excited. "Maybe we'll have water in our homes," I tell mother. She smiles and hands me the kettle.

A Visit from the Red Cross

Yuki and I walk with care along the path.
The snow-covered ground feels soft under our feet.
I carry a kettle full of water; Yuki, two buckets.

In the distance I see the Red Cross people and another
man, all in smart winter overcoats with briefcases.
They stop to watch us with our buckets of water.
We walk past them. The sharp-faced man with glasses
and dark, wavy hair stares at us, turns
to his companion, and says: "And they have no light?"

The old, dark Japanese man, the veteran who had shouted
at father, comes towards the small group of men.

He says aloud in English, "And we have to read and work
with candles, and they're rationed. Our eyes are ruined."

Several days later, father brings home a lamp.
So does Mr. Kono. One coal-oil lamp
has been given to each family by the Security
Commission. It is hard to believe. Father has a
triumphant smile on his face as he carries it in.
He places it gently on our table, "Well, this
will give us better light to cook and read."
Seeing me staring, he adds: "Since you do most
of the cooking, Shichan." I laugh and look at
the new lamp. Its metal parts shine, the round
glass part looks lovely. I touch it with my hands.

Mother comes closer, smiles. She too looks happy.

That night the lamp glows merrily on our dinner table.
The sharp smell of oil is pleasant. I look across
the room. Mrs. Kono's lamp is glowing on her table
too. Kay-ko is staring at it. She turns, smiles and
presses her eyes together. "I have one too!"
she shouts from her seat. Her father says,
"They're eating. You mustn't shout." I only nod.
Father says, "One step at a time. Next comes
water . . . in the spring."

Early Summer 1943
Water at Last!

June arrives, and with it, water! At last, water is piped into the
main streets of the whole camp. It is hard to believe. All spring
I watched the men lay the long, shining pipes, then put in little
taps, one for each eight or nine houses. We still have to go outside
to draw water but now we do not have to walk so far. Our
tap is quite close to our house. It will be especially good for the
old people. They found it so hard to fetch water. Often, the
younger boys brought it for them. Father is pleased. He fought
so hard for this.

I look at the pipe with the small, shining tap.
It appears from the ground like a metal snake.
I wonder if it will really work. Slowly, I turn it.
A pause, then the clear water gushes out.
It crashes down into the narrow wood sink
placed flush to the ground. I shout, "It works!" The water
keeps pouring out. Mrs. Kono is standing
with her two buckets. "My," she exclaims, "it's like
a dream. One forgets so quickly that we had water
in our homes at one time. Isn't this wonderful,
Shichan?" We smile at each other with pure happiness.
I touch it with my hands, let it flow through my fingers.

A Child in Prison Camp

Before You Read

Shichan and her family remained in New Denver for three years. In August 1945, they heard the terrifying news that the United States had dropped an atomic bomb on Hiroshima and Nagasaki. The war was over. Again the family waited to see where they would be sent. Would they have to go to Japan? Could they return to their home in Vancouver?

Try This

View and read pages 226 to 229, *After the War.* Pay special attention to the dates of the newspaper articles. Find out what happened to the Japanese Canadians.

Ottawa, June 13, 1950. On the recommendation of royal commissioner Justice H.I. Bird, the government announces it will pay $1,222,829 in conscience money to Japanese forcibly evacuated from their west coast homes during WWII.

Japanese won't be deported after all

Jan. 24, 1947

OTTAWA—The Liberal government today revoked the 1945 orders-in-council permitting the deportation of Japanese Canadians, despite vehement opposition by MPs from British Columbia. While Japanese Canadians and white liberal-minded activists alike consider revocation of the arbitrary orders a moral victory, a larger hurdle still remains to be conquered.

The controversial exclusion order restricting Japanese Canadians from changing place of residence without a permit remains in effect, and they are still prohibited from fishing off B.C.'s coast. In 1941, 90 percent of Canada's Japanese lived there. Now, only 33 percent do.

THE WAR

Japanese Canadians to get compensation

Sept. 21, 1988

OTTAWA—After four long years of negotiations, the federal government today agreed to terms of compensation for 21,800 Japanese Canadians forcibly removed from the west coast during the Second World War. The settlement, signed by Prime Minister Brian Mulroney and Art Miki, president of the National Association of Japanese Canadians, could pay as much as $300 million in individual compensation. It provides those still living whose property was expropriated or who were interned with $21,000 each. The government has also agreed it would provide a $12-million community fund.

A Child in Prison Camp

Try This

As you read, think about Shichan's feelings as she and her family are forced to move again.

August, 1945

We hear the terrifying news. The atomic bomb! Father and mother are silent. The end of the war.

At last the war with Japan is at an end! We are not surprised, we have been expecting it for months now. It hits the older people very hard. They are given two choices by the Canadian Government: to sign a paper and renounce their Canadian citizenship and return to Japan, or to remain here and be relocated elsewhere.

My mother and I just wait, hoping. Then one day,
out of the blue, father says quietly: "We go east!
I've placed an application. We sign to go to Toronto."
He speaks quietly, more to mother than to me.
"It is useless to return now. My family, God knows
where they are, if any are still alive. I'm glad it's over.
We'll just have to start again. It won't be easy for us."
He looks strange. He rises from his chair quickly
and walks out. I feel sorry for him. The atomic bomb
has upset everyone deeply, too. It seems so wrong.
Mother looks at me, smiles. Her eyes beam.
"See, I told you, I told you he would see the sense
in remaining here. We can't return to Japan.
They have nothing now, no food, clothes,
houses for their own people. Here, we have each other.
Write to Yuki and David." I write immediately.

Yuki is in Hamilton, Ontario, living with another friend. I am so happy, so is mother. Father is quiet.

Mother and I begin to pack. I have to leave many things I have grown to love behind.

September 1945

It is almost three years to the day since we left Vancouver. The papers for us to leave for the east come through. This is our last week in New Denver.

I go to the lake for the last time with mother
to rinse our clothes. The water is still warm.
I swish the white sheets in the clear water.
Mother is wringing the clothes. She is singing,
she looks so happy. I wonder what David will
look like. I say, "We won't be doing this in Toronto."
Mother sighs, stops, looks at the mountains.
"All in all, Shichan, the three years have not been very hard,
when you think of all the poor people who have been
killed and hurt, and now the suffering in Japan."

Mother and I look out into the distance.
The morning mist is slowly
rising from the lake. It looks like it is on fire.
The sun's rays try to seep through the mist.
Everything looks all misty and gray-yellow. I know
I shall remember this beautiful scene,
doing our chores for the last time, with nature
all-giving and so silent. Mother bends her frail body,
continues to rinse the clothes. I go back to helping her.
There is warmth between us, and I feel her happiness.

Moving Away

We are moved east from the camp, only to find that the
quota of Japanese permitted to live in Toronto is filled, and
there are no jobs.

My parents go to work as domestic servants
for an American family in Oakville, father to do the gardening
and cooking and mother to clean and care for their small
child. I cannot join them, father tells me gently, for the estate
is in the country and there are no schools nearby. He talks it
over with mother and David, and I am to go to Hamilton to
stay with Yuki. David will send the money for me to continue school.

An Afterword

This story is based on what actually happened to me and other
people of Japanese origin living in Canada. Names of individuals and
certain incidents have been altered, in some cases to give anonymity to
those involved (not all of us care to be reminded or questioned about
those painful years); in other cases to keep the account simple.

Nineteen years passed following World War II before that night in
1964 when Prime Minister Lester Pearson admitted the "black
mark" against Canada that the internment of Canadians of Japanese
origin represented. It would take another twenty-four years before
another Prime Minister, Brian Mulroney, speaking officially in the
House of Commons condemned the internment and offered financial redress.

The compensation was long, long overdue. Of the 22,000 unjustly
interned, only 12,000 were alive to be "compensated."

At war's end, almost 4,000 of us were expelled from Canada or
chose to go to war-ravaged Japan rather than remain in the uncertain
hostile climate here. Their citizenship was revoked.

My parents and most of their generation are gone. It is for us to
remember and never allow such injustice to occur again.

Shizuye "Shichan" Takashima
Toronto, Canada, 1989

First Reaction

1. Did you know about this time in Canadian history before you read *A Child in Prison Camp*? Write some of your thoughts. You may want to use the following statements to get you thinking.

   - I didn't know that . . .

   - I was surprised to find out . . .

   - I'm still wondering about . . .

   - The part I want to find out more about is . . .

Look More Closely

2. Reread Shichan's story. Make a list of the significant events that occur in Shichan's life from 1942 to 1945. Graph these events on a positive and negative chart like the one below. You may want to add sketches to the graph.

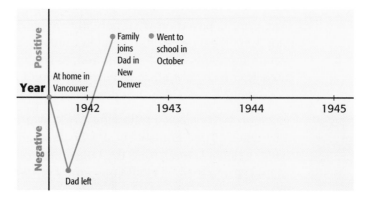

3. Visuals such as pictures and charts can often give a reader more information than a page full of words. Select one visual that provided you with new information or that really made you think about this time in history. Examine it closely. Make a list of the facts that you learned from it and the ideas it gave you.

4. Reread the headlines on the viewing pages. Write five of your own headlines about different events that took place. Be brief and use words that will catch the reader's attention.

5. Reread Shichan's story and select lines where she expresses her feelings. Divide your paper in half and record your favourite lines on the left side. On the right side, give the reason why you selected each line.

Favourite Lines

1.

2.

3.

My Reasons

1.

2.

3.

Develop Your Ideas

6. At the end of her story, Shichan writes, "My parents and most of their generation are gone. It is for us to remember and never allow such injustice to occur again." Today, the story of the Japanese Canadians is kept alive in the town of New Denver. There is a small museum where people can go to see the houses and artifacts of the relocation camp. You might want to write for information to:

Nikkei Memorial Center
Kyowakai Society
Box 273
New Denver, B.C.
VOG 1SO

7. The expression "Time heals all wounds" suggests that everything will be fine and forgotten once a period of time has passed. This event told by Shichan took place over fifty years ago. Do you think time will heal all wounds in this case? Write your explanation.

Make Connections

Now you can demonstrate what you've learned in *Young People in History*. Read and think about the questions below.

Ask Yourself . . .

 Did you use various strategies to view and interpret materials such as photos, diagrams, pictures, and maps?

 Did you use the characters' points of view to help you understand the meaning of the stories and the times in history?

GOAL 3 Did you extend your own background knowledge and link this to new information to help you understand what you read?

GOAL 4 Did you organize and represent information and ideas in a variety of ways?

The following activities can help you think about your work in this unit and plan how to use what you've learned in the future. Each activity is keyed to the questions in *Ask Yourself . . .*

Look Back . . .

1. Review the *Tips On: Viewing*, page 199. Make a list of the strategies. Use the following symbols to indicate your use:

   *   Used often.

   ✓   Used sometimes.

   χ   Have not used this strategy yet. ❶

2. Which personal story (Jack Thayer or Shichan) did you learn more from? Which were you able to understand best? Which story appealed to you? Give your reasons. ❷ ❸

3. Think about what you knew before you read this unit. Think about what you know now. Use the following sentence structure to show how your thinking changed about the *Titanic* disaster and the relocation of Japanese Canadians.

   I used to think, . . . but now I know . . . ❷ ❸

4. Look at the different ways you represented your ideas in this unit. What two representations are your best? Explain why. What other ways of representing would you liked to have seen as choices? ❹

Show What You've Learned . . .

5. Think of visual materials you view and read outside of school. Describe the strategies you use to view and interpret these materials. Compare your strategies with a partner's strategies. ❶

6. If you had to choose between reading the personal stories of survival or looking at and reading the viewing pages, which would you choose? Explain why. ❷

7. Select a topic that interests you.

- Record what you know about the topic and any questions that you have.

- Collect and organize your information.

- Decide on the best visuals to convey your ideas.

- Display your visual representation for others to see.

    Refer to *Focus On: Representing Using Visual Forms*, on page 212, and complete a self-assessment of your work. ❸ ❹

Imagined Worlds

What kind of poem captures your attention? What type of poem could make you laugh? What kind could make you cry? What poems trigger your imagination?

Poets have a way of reaching a world that is inside all of us — a world of emotions, thoughts, and imagination. One way poets help readers connect to this inner world is by creating powerful word pictures. They also use techniques to emphasize what they want their readers to imagine, think about, and understand.

In *Imagined Worlds*, poems are arranged in three clusters. Two are on specific topics — sports and animals. The third cluster presents a variety of forms of poetry.

SETTING GOALS

In this unit you can:

- Use a variety of strategies to understand and enjoy different poems.

- Recognize when and why poets use techniques including imagery, personification, simile, alliteration, rhythm, and rhyme.

- Write your own poems expressing your feelings, thoughts and observations using a variety of forms and experimenting with techniques poets use.

- Select, present, and share favourite poems with others.

Sports 235

Though the Afternoon Was Freezing Cold 236
by Arnold Adoff

Photo Finish 237
by Lillian Morrison

Foul Shot 237
by Edwin A. Hoey

Sometimes In Centre Field on a Hot Summer Evening 238
by Arnold Adoff

The Sidewalk Racer or On the Skateboard 239
by Lillian Morrison

A View From the Mound 239
by Gordon and Bernice Korman

High Jumper 239
Don Welch

Animals 242

Mosquito 242
by Veronica Eddy Brock

Polar Bear 243
by Iglukik

Cat 243
by Valerie Worth

Whalesong 244
by Judith Nicholls

Lone Dog 245
by Irene McLeod

Something Told the Wild Geese 245
by Rachel Field

Flies 245
by Valerie Worth

Form 248

My Room is a Mess . . .248
by Sharon Lange

Life Lesson 248
by Don Raye

Kite 249
Anonymous

Concrete Cat 249
by Dorthi Charles

Young and Old 250
by Robert Bennett

Galaxies and Atoms . . .250

A lady from near Lake Louise 251

So you found some fresh tracks in the snow 251
by David McCord

Desert 251
by Brian Powell

Depression 251
by Dale McMechan

Tips On

Here are some strategies to help you understand and enjoy the poetry you read.

- **Think about personal experiences, thoughts, and feelings.** Does this poem remind me of anything I know about? How does the poem make me feel? What part expresses how I feel and what I believe?

- **Notice poetic forms and techniques.** What images come into my mind when I read the poem? What words or sounds stand out for me?

- **Read a poem more than once.** What new ideas and questions do I have now? What parts don't I understand?

- **Consider different meanings for the poem.** What might this poem be about? Does the title or the ending give me any special clues? Could the poem have other meanings?

Before You Read

Poets choose their words carefully to create pictures in the mind of the reader. This technique is called *imagery*. Poets appeal to the senses and emotions to let the reader see, hear, and feel what they have experienced.

Think of a time when you played or watched a particular sport. What sounds did you hear? What do you remember? What feelings did the athletes and spectators show? What happened before and after the game?

Try This

As you read, think about the images the poet uses to help you picture the sport. Reread each poem, noticing specific words the poet selects and the pictures you imagine.

SPORTS

Though the Afternoon Was Freezing Cold

by Arnold Adoff

Though the Afternoon
Was Freezing Cold,
there was a place
in front of the
                    nets
that was soft and
            dug out.

When the cleats
on my right foot
caught in that
            soft
                    mud,
my body was
already turning
    and following
        into the play.
My right knee
                    was
            turning
                too.

Only my foot
remained
            unmoving
in its unmoving
            shoe.

This was definitely not a good day.

Photo Finish

Lillian Morrison

Two track stars ran a race
and neither knew defeat.
Both perished at the tape;
they called it a dead heat.

IMAGERY

Creating vivid word
pictures for the
reader by:

- Choosing words
  carefully.
- Capturing the
  imagination.
- Triggering
  emotions.
- Appealing to the
  senses — sight,
  smell, sound,
  touch, and taste.

Foul Shot

Edwin A. Hoey

With two 60's stuck on the scoreboard
And two seconds hanging on the clock,
The solemn boy in the center of eyes,
Squeezed by silence,
Seeks out the line with his feet,
Soothes his hands along his uniform,
Gently drums the ball against the floor,
Then measures the waiting net,
Raises the ball on his right hand,
Balances it with his left,
Calms it with fingertips,
Breathes,
Crouches,
Waits,
And then through a stretching of stillness,
Nudges it upward.

The ball
Slides up and out,
Lands,
Leans,
Wobbles,
Wavers,
Hesitates,
Exasperates,
Plays it coy
Until every face begs with unsounding screams —

And then
        And then
                And then,

Right before ROAR-UP,
Dives down and through.

Sometimes in Center Field On A Hot Summer Evening,

Arnold Adoff

Sometimes   in   Center   Field   On   A   Hot   Summer   Evening,

when the air is so still   you almost think you hear
                        the mosquitos warming up their engines,
and
our pitcher is getting
the o p p o s i t i o n
to dribble grounders
        to the infield.

                    . .

Sometimes in center field
I have a hard time staying
                    awake.

I never
close my eyes and fall asleep standing
            but my mind will m o v e
                        o v e r
to last week's extra-inning loss
and my wild toss to third to
                    help
them score and help *us* lose that g a m e .

My throat is always too dry
    and there is always an ice
                    cold
                    can
    of pop waiting at the cold
                    pop
                    stand.

One   time a   well-hit   ball   popped into   my   outstretched   hand
                before I could remember my name.

The Sidewalk Racer or On the Skateboard

Lillian Morrison

Skimming
an asphalt sea
I swerve, I curve, I
sway; I speed to whirring
sound an inch above the
ground; I'm the sailor
and the sail, I'm the
driver and the wheel
I'm the one and only
single engine
human auto
mobile.

A View From the Mound

Gordon and Bernice Korman

Two cunning pitches are all that I've got.
One is a fastball; the other is not.

My first is like lightning; the speed is intense;
My second the batter pokes over the fence.

But I do not fear this, for he'll never know
Which one of my pitches I'm planning to throw.

High Jumper

Don Welch

Looking at the standards,
he closes his eyes,
imagining himself
a pure figure following
a precise mathematical arc
away from the bar,

    and everything slows,

then he begins to close,
whip back,
gathering speed
as he shoves the weight
of the universe down through
his foot, his right arm
shot upward in a victory signal
toward heaven,
his right shoulder suddenly liquid
bending in on itself,
his hip bones thrust out —

    then everything stops,

and his body, floating,
knows nothing more
than itself,
is calm, severe, solid, yet light

    (what *is* the sum of the length
    of ourselves?)

and stays that way,
with no time over it,
hurrying.

First Reaction

1. Write the numbers from one to six down the side of your paper. Beside the number *1*, write the title of the poem that gives you the clearest picture of the sport it describes. Rank all the poems in order from clearest to the least clear.

Look More Closely

2. Look back at the poems in this cluster and think about the type of designs, sketches, logos, photos, or cartoons that might add to a reader's enjoyment and understanding. Create your own illustrations for this cluster.

3. Poets create images by appealing to our senses. Draw an outline like the one below. Fill in the spaces with words and lines from any of the poems that connect to a particular sense.

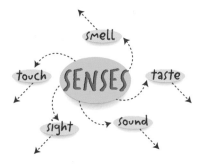

4. Record five of your favourite lines from the poems you have read. Include the titles of the poems. Work with a partner and talk about the lines that each of you preferred.

Develop Your Ideas

5. Work by yourself or with a partner to write a sports poem. You might begin by finding a picture of a favourite sport, observing a game, or remembering a sport you participated in. List all the ideas that come to mind about the action, equipment, feelings, sounds, and movement. Arrange your ideas on a page to look and sound like a poem.

6. Poems are meant to be read aloud. Find a sports poem that you like. Practise reading it aloud, then share it with a small group. Ask your audience to draw pictures of what they are thinking about as you read the poem.

Think About Your Poem Presentation

7. After you present your sports poem to a small group, answer the following questions. Ask someone who listened to your poem presentation to do the same.

- Did I read the poem at a pace the audience could follow?

- Did I pause at appropriate places within the poem?

- Did I read the poem with feeling, but without overdramatizing?

- Did I use a natural voice?

Write a personal goal for the next time you present a poem.

Next time I present a poem, I will remember to . . .

Aimals

Poets choose words with care. They pay special attention to the sound as well as the meaning of the words they select for their poems. They use poetic techniques to help the reader imagine and bring their subjects to life.

Recall a time when you have observed an animal. It could be a pet, an animal you have watched in the wild, or one you have seen on television. Think of what this animal:

• Reminds you of.

• Can be compared to.

• Makes you think of.

Tell a partner about the animal you are thinking about.

Try This

As you read, pause and think of details the poet observed about the animal. Read the information box *Techniques for Writing Poems*. Reread the poems and notice how the techniques help your understanding.

Techniques for Writing Poems

Simile
Makes a comparison using *like* or *as*.

Personification
Gives human qualities to an object, an idea, or an animal.

Alliteration
Repeats beginning consonant sounds.

Rhyme
Repeats the same sounds at the end of two or more lines of poetry. Words can also rhyme within a line of poetry.

Rhythm
Repeats a stress or beat in a regular way in a line of poetry.

Mosquito

Veronica Eddy Brock

The mosquito is a hateful pest
Who'll never give you any rest.
He'll put your bravery to the test,
In his not so silent quest.

He buzzes round; you know he's near.
He's in your hair; he's in your ear.
His stinger's sharp, just like a spear.
He bites so deep it brings a tear.

When weather's hot and damp and still,
They hurry out to drink their fill.
I longed for summer with a will,
So when they bite I shall kill.

Polar Bear

Iglukik
Translated by T. Lowenstein

I saw a polar bear
on an ice-drift.
He seemed harmless as a dog, — Simile
who comes running towards you,
wagging his tail.
But so much
did he want to get at me
that when I jumped aside
he went spinning on the ice.
We played this game of tag
from morning until dusk.
But then at last, I tired him out,
and ran my spear into his side.

cat

Valerie Worth

The spotted cat hops
Up to a white radiator-cover
As warm as summer, and there,

Between pots of green leaves growing,
By a window of cold panes showing
Silver of snow thin across the grass,

She settles slight neat muscles
Smoothly down within
Her comfortable fur,

Slips in the ends, front paws,
Tail, until she is readied,
Arranged, shaped for sleep.

Whalesong

Judith Nicholls

I am
ocean voyager,
sky-leaper,
maker of waves;
I harm no man.

I know
only the slow tune
of **turning tide,** — `Alliteration`
the heave and sigh
of full seas meeting land
at dusk and dawn,
the sad whale song.
I harm no man.

Lone Dog

Irene McLeod

I'm a lean dog, a keen dog, a wild dog and lone,
I'm a rough dog, a tough dog, hunting on my own!
I'm a bad dog, a mad dog, **teasing silly sheep;** — `Personification`
I love to sit and bay at the moon and keep fat souls from sleep.

`Rhyme`
I'll never be a lap dog, licking dirty feet,
A **sleek** dog, a **meek** dog, cringing for my meat.
Not for me the fireside, the well-filled plate,
But shut the door and sharp stone and cuff and kick and hate.

Not for me the other dogs, running by my side,
Some have run a short while, but none of them would bide.
O mine is still the lone trail, the hard trail, the best,
Wide wind and wild stars and the hunger of the quest.

Something Told the Wild Geese

Rachel Field

Something told the wild geese
      It was time to go.
Though the fields lay golden
      Something whispered — 'Snow'.
Leaves were green and stirring,
      Berries, lustre-glossed, — `Rhyme`
But beneath warm feathers
      Something cautioned — 'Frost'. — `Rhyme`

All the sagging orchards
      Steamed with amber spice,
But each wild beast stiffened
      At remembered ice.
Something told the wild geese
      It was time to fly —
Summer sun was on their wings,
      Winter in their cry.

Flies

Valerie Worth

Flies wear
Their bones
On the outside.

Some show dead
Gray, as bones
Should seem,

But others gleam
Dark blue, or bright
Metal-green,

Or a polished
Copper, mirroring
The sun:

If all bones
Shone so, I
Wouldn't mind

Going around
In my own
Skeleton.

First Reaction

1. Using the following questions as a guide, write a brief paragraph giving your overall impression of this cluster of poems.

   - Which of the poems caught your interest and imagination?

   - Which lines stand out for you?

   - Which of the techniques is the easiest to recognize?

   - Which poem might be the best to read aloud? Why?

   - Which poem can you connect to your own experiences, thoughts, or feelings?

Look More Closely

2. Sketch one of the animals from the poems you have read. Select the specific words that bring this animal to life for you and record them on the page with your sketch.

3. Reread the definitions of *simile, personification, alliteration, rhyme,* and *rhythm.* Choose a favourite example of each of the techniques and record them in your notebook.

4. Write your own examples of alliteration, personification, and simile. You may want to use the following ideas as a guide.

   Alliteration. Name an animal and write three descriptive words beginning with the same letter.

   Personification. Think of a pet you had or would like to have and list words that describe its human characteristics and personality.

   Simile. Use the words *like* or *as* to make a comparison.

Develop Your Ideas

5. Write a poem about an animal you have strong feelings about. It may be an animal you have observed, owned, or imagined. As you plan and write your poem, use the following ideas to guide your thinking.

Prewriting

- List animals you know and admire.

- Decide which animal you are going to write about.

- Make a web of the details such as size, colour, action, and habits of the animal.

- Add words that express your feelings about the animal.

Drafting

- Write your thoughts and feelings about the strongest images in your web.

Thinking About Your Animal Poem

6. Revising is a way to self-assess your written work. Follow the steps described in *Focus On: Revising Your Poem*, page 253. After you have revised your poem, complete the following sentences.

The biggest improvement I made during revision was . . .

The next time I write a poem, I want to remember to . . .

When poets write, they sometimes decide to use a particular form. They arrange words into a specific pattern and structure that follow the rules for the form. In this cluster, five forms are presented: *cinquain, concrete, haiku, diamanté,* and *limerick.*

In your notebook, list the five different forms. Record one of these symbols after each form.

R = I have read this form before.

W = I have written this form before.

? = I'm not sure if I've seen this form before.

There are many other forms of poetry beyond these five. Add any other forms you know to the list and record the appropriate symbol.

Try This

Read each poem, then read the rules for the forms in the boxes. Reread each poem noticing how the poets have followed the rules.

My room is a mess,
Clothes are scattered on the floor,
I can't find my bed.

Sharon Lange

Life Lesson

The fierce wind rages
And I see how trees survive —
They have learned to bend.

Don Raye

Rules of the Form Poem

HAIKU

- Traditional Japanese poetry.
- Tells about one experience or impression.
- Is a three-line poem with 17 syllables.

  Line one: 5 syllables.
  Line two: 7 syllables.
  Line three: 5 syllables.

Kite

I
wish
I were a
kite on high
I could fly up to the sky
Up to the blue sky
High as a cloud
I wish I were
A kite
High
Up
Up
Up
Up
+
+
+
+
+
Anonymous +

Concrete Cat

A   A
e r   e r

eYe   eYe
whisker   whisker
whisker   m   h whisker
          o   t
          U

stripestripestripestripe   t a i l t a i l
stripestripestripe
stripestripestripestripes
stripestripestripe
stripestripestripestripe

paw paw   paw paw   ǝsnoɯ

dishdish   litterbox
                            litterbox

Dorthi Charles

Young
Happy, Lively
Living, Wrestling, Waking
Work, Machines, Bed, Paper
Retiring, Resting, Sleeping
Sad, Weary
Old.

Robert Bennett

Galaxies —
Distant, huge
Glowing, turning, going
Space, mystery — energy, life
Growing, circling, building
Tiny, basic
Atoms.

Rules of the Form Poem

DIAMANTÉ

- A seven-line poem.

- Has lines arranged in a diamond form.

- Tells about opposites.

  Line one: one-word title.

  Line two: two adjectives describing the title.

  Line three: three action words about the title ending in *ing* or *ed*.

  Line four: four nouns, two words relate to the title and two words relate to the opposite of the title.

  Line five: three action words the opposite of the title ending in *ing* or *ed*.

  Line six: two adjectives describing the opposite of the title.

  Line seven: one word describing the opposite of the title.

  A variation of the diamanté form does not deal with opposites. Instead, it describes the same topic throughout the poem.

FORM

A lady from near Lake Louise   (a)
Declared she was bothered by fleas.   (a)
     She used gasoline   (b)
     And later was seen   (b)
Sailing over the hills and the trees.   (a)

Limerick

Rules of the Form Poem

LIMERICK

- Is a five-line poem.
- Is humorous.
- Has a regular rhyme — a a b b a.
- Has a regular rhythm.

  Line one: 7-9 beats with 3 stresses.
  Line two: 7-9 beats with 3 stresses.
  Line three: 4-6 beats with 2 stresses.
  Line four: 4-6 beats with 2 stresses.
  Line five: 7-9 beats with 3 stresses.

So you found some fresh tracks in the snow?
And what made them? You say you don't know!
Were they two pairs of skis?
Rabbits down on their knees?
Or a skunk with a splint on his toe?

David McCord

Rules of the Form Poem

CINQUAIN

- Is a five-line poem.
- Has lines arranged by number of words.
- Tells about one idea.

  Line one: one-word title.

  Line two: two-word description of the title.

  Line three: three action words about the title (*-ing* words).

  Line four: four-word phrase about a feeling.

  Line five: one-word synonym for the title.

  Variation for line five: repeat the title.

Desert
hot, sandy,
sweaty, thirsty, treeless,
bitter cold at night,
desert.

Brian Powell

Depression
Very lonely
Having no friends
Feeling downcast, frightened, unwanted
Frustration. . . .

Dale McMechan

First Reaction

1. Record the title of the poem and the form that you:

   - Like the best.

   - Think would be the easiest to write.

   - Think would be difficult to write.

   Give reasons for your choices.

Look More Closely

2. Choose one haiku and find or draw an illustration that shows the main idea of the poem.

3. List three topics that would work well as concrete poems.

4. Choose one of the diamantés. Fold a piece of paper in half and illustrate the first three lines on one side of the paper and the last three lines on the other. Find a way to show how line 4 is about both ideas.

5. Quote a line from one of the limericks that made you smile.

6. The last line of a cinquain can be a repeat of the first line or it can be a *synonym*, a word that means the same thing. Which variation do you prefer? Why?

7. Reread the poems and decide which is your favourite form. Review the rules for writing this form. Write your own poem. Try writing several different forms on the same topic to see if one is more appropriate than another. Read your poems to others and ask them to tell you which form they prefer.

Develop Your Ideas

8. Most forms of poetry have been changed slightly by poets over the years. Choose one form and adapt or change the rules to create your own version. Write a poem and list the new rules you have followed. Share your poem and rules with others.

Revising Your Poem

Here are three steps to help you revise a poem.

1. Select a poem you have written that you like or that has potential. Make a second copy of the poem.

2. Ask a partner to read your poem to you.

3. Listen to your partner read it. On your copy, mark places where you might make changes. You could use the first letter of the editing ideas below to indicate the changes you might make. For example: If you are changing a word, write *W*.

Editing Issues	You Could . . .
Word Choice (W) Are there any words you want to change?	Circle any words that are boring or that you overused. In the margin, brainstorm more original words.
Main Idea or Feeling (M) Do you want to emphasize a main idea or feeling? Would your audience understand the point(s) you want to get across?	Try using a poetic technique such as simile or personification that might make the idea or feeling clearer for your reader.
Reorganize Your Ideas (R) Would reorganizing lines makes a difference?	Rearrange the words, the lines, the way the poem looks on the page, the beginning, the ending, or the punctuation.
Powerful Images (P) Are you showing the reader a vivid picture?	Are there gaps between the images you are thinking about and what you have written? Include details to give a more complete picture.
Delete (D) What words, lines, or ideas don't fit with your poem or seem out of place?	Try reading your poem aloud, leaving out the words or lines that don't seem to fit. Then read your poem again as it originally was. Decide which sounds better to you.

Make Connections

Now you can demonstrate what you've learned in *Imagined Worlds*. Read and think about the questions below.

Ask Yourself . . .

GOAL 1 Did you use a variety of strategies to understand and enjoy different poems?

GOAL 2 Did you learn how to recognize when and why poets use techniques including imagery, personification, simile, alliteration, rhythm, and rhyme?

GOAL 3 Did you write poems expressing your own feelings, thoughts, and observations, using techniques and forms that poets use?

GOAL 4 Did you select, present, and share favourite poems with others?

The following activities can help you think about your work in this unit and plan how to use what you've learned in the future. Each activity is keyed to the questions in *Ask Yourself* . . .

Look Back . . .

1. Think about the strategies you use when you read poems. Refer to *Tips On: Reading Poetry*, page 235. What strategies did you use most frequently? What strategies did you use rarely or not at all? What strategies did you use that were not mentioned in the tips?

2. Recall the techniques that you examined in this unit. Make three lists: ❷ ❸

   • Techniques you recognize.

   • Techniques you know so well that you could explain them to someone else.

   • Techniques you use in your own writing of poems

3. Reread the poems that you've written in this unit and write point-form answers to these questions. ❷ ❸

   • What kinds of poems do you usually write? Are they long or short? Do they rhyme or not rhyme? Do you use a particular form?

   • What are you really good at? In the poems you write, do you express your own feelings? Do you use interesting words? Do you write catchy titles? Do you create images? Do you use poetic techniques?

   • What causes you problems? Where do you have difficulty when you write? What do you do when you have difficulty? What would you like someone to show or teach you about writing poetry?

4. Think about the poems you've shared and presented in this unit. Make a list of the techniques that worked well when you presented your work. List techniques you tried, but won't use again. List new techniques you will try the next time you present and share. ❶

Show What You've Learned . . .

5. Make a list of the strategies you would suggest to someone who is struggling to understand or enjoy poetry. Use words you think others your age will understand. Ask several friends to try your ideas and tell you what worked, what didn't work, and what you might add. ❶

6. Work with a partner to find one or two new poems you like. Read the poem(s) together. On a copy, identify and label any poetic techniques you recognize. Write a brief explanation of how each technique adds to your understanding of the poem(s). ❷ ❸

7. Select a poem you've written or write a new one that expresses your feelings and shows your ability to use poetic techniques and forms. Work by yourself or with a partner and decide on a way to share your poem. ❷ ❸ ❹

Making Things Happen

Why do some good ideas catch on and others fizzle? Often, the only difference is how well the idea is communicated. If you want people to do something, you have to *explain* what they need to do and *persuade* them to act.

In *Making Things Happen* you will look at many different ways to explain and persuade — from poetry to business letters. You will read about a group of people who are working to encourage schools to use some of their grounds in more environmentally friendly ways. This might give you some ideas of ways you could spread the word about an environmental issue important to you.

SETTING GOALS

In this unit you can:

■ Learn different ways to explain your ideas and persuade people to act.

■ Learn about oral, visual, and written communications that groups use to organize their work and share their ideas.

■ Practise choosing the right form and the right words and pictures, depending on your purpose and audience.

■ Create T-shirt designs and pamphlets, write correspondence, and conduct meetings.

A Vision of the Coming Revolution of the Earth *258*
by Jamaal Haidar

A teenager uses poetry to express his hopes for the future.

Food Fun *262*
by Sharon Sterling

In this interview, Mark Bomford explains how his group is putting its beliefs into action.

Worm Composting *269*
A worm composting pamphlet is a starting point for your own pamphlet ideas.

Correspondence *274*
Letter? E-mail? Fax? Selecting the best form to suit your needs.

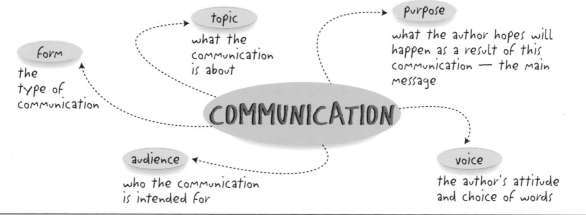

Tips On Understanding Communications

Communication is information passed between people. There are many types of communications, including: poetry, e-mail, videos, and speeches. When you communicate, there are five elements to think about.

- **topic** — what the communication is about
- **purpose** — what the author hopes will happen as a result of this communication — the main message
- **form** — the type of communication
- **audience** — who the communication is intended for
- **voice** — the author's attitude and choice of words

COMMUNICATION

A Vision of the

Before You Read

To communicate an idea well, it helps to believe that you have something important to say. It also helps to think that people are willing to listen to you.

A Vision of the Coming Revolution of the Earth is thirteen-year-old Canadian Jamaal Haidar's opinion of the ability of his generation to make a difference. This poem was selected in 1997 by an environmental action group as part of a publication they put out during Earth Week — a time set aside in many countries to celebrate the environment. That year the theme for Earth Week was "listen to our children and youth."

Jamaal Haidar wrote his poem especially for Earth Week. He chose poetry to express his view of the future because "my ideas were too abstract to be contained in a short story." Jamaal believes that we need to "go back and see how they did things in the past and use those ideas for the future. Environmental degradation is a recent problem, if you look back at the history of the planet. We've forgotten our roots and that has lead to our current problems."

> What do you think? Are adults willing to listen to the ideas of young people? Do you think the way you present your ideas can make a difference? For each question, briefly state your opinion and an example to support it.

Try This

When you read *A Vision of the Coming Revolution of the Earth* for the first time, think what the main message might be.

Mood and *persona* are two important clues to understanding the main message in poetry.

- *Mood* is the general feeling you get when you read the poem — joyful, angry, or mysterious are three possible moods. Imagine how the poem would sound read aloud.

- The *persona* is the role the author took while writing the poem — the person or group who is speaking in the poem. Ask yourself, "What is the person's attitude?"

Coming Revolution of the Earth

by Jamaal Haidar

we are here now
we are now
we are the moment
and we make words fly

home
where is home
home is here
here is earth
earth is home

we pulsate a collective consciousness
and joy

correlated thought
we are all hooked
into another
brother
sister

do you make words fly

different forms
one idea amalgamated

we are now
we are the instinct
in all forms of life
to MOVE
we are self
we are tribe
we are the tower
we are the future
and we are Now

we are the old religion in the new world
we are going to find a new way of being
from the old way of knowing
we will sow the seeds of the
now song
cannot be kept down any longer
cannot be housed any longer
the structure has become too small
to house what is inside
we grew too much
in that old structure
and now it's gonna'
explode
and that explosion is gonna' send all us
out all over to build a new world.

---

pulsate Expand and contract rhythmically — throb.
collective conscience The shared thoughts and feelings of a group of people.
correlated Related to one another.
amalgamated Combined to form one whole.
old religion in the new world Applying traditional ideas to solve new problems.

First Reaction

1. What do you think is the main message of *A Vision of the Coming Revolution of the Earth*?

Look More Closely

2. Answer each of these questions in one or two sentences. Reread the poem to find the lines quoted.

   • What mood is set by the word *revolution*?

   • Who is the author referring to when he says "we are now"?

   • What images of the future are suggested by these lines:

     - "earth is home"

     - "we are all hooked into/one another/brother/sister"

     - "we are going to find a new way of being"

3. Make a list of two or three possible reasons why the environmental action group chose to publish this particular poem to communicate its ideas.

4. To communicate an idea, a poet uses mood and images to create a detailed picture. Sometimes you want to communicate an idea in a few powerful words or images. Bumper stickers and posters are two examples of short-form ways to communicate a strong opinion.

   Create a design for a T-shirt that summarizes Jamaal Haidar's vision of the role of youth in the future of the earth. Your T-shirt design might include images as well as words, or just words. Decide whether you want something on the back and the front, or just on one side.

   Use the chart on the next page to help you think about your design.

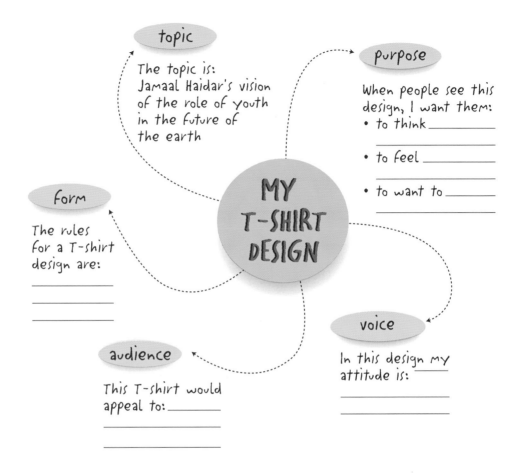

topic

The topic is: Jamaal Haidar's vision of the role of youth in the future of the earth

purpose

When people see this design, I want them:
- to think _____
  _____
- to feel _____
  _____
- to want to _____
  _____

form

The rules for a T-shirt design are:
_____
_____
_____

MY T-SHIRT DESIGN

voice

In this design my attitude is: _____
_____
_____

audience

This T-shirt would appeal to: _____
_____
_____

Develop Your Ideas

5. Quote a line from *A Vision of the Coming Revolution of the Earth* that is appropriate in poetry but would not be a good choice of words to explain the same idea in a letter to the editor of a newspaper. (Don't forget to put your quotations in quotation marks!)

Rewrite the idea in one or two sentences you *could* include in a letter to the editor of a newspaper.

6. Research poems that have a concern for the environment as a theme. Make an anthology of the ten best poems you find. For each poem, summarize the author's main message. Give your anthology a cover, title page, and table of contents.

Before You Read

To get things done in a group, the members must communicate clearly with each other. If the group wants to share its ideas with others, then there are decisions to make about the best ways to do this.

Food Fun is an interview with Mark Bomford, a young British Columbian who is one of five members of the Growing Schools project, a project that encourages schools to plant vegetable gardens.

> Does your school have a vegetable garden? Probably not. Most school grounds have features such as parking lots, play areas, and shrubs. Sketch a map that shows how the outdoor space is used at your school.

Try This

When you read *Food Fun* for the first time, try to determine how the project is organized and its overall goals.

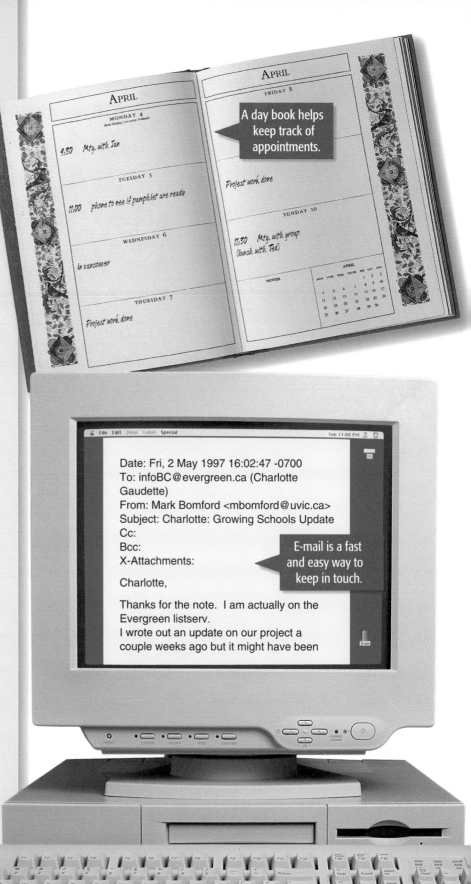

A day book helps keep track of appointments.

E-mail is a fast and easy way to keep in touch.

Food Fun

by Sharon Sterling

INTERVIEWER: So, what do a room full of Grade 1 and Grade 2 students pretending to be carrots have to do with taking care of the environment?

MARK: Well, they weren't all the same sort of carrots. Some kids were carrots grown in California, some kids were carrots grown right here, and some kids played the part of the food shipping and processing industries.

INTERVIEWER: This was the lead-in to a school garden project?

MARK: Right. The idea was that they got to have a little fun and learn about where food comes from at the same time. Of course, we wouldn't do that sort of thing with Grade 7 students.

INTERVIEWER: Why is it important for kids to understand that? Shouldn't you just be describing environmental problems?

MARK: Personally, I don't think there are problems with the environment. I think there are problems with society that lead to environmental problems.

INTERVIEWER: Could you explain that a little more?

MARK: Sure. It's like this. Plants, people, and wildlife are all part of a web of life — the biosphere. If our society has the attitude that food is something you buy at the supermarket, then we won't take care of the land we have that could be used for growing food. In time, that becomes an environmental problem. We're working to change society's attitudes. ✻ This is the only way environmental change will happen.

INTERVIEWER: How did you get from that general idea to having gardens in five schools in Victoria?

MARK: It wasn't easy. We chose a first-year objective of five schools because it seemed like a reasonable number. But when I started as the coordinator, I didn't have a clue how to go about a project like this.

✻ Pause and Think
What is the group's overall goal?

INTERVIEWER: Time to do research?

MARK: Yes. I used the Internet to collect information from any place in the world that had school garden projects. I got a lot of information, but I had to sort through it to find the valuable bits. I also talked to anyone locally who I thought might know about gardens on school grounds. I quickly learned that we'd have to adapt our ideas to fit with the schools' educational goals.

INTERVIEWER: And that's how you came up with your basic approach to the projects?

MARK: Right. We work with the teachers, parents, principal, and grounds maintenance people to come up with a project that will work for each school. We make presentations to the students, then work with them to build gardens and plant seeds or seedlings. As the school year comes to a close in the spring, we help the interested parents put in place a plan for maintaining the gardens over the summer. In the end, we hope that everyone involved has had a chance to think a little about where food comes from. ✳

GETTING THINGS DONE

INTERVIEWER: How do you manage to keep everything organized?

MARK: There are five of us, so each project member is responsible for one school. Each person keeps a binder of information on her or his school. We also have a calendar on the wall that shows all the meetings and work dates. And there is a call log to record phone messages. I personally have a work diary where I record all my appointments and the names of important contacts. I also have a day book that I take to every meeting. In my book I note the decisions made at the meeting and the things I've promised to do.

INTERVIEWER: Are there a lot of meetings?

MARK: Yes. We try to work things out as a group whenever possible, so that means getting together to talk. Let's say we have a meeting and decide we need to come up with a worksheet that explains how to build a plant box. One person will volunteer to come up with something. At the next meeting we'll all look at the ideas and comment. ✳

INTERVIEWER: Do you ever have trouble agreeing?

MARK: Sometimes. Because we've made commitments to the schools, we can't take so long over a decision that we get late with the project. Because I'm the project coordinator, I sometimes have to say, "Well, we can't take anymore time for this. Here's what we'll do." But not very often.

✳ Pause and Think
How do school garden projects help the group achieve their overall goal?

✳ Pause and Think
How does the group make important decisions?

PROPOSED LAMPSON STREET GARDEN PLAN

YOUNG TREE (FIR?) WITH REBAR SUPPORT

THREE BOXES, TERRACED DOWN SLOPE

1'
3'
3'
6' 2 m

OF LARGE TREE

HERE IS A SITE PLAN FOR THE
RAISED BED BOXES AS
DISCUSSED WITH AL HOOD AND
JIM LOCKE ON TUESDAY, APRIL 22
THERE ARE SIX SMALL (3' X 3')
BOXES IN TOTAL, TERRACED IN
TWO ROWS DOWN THE SLOPE.

SOME LEVELLING OF THE GROUND
BENEATH THE BOXES WOULD BE

> Faxes are useful for sending diagrams.

Sent Friday, May 2nd, 1997.
Mark Bomford
DIGS Youth Coordinator
Lifecycles Community Gardening Project
2175 Dowler Pl.

Office: tel.386.3447 fax.386.3449
home: tel.995.1852
email: mbomford@uvic.ca

> A friendly letter is a more formal way to say "thank you".

Dear Ann,

Just a short note to thank you once again for the
tools you donated to the Growing Schools project.
This helps both our program and the community
— they are all guaranteed to be well used by
many hands. We should get our first field tests
of them this Friday, and the pots will be holding
classroom transplants by next week. Because
Lifecycles is a registered charity, I can make up
a charitable donation tax receipt for you, based
upon an estimated value of the tools. This takes
a bit of time though, and I wanted to express my
gratitude before I got through the paperwork.

This is an immense help to us.
Sincerely, The Growing Schools Team

Emily Darren Lara Mike Mark

Press Release
For Immediate Release

Youth Acting Locally:
Open House Celebrates Successful Urban Sustainability Projects

The LifeCycles Project Society and the West Coast Ecological
Youth Alliance are holding an open house in their new office. The
celebration happens on Wednesday, May the 7th between 11:00 AM
and 2:00 PM at 2175 Dowler Place, and will include food and
entertainment.

The West Coast EYA creates and participates in projects which
promote biodiversity, and educates the public about environmental
issues and awareness. Our projects include native plant salvage,
community ecosystems restoration, native plant gardens, a native
plant nursery, and alternative transportation. Lifecycles promotes
and creates awareness about food, through public education and
garden building. We are currently creating community gardens,
garden for low-income families, gardens in schools, and running the
"Sharing Backyards" program linking enthusiastic gardeners with no
space to property owners with no time to garden. Both organizations
are currently working on the DIGS II project, funded by Human
Resources Development Canada and Environment Canada, Action
21, which involves 19 youth participants in a very active 6 month
skills development program. Both Lifecycles and the West Coast
EYA have local and international partners.

"This is a great opportunity for us to thank everyone who has
helped us out, and a good place for [...]   neet,"
says LifeCycles member Kristl [...]   with
Edward May from the West Coast [...]   t
projects on the go, check out the ne[...]
celebratory planting, and see some

> Press releases go to newspapers — maybe the newspaper will want to do an article about the project.

If you have any questions, please contact [...]o at Lifecycles office (383-5800) or
Antonio at West Coast EYA (383-2062).

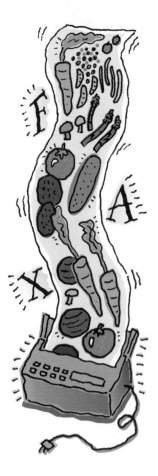

INTERVIEWER: Do you keep formal minutes of your meetings?

MARK: Only the really important ones. We really should keep minutes of more meetings, I guess, but we're a fairly new group and are just working out all the pieces.

INTERVIEWER: Do you use e-mail much?

MARK: Not for local communication, but almost all my contact with people working on similar projects in other places is by e-mail.

INTERVIEWER: I guess you also have to keep in touch with the people at the schools.

MARK: We use faxes a lot for that — for things such as work plans or information on how the beds will be put together.

INTERVIEWER: Any letters?

MARK: Well, there are official forms and things we have to fill out — lots of those. But the letters we write are usually thank-you letters to people who have donated something to the project.

SPREADING THE WORD

INTERVIEWER: I see you have a pamphlet — on recycled paper, of course — explaining your project. What was this developed for?

MARK: We use it to hand out at displays, give to teachers and parents, send to people who want to know about the project — it comes in handy for giving people a quick idea about what we're doing. We take every chance we get to spread the word about the importance of urban gardens. ✶

INTERVIEWER: Anything else you do for publicity?

MARK: We put up displays at events such as Earth Week. And we send out press releases when we are going to do something that the local papers or radio station might be interested in writing a story about.

INTERVIEWER: It sounds like a lot of work.

MARK: It is.

INTERVIEWER: Do you think it will make a difference?

MARK: Yes. I really do. On the days when I start to doubt that, I think about other projects that started with just one or two people with an idea and grew into a change in social attitudes. Just think — there was a time when no city would even think of a recycling program. Now they're everywhere.

INTERVIEWER: Gardens next?

MARK: I hope so!

✶ Pause and Think
How do pamphlet and displays help the group achieve its goals?

First Reaction

1. What do you think of the Growing Schools group's goals? What do you think of their chances of achieving their goals?

Look More Closely

2. Mark and his group require a variety of written communications to achieve their goals.

   - Some of their written communications are for their own use. These communications help track their progress and let everyone know what is going on in the group. The communications must be neat and readable. They are like a first draft of writing. The writing in these communications is *informal* — it might not follow all the rules of grammar.

   - Other communications are written to persuade people outside the group to listen to the group's ideas. These communications must be revised and polished so that they are top-quality, error-free presentations. This is *formal* writing.

   Make two lists. Title one list *Inside Communications* and the other *Outside Communications*. Reread the interview and put each communication mentioned in one of the lists. You might find it helps to look at the visuals included with the interview.

DIGS is a partnership project between: The Lifecycles Project, a non-profit organization which initiates action around food, health, and urban sustainability in the Greater Victoria Community, and The West Coast Ecological Youth Alliance (WCEYA), which works in constructive, life-affirming ways towards the vision of a just, ecological and sustainable society.

This project is made possible through grants from Youth Services Canada and Action 21.

Develop Your Ideas

3. Mark Bomford and the Growing Schools group are interested in making sure we keep some land for growing food. What environmental challenge interests you the most? What should people in your community do differently to solve this problem?

Draw a cartoon that illustrates your concern and your suggested solution.

4. Interview three people to get brief statements on their concerns about the environment. For example, you might want to ask people their opinions of the future of the planet. Ask each person to give you reasons for her or his opinion.

Make this a very short interview, just one question. You can conduct your interview in person, by telephone, or by e-mail.

Here is a sample statement from one student:

My concerns are the number of species that have become extinct every day and the constant increase in pollution. My generation's future is unsure, as there is no way to be sure how much longer Earth will hold up against the ever-increasing pollution and other problems.

Once you have your three interview statements, write down your own answers to the interview question. Compare the opinions of the people you interviewed with your opinion. Decide if it is similar to any of the others, or if it is quite different.

Before You Read

A pamphlet is a useful form for many purposes. It can be used to persuade people to act, to give instructions, or to provide general information. For example, the *Worm Composting* pamphlet you are about to read explains why it is a good idea to compost with worms and how to do it. This pamphlet was written by a community group to encourage people to compost in their yards or homes.

A pamphlet is a common type of advertisement for businesses such as hotels, tourist attractions, and recreational programs. A park might have a pamphlet that includes a map of the hiking trails and a list of *Do's and Don'ts* for hikers.

A pamphlet is often just one piece of paper folded to a convenient size that fits into a purse or pocket. We're now going to take a closer look at how to design a pamphlet so you can design your own.

> Name two places that you think would carry pamphlets to describe what they do. For each place, describe two or three types of information you think the pamphlets would contain.

Try This

A pamphlet is usually easy to read — the whole point is to catch a person's attention and give information quickly. Here are three pointers for reading a pamphlet.

- Look for a title to tell you what the pamphlet is about.

- Skim the headings for an idea of the main points.

- Decide if the illustrations are for information or decoration.

Worm Composting

Worm composting is a great way to turn your food waste into valuable fertilizer. It can be done year-round, indoors and outdoors, by apartment dwellers and householders. The compost is a good soil conditioner for houseplants, gardens, and lawns.

What You Need

- A Container (made of wood or plastic)
- Worms (500 to 2000 redworms)
- Bedding (shredded newspaper will do)
- Food Waste (fruit and vegetable waste)

How You Do It

Fill the container with damp bedding. Add the worms. Pull aside some of the bedding, bury the food waste, and cover it up with the bedding.

What Happens

Over a period of two to three months the worms and microorganisms eat the organic material and bedding, producing rich compost.

Worms are Living Creatures

Taking worms out of their natural environment and placing them in containers creates a human responsibility. Worms are living creatures with their own unique needs, so it is important to create and maintain a healthy habitat for them to do their work. If you supply the right ingredients and care, your worms will thrive and make compost for you. Happy and successful composting!

To learn more:

- Come to one of the Compost Seminars held at the Worm Centre on the last Saturday of each month.
- Read *Worms Eat My Garbage* by Mary Appelhof, Flower Press: Kalamazoo, 1982. (Provides instructions for building a worm bin.)
- Call the WormLine at:

386-3030

Worm Composting

Worm composting is a great way to turn your food waste into valuable fertilizer. It can be done year-round, indoors and outdoors, by apartment dwellers and householders. The compost is a good soil conditioner for houseplants, gardens, and lawns.

What You Need

- A Container (made of wood or plastic)
- Worms (500 to 2000 redworms)

Worm Bins
- Four Key Ingredients

1. The Container

The container should be between 20 to 30 cm deep. An old dresser drawer works well. You need .2m² surface area for every kilogram of food waste per week.

Drill holes in the bottom of the container for drainage and air. Place a tray underneath to catch excess liquid. You can use this as liquid plant fertilizer! Cover the bin to preserve moisture and provide darkness for the worms. Indoors, cover with dark plastic or burlap. Outdoors, you need a solid lid to protect your compost from rodents and rain.

Worm bins can be located indoors or outdoors. Keep them out of hot sun, heavy rain, and extreme cold. When temperatures drop below 4°C, move the bins indoors or insulate them.

2. The Worms

Redworms are the best for composting. Officially known as Elsenia foetida and Lumbricus rubellus, they are commonly known as red wigglers, brandlings, or manure worms. For every kilogram per day of food waste you'll need two kilograms of worms.

You can get worms from a friend's compost or purchase them. Contact the Worm Line (386-3030) for sources of worms.

3. The Bedding

Bedding can be made of shredded newspaper or cardboard, shredded fallen leaves, chopped straw and other dead plants, seaweed, sawdust, dried grass clippings, peat moss, or aged manure. Vary the bedding somewhat to provide more nutrients for the worms. Add a couple of handfuls of sand and soil to provide the worms with the grit they need for digestion.

The bedding should be slightly damp. Lift it gently from time to time to create air spaces.

4. The Food Waste

Your worms will eat food scraps such as fruit and vegetable peels, pulverized egg shells, tea bags, and coffee grounds. To avoid potential rodent problems do not compost meats, dairy products, oily foods, or grains.

The bedding should be slightly damp. Lift it gently from time to time to create air spaces.

Bury the food waste by pulling aside some of the bedding, dumping the waste, and then covering it up with the bedding again. Bury successive loads in different locations in the bin.

Harvesting Your Compost

After two and a half months have passed there should be little or no original bedding visible in the bin, and the contents will be brown and earthy-looking. It is time to remove some of the finished compost.

The quickest method is to move the finished compost over to one side of the bin, place new bedding in the space created, and put food waste in the new bedding. The worms will gradually move over and the finished compost can be

First Reaction

1. Do you think the *Worm Composting* pamphlet effectively *explains* and *persuades*? Explain.

Look More Closely

2. Rate the *Worm Composting* pamphlet.

Use this scale to rate your pamphlets.

Key: 3 — Well done!

2 — The basics are there.

1 — Needs work.

0 — Not included.

The content includes:

- A clear title.
- Attention-grabbing key points.
- Summary of main points.
- Sufficient detail.
- Useful or attractive illustrations.
- Clear information on how to contact the organization.

The design:

- Is well organized and easy to follow.
- Uses colour, lettering, and shapes to communicate a mood.
- Fits onto a standard-sized piece of paper.
- Folds to make a convenient pamphlet.

The writing:

- Is free of errors.
- Is written in a voice suitable for the audience.
- Stays in the same voice throughout the pamphlet.

3. Would you describe the language in the pamphlet as *formal* or *informal?* Quote words or phrases to support your opinion.

Develop Your Ideas

4. Create a pamphlet to persuade people in your community to do something positive for the environment. Your topic can be anything that interests you — you might want use the idea you thought of for your cartoon. Here are the steps to follow.

- Select a topic, purpose, and audience.
- Sketch out some rough ideas for what your pamphlet might look like.
- Make notes about what you already know and what you need to find out.
- Research information and illustrations.
- Decide on the voice. What attitude will you take? What types of words will help you explain or persuade?
- Write a first draft. Ask a partner to read it. Revise where necessary.
- Plan a final design.
- Arrange your content according to your design.
- Carefully proofread your final copy.

Meetings

Meetings are a useful way for people to come together and exchange ideas. A badly run meeting can be a waste of everyone's time. Here's how to make sure your meetings go well.

Before the Meeting

- Decide who needs to come to the meeting and make sure everyone knows when and where the meeting will be held.

- Decide who will *chair* the meeting and who will take *minutes*. It's the chairperson's job to make sure all the important topics are covered and that everyone gets a fair chance to speak at the meeting. The minutes of the meeting are a point-form record of what was decided about each agenda item.

- Write out an agenda. An agenda is a list of the topics that will be discussed at the meeting. You can make copies of the agenda to give to everyone coming to the meeting. To save paper, you can write out the agenda once on a large sheet of paper or on a chalkboard.

  An agenda is usually divided into three parts.

    - Reading the minutes of the last meeting.

    - Follow-up to decisions made at the last meeting.

    - New items to discuss.

Sometimes a meeting will also have an overall goal, such as *get ready for the horse show*.

During the Meeting

During the meeting, different people have different jobs to do. When you attend a meeting, listen to others and speak up when you have a good idea or a question.

- The chairperson begins by asking if there is anything that needs to be added to the agenda.

- Once the agenda is complete, then the group discusses each item on the agenda. Each member of the group should be allowed to give her or his opinion.

- Before moving on to the next item on the agenda, the chairperson should sum up the current item. This is usually a decision to do something or a plan to get more information. Sometimes the group might want to vote on the best thing to do. If something has to be done, make sure to decide who will be responsible and when the work needs to be finished.

- At the end of the meeting, the chairperson should check that everyone thinks all the important topics have been covered.

Now Practise

Conduct a meeting of five to ten people. Your overall goal for the meeting is to make plans to produce a large poster or mural that shows how your community fits in the "web of life" that Mark Bomford talks about in the *Food Fun* interview.

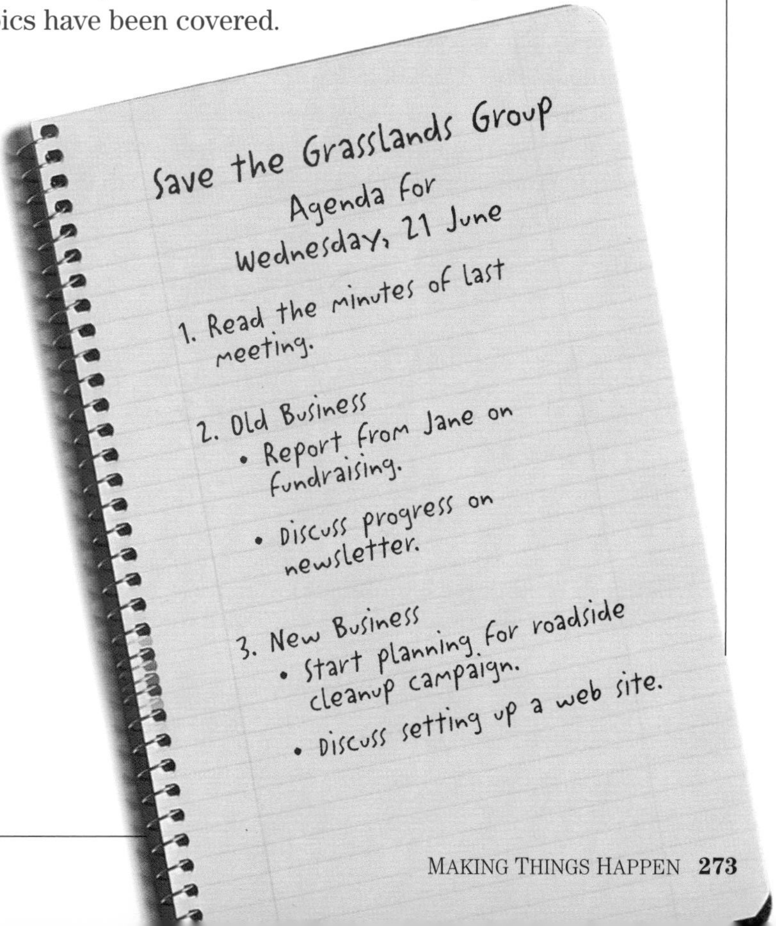

Save the Grasslands Group
Agenda for
Wednesday, 21 June

1. Read the minutes of last meeting.

2. Old Business
   - Report from Jane on fundraising.
   - Discuss progress on newsletter.

3. New Business
   - Start planning for roadside cleanup campaign.
   - Discuss setting up a web site.

Correspondence

Correspondence Correspondence

Before You Read

Correspondence is a two-way communication using written words.

When you correspond with someone, you have to think of topic, audience, and purpose in order to choose the best form. The most common forms for correspondence in businesses and organizations are letter, fax, and e-mail. In *Correspondence* you can look at a sample of each so that you can decide which one would be the best way for you to tell people about your idea for protecting the environment.

Not everyone has the same communication technologies. For example, most people can send mail through the postal service, some people have fax machines, and some have computers with modems that allow them to send e-mail. Even common technologies such as the telephone can have special features, such as a telecommunications device for the deaf that makes it possible for one person to speak and another person to see written words.

How about you? Create a chart that shows ways you have to communicate with others.

ME → pizza delivery
ME → grandma
telephone → friends

Try This

When you read correspondence in this section notice:

- The parts required for each form.

- How the parts are arranged.

- Use of punctuation.

FAX COVER SHEET

From: Sarah McMillan
Lady Caroline School
Fax: 489-3958

To: Mary Smith
Joe Mountain Preservation Society
Fax: 345-9879

1 page plus Cover Sheet.

11 June 1998

Here's our plan for the trail marker design. I've included a sketch of how it would look at the edge of a trail, and detailed plans for making each one. Jenny is still working on the cost of the materials.

I understand we'll discuss the plan in detail at our next meeting. I'll have the costs by then.

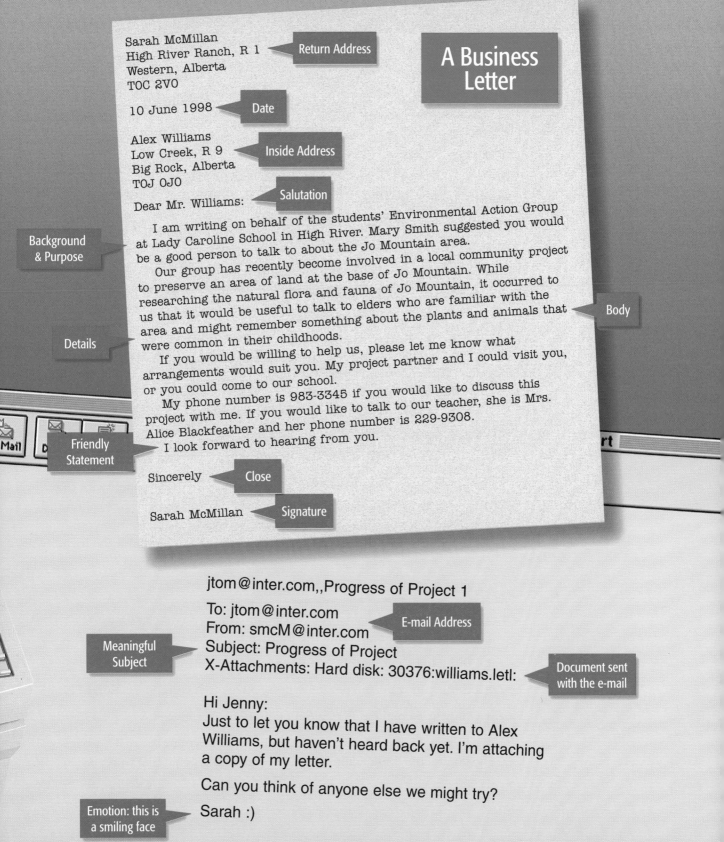

A Business Letter

Sarah McMillan
High River Ranch, R 1
Western, Alberta
TOC 2VO
Return Address

10 June 1998
Date

Alex Williams
Low Creek, R 9
Big Rock, Alberta
TOJ OJO
Inside Address

Dear Mr. Williams:
Salutation

Background & Purpose

I am writing on behalf of the students' Environmental Action Group at Lady Caroline School in High River. Mary Smith suggested you would be a good person to talk to about the Jo Mountain area.

Our group has recently become involved in a local community project to preserve an area of land at the base of Jo Mountain. While researching the natural flora and fauna of Jo Mountain, it occurred to us that it would be useful to talk to elders who are familiar with the area and might remember something about the plants and animals that were common in their childhoods.

Body

Details

If you would be willing to help us, please let me know what arrangements would suit you. My project partner and I could visit you, or you could come to our school.

My phone number is 983-3345 if you would like to discuss this project with me. If you would like to talk to our teacher, she is Mrs. Alice Blackfeather and her phone number is 229-9308.

Friendly Statement

I look forward to hearing from you.

Sincerely
Close

Sarah McMillan
Signature

jtom@inter.com,,Progress of Project 1

To: jtom@inter.com
From: smcM@inter.com
E-mail Address

Meaningful Subject
Subject: Progress of Project
X-Attachments: Hard disk: 30376:williams.letl:
Document sent with the e-mail

Hi Jenny:
Just to let you know that I have written to Alex Williams, but haven't heard back yet. I'm attaching a copy of my letter.

Can you think of anyone else we might try?

Emotion: this is a smiling face
Sarah :)

First Reaction

1. What is the purpose of each piece of correspondence shown in this section of *Making Things Happen*?

Look More Closely

2. Reread each sample in *Correspondence* carefully, then decide which one:

   • Almost all people are able to receive.

   • Is good for quickly sending pictures.

   • Is most like a conversation in writing.

3. Compare the words used in the e-mail with the words used in the letter. Write down one or two examples of phrases that show which is most formal.

Develop Your Ideas

4. Decide on a person or organization you'd like to tell about your idea for protecting the environment. Research how to get in touch with the person or organization, then write a letter, fax, or e-mail that explains your ideas and persuades the organization to use them. Before you start, look back at the samples to make sure you understand the form.

Think About Your Correspondence

5. Trade correspondence with a classmate. Each of you can assess the other's work by completing the following sentences.

   • I think the topic of this communication is . . .

   • I think you want the person who receives this communication to . . .

   • One way to make this communication clearer is . . .

   When you get your correspondence back from your classmate, review the comments and decide if there is something you'd like to revise.

Make Connections

Now you can demonstrate what you've learned in *Making Things Happen*. Read and think about the questions below.

Ask Yourself . . .

 Have you learned a variety of ways to explain your ideas and persuade people to act?

 Have you learned about the oral, visual, and written communications that groups use to organize their work and share their ideas?

GOAL 3 Did you practise choosing the right form and the right words and pictures depending on your purpose and audience?

GOAL 4 Did you create t-shirt designs and pamphlets, write correspondence, and conduct meetings?

The following activities can help you think about your work in this unit and plan how to use what you've learned in the future. Each activity is keyed to the questions in *Ask Yourself . . .*

Look Back . . .

1. Use the *Pamphlet Rating Scale* on page 271 to rate the pamphlet you created in this unit.

2. Make a list of three things you learned in this unit about participating in meetings. Select one idea from your list and use it to make a poster that would help students conduct better meetings. ②

Show What You've Learned . . .

3. Research three examples of excellent written communications. You might find examples in the library, on the Internet, or in your home. Review *Tips On: Understanding Communications*, page 257. For each communication you find, summarize the topic, the purpose, the form, the audience, and the voice. ❶ ❸

4. Meet with three to five people. As a group, decide on three goals for improving your meetings. Encourage all members of the group to discuss ways to make sure your meetings get things done. At the end, review the goals you've decided on. How well did you do at this meeting? ❷ ❹

5. Use a word-processing program to create a general form (called a *template*) you could use every time you wanted to write a business letter.

or

Design an attractive hand-drawn fax cover sheet that could be used to send faxes from your school. ❷ ❹

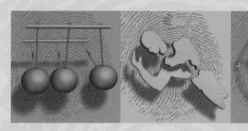

Help
YOURSELF

Proofreading

Use one or more of these techniques to make sure your final work is correct and readable.

- Make a separate pass through your work for each of the items on the *Proofreading Checklist.*

- Trade work with a partner and proofread each other's work.

- Keep a dictionary and writer's handbook (such as *Writing Reminders*) handy — and use them.

Proofreading Checklist

What to Check	What to Do
spelling	*Circle words you're not sure of, then find the correct spelling on your personal spelling list, in a dictionary, or by asking someone.*
capital letters	*Check for capital letters:* • at the beginning of sentences • for the main words in titles • for names of people or places
commas	*Do use a comma to separate items in a list.* ✗ I can send you a fax an e-mail or a letter. ✔ I can send you a fax, an e-mail, or a letter. *Do use a comma to join the main clauses in a compound sentence.* ✗ I would like a garden at our school but my friend thinks it would be too much work. ✔ I would like a garden at our school, but my friend thinks it would be too much work.
end punctuation	*Check that every sentence ends with a period, exclamation mark, or question mark.*
quotation marks	*Enclose direct quotations from books or articles in double quotation marks.* ✗ The author describes his grandfather as an excellent teacher. ✔ The author describes his grandfather as "an excellent teacher."

subject—verb agreement	*Check that your singular subjects have singular verbs.* ✗ The Defender are tired of playing the game. ✔ The Defender is tired of playing the game. *Check that your plural subjects have plural verbs.* ✗ The Challenger and the Defender is on opposite sides. ✔ The Challenger and the Defender are on opposite sides.
apostrophes	*Use an apostrophe to show possession.* ✗ Here is Rajeets definition of a hero. ✔ Here is Rajeet's definition of a hero. *Use an apostrophe to show missing words in a contraction.* ✗ Its the best animal hero story Ive ever read. ✔ It's the best animal hero story I've ever read. *Don't use an apostrophe for* its *when the meaning is "belonging to."* ✗ The group handed in it's definition of the term *unsung hero.* ✔ The group handed in its definition of the term *unsung hero.*
pronouns	*Use the correct class of pronoun when it is the subject of the sentence.* ✗ Gary and me made a booklet of the character sketches. ✔ Gary and I made a booklet of the character sketches. *Use the correct class of pronoun when it is the object of the sentence.* ✗ She gave the character sketches to Gary and I. ✔ She gave the character sketches to Gary and me.
homonyms	*Use the correct choice for words that sound the same but are spelled differently and have different meanings.* ✗ When we went their to see the play, we past buy your school. ✔ When we went there to see the play, we passed by your school.

The Reading Process

There are three basic stages to reading a piece for the first time. To find out more about a work, you often need to reread.

Before Reading

- Set a purpose for reading. Do you want to find information? Enjoy yourself?

While Reading

- Look at the title and illustrations for a general idea of what the piece might be about.

- Pause and think about what you are reading from time to time.

- Look for connections between what you are reading and what you know and feel about the topic or the situation.

Reread

Need more information?

After Reading

- Respond honestly to what you've read. Did you like it? How did it make you feel?

- Think of connections between what you've just read and what you already know.

- Think about it, talk it over with friends, and ask questions to make meaning of what you have read.

More Information

For more information on reading strategies and techniques, see:

Tips On: Reading (general information on reading), page 11

For specific techniques for reading different genres or forms, see:

Tips On: Reading Short Stories, page 75

Focus On: Interpreting Fiction, page 86

Tips On: Reading for Information, page 133

Tips On: Reading Poetry, page 234

Representing

Representing is what you do to show what you know about something, share an idea, or communicate with another person.

Types of Representations

There are many ways to represent your ideas. You can choose from:

- Written Forms
  These include poems, paragraphs, and short stories.

- Visual Forms
  These include charts, maps, and drawings.

- Oral Forms
  These include speeches, debates, and songs.

- Movement
  This includes dance and mime.

Some representations combine two or more forms. For example, drama combines oral work and movement.

Elements of Representations

When you decide to represent something, there are five things you have to think about:

- Topic
  What the work is about.

- Purpose
  What you hope will happen as a result of the work — the main message.

- Voice
  Choosing the right words and images to express your attitude toward the topic.

- Audience
  Who the work is intended for.

- Form
  The type of representation.

More Information

For a web that shows how understanding the elements of representation can help you communicate effectively, see:

Tips On: Understanding Communications, page 257

For specific techniques for representing in various ways, see:

- *Help Yourself: The Writing Process*, page 282

- *Focus On: Representing Using Visual Forms*, page 212

- *Tips On: Nonverbal Communication*, page 173

- *Focus On: Debate*, page 60

- Think About Your Poster, page 10

- Think About Your Presentation, page 13 (with visuals, page 144)

- Storyboard, page 69

- Think About Your Poem Presentation (oral), page 241

- Pamphlet, page 269

The Writing Process

When you write, you might find it helps to think of five stages to the process. Sometimes you'll get it right in one or two drafts.

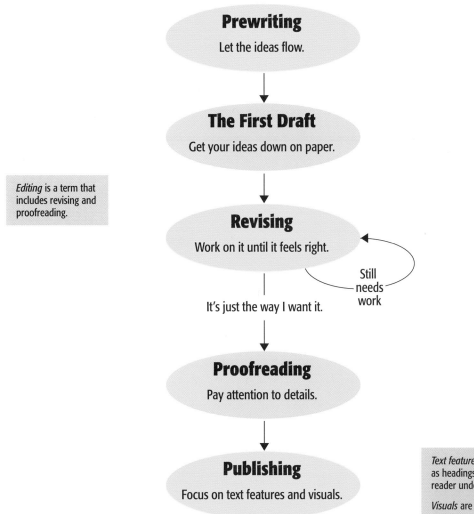

Prewriting
Let the ideas flow.

The First Draft
Get your ideas down on paper.

Editing is a term that includes revising and proofreading.

Revising
Work on it until it feels right.

Still needs work

It's just the way I want it.

Proofreading
Pay attention to details.

Publishing
Focus on text features and visuals.

Text features are elements such as headings that help the reader understand the piece.

Visuals are images that accompany your writing.

Helpful Hints

Word Processing Tip
Create and keep a file that contains text features you often use. These files are called templates.

Prewriting

- Decide on the audience, purpose, topic, form, and voice of the piece.
- Think creatively: imagine, recall, elaborate, and make connections.
- Decide what you know and what you need to find out.
- Think about how this form is usually presented, including text features and types of visuals.

Word Processing Tip
Start a new folder for a new project.

The First Draft

- Write write, write, write — don't worry about getting it perfect in the first draft.

Word Processing Tip
Copy your file to start a new draft. Keep your earlier draft in case you want to go back to those ideas.

Revising

- Rewrite to make your main message clearer to the reader.
- Get another person's opinion of your work.

Word Processing Tip
Don't trust the spell checker to do your job for you! Many people find they proof best by reading a print-out of the file.

Proofreading

- When you are sure you've expressed your ideas clearly, check your work for errors of grammar, spelling, and punctuation.

Word Processing Tip
Sometimes hand-drawn pictures or hand lettering is more effective than art or type copied from a computer program. Be original!

Publishing

- If there are rules for ways to present the form, make sure you follow them.
- Arrange your text and any visuals in a way that is pleasing and easy to understand.

More Information

For information on writing specific forms, see:

Focus On: Writing a Memoir, page 31

Focus On: Writing Historical Fiction, page 154

Focus On: Revising Your Poem, page 253

For information on the elements of specific forms, see:

Think About Your Found Poem, pages 25 and 99

Newspaper Headlines, page 45

Want to write a television script?, page 51

Think About What Makes an Effective Parody, page 85

Think About Your Responses, page 111 (writing responses to questions)

The Parts of a Script, page 174

Rules of the Form Poem Haiku, page 248

Rules of the Form Poem Concrete, page 249

Rules of the Form Poem Diamanté, page 250

Rules of the Form Poem Cinquain, page 251

Rules of the Form Poem Limerick, page 251

Friendly Letter, page 265

Press Release, page 265

Meeting Agenda, page 273

Fax, page 274

E-mail, page 275

Business Letter, page 275

Research

Research is what you do when you want to find information on a topic. There are many reasons for researching. You might want to collect information to write a report, check a fact, or find out how to do something.

The Research Process

Following these steps will help make sure your research time is well spent.

1. Select a Topic
- If your teacher hasn't assigned a topic, select something that really interests you.

2. Make a Chart of What I Know/What I Need to Find Out
- Decide whether you need to *confirm* information you think you already know.

3. Take a Quick Look for Sources
- Review your chart to come up with a list of nouns and verbs that would be useful key words to help you search in a card catalogue or computer database.

4. Focus Your Topic
- Try to find three to six books or articles on your topic. If you can't, ask a librarian for help. Sometimes you might have to select a new topic. Look for recent sources of information.

5. Select Sources
- To focus your topic, write a *thesis statement*. This is a one-sentence summary of your main idea.

6. Make Notes
- Start your research by reading the most general article you can find on the topic. This might be an entry in an encyclopedia.
- Keep your notes organized. Use a separate sheet of paper or file card to record information from each source. Always write down the full title and author of the material, and the information you need to find the source again. In the library, this would be the *call number*. For on-line research, this would be the *URL* (location information needed to access the web site).
- When you write your notes, put direct quotations from the books or articles in quotation marks. Copy carefully. Write your own ideas in point form, using heads to organize the information.

7. Review Your Chart
- You might find you need to collect more information. If your notes are in good shape, that should be easy!

8. Show What You Know
- Do a draft of your project. You might find you need to do a little more research.

Research or Plagiarism?

If you collect the ideas of several people and use their ideas to help you form your own ideas, that's research. Always give credit to the person whose ideas you are using. If you copy or download other people's ideas and present them as your own, that's *plagiarism*. Plagiarism isn't fair to the person whose ideas you have stolen, and it doesn't help you learn to form your own ideas and opinions.

Writing Reminders

1. Sentences

A sentence expresses a single, complete idea. Here are the main types of sentences:

Declarative	This is a mystery.
Interrogatory	Is this a mystery?
Exclamatory	This is quite a mystery!
Imperative	Call Sidney Stalwart.

Simple Sentences

A simple sentence has two parts: a *subject* and a *predicate*.

The simple subject of the sentence is the *noun* — person, place, thing, or idea — the sentence is about. The simple predicate is a verb. Verbs are either *action words* that tell you what the subject is doing, or *linking words* that connect the subject to words that describe it.

Simple Subject	**Simple Predicate**	
The detective	hid.	(*hid* is an action verb)
The key	was important.	(*was* is a linking verb)

Two- or three-word sentences don't give you a lot of information about the subject or what it is doing, so writers usually *modify* the subject and predicate by adding additional information.

Complete Subject	**Complete Predicate**
The clever detective	hid quietly in the closet.
The key to the closet	was very important.

These are both still simple sentences, but they tell you a little more about what is going on. In these sentences you can still find the simple subjects *detective* and *key*, and the simple predicates *hid* and *was*.

✔ *Sentence check*: If you're not sure you've got a complete sentence, decide if your sentence includes a person or thing *doing* something and a verb that tells you *what*.

Compound Sentences

A long piece of writing consisting of a series of simple sentences can become difficult to read. For this reason, writers often combine two sentences that have related ideas. When a simple sentence is combined with another simple sentence, each sentence becomes a *main clause*. The result is a *compound sentence*.

The most common way to combine two sentences is to use a comma and a *coordinating conjunction* between them.

Three useful coordinating conjunctions are: *and, or,* and *but.*

Two Sentences	**Compound Sentence**
The closet is to the audience's left. The doorway is to the audience's right.	The closet is to the audience's left, and the doorway is to the audience's right.
Dr. Chilling might succeed with his evil plan. He might get caught.	Dr. Chilling might succeed with his evil plan, or he might get caught.
Sidney thought Dr. Chilling was nice. Amy knew the truth.	Sidney thought Dr. Chilling was nice, but Amy knew the truth.

Another way to create a compound sentence is to join the two clauses with a semicolon.

Two Sentences	**Compound Sentence**
The iced tea was tasty. It was also poisoned.	The iced tea was tasty; it was also poisoned.

✔ *Sentence check*: Does each clause in your compound sentence have a subject and predicate? Are the ideas in the two clauses very closely related?

Run-On Sentences

An incorrectly built compound sentence is called a *run-on* sentence. Run-on sentences make it hard for the reader to understand what you're saying. Avoid them at all cost!

There are three main causes of run-on sentences:

• too many unrelated ideas in one sentence

• a missing coordinating conjunction

• a comma where there should be a period or a semicolon

Run-On Sentence	**Possible Solution**
The director selected the cast, and the cast memorized the script, then on Saturday they started rehearsing.	The director select the cast. The cast memorized the script, then started rehearsing on Saturday.

| The curtain fell down, the cast kept performing. | The curtain fell down, but the cast kept performing. |
| The set designer brought in the props, everybody helped put them in the right places. | The set designer brought in the props. Everybody helped put them in the right places. |

✔ *Sentence check*: Would your ideas be clearer if the sentence were divided into two?

Sentence Fragments

A sentence fragment is a sentence that is missing either a subject or a predicate. Sometimes this occurs when the writer has one complete sentence, then adds a fragment of additional information.

Fragment	**Possible Solution**
• Missing a subject:	
Amy Truegood is brave. Also smart.	Amy Truegood is brave and smart.
• Missing a predicate:	
Dr. Chilling's evil plan. It came to nothing.	Dr. Chilling's evil plan came to nothing.

A fragment is usually considered a mistake. Sometimes, however, sentence fragments are used to achieve a particular effect in speeches or creative writing. For example: "An evil scientist. A secret formula. Can the two detectives solve the case?"

Sentence fragments may also be used in lists when writing out full sentences would make the list difficult to read. To make the list look neater, the fragments are sometimes punctuated as though they are sentences.

✔ *Sentence check*: Don't use sentence fragments unless you want to create a special effect in a speech, a story, or a poem.

2. Point of View

The point of view in a sentence tells you who is speaking or writing. In the *first person*, the subject of the sentence is the person speaking. In the *second person*, the subject is the person spoken to. In the *third person*, the subject is the person or thing spoken about.

In these examples, notice that the form of verb changes for third person, but only the pronoun changes for first and second person. This is a common pattern for verbs.

First Person	I dig for bones.
Second Person	You dig for bones.
Third Person	She digs for bones.

With the verb *to be*, the form of the verb changes each time.

First Person	I am an anthropologist.
Second Person	You are an anthropologist.
Third Person	She is an anthropologist.

✔ *Point of view check*: Is there more than one point of view in your writing? Unless you are writing fiction or poetry, the point of view should usually stay the same throughout the whole piece.

3. Subject-Verb Agreement

Number tells you how many things or people you're talking about. In a sentence, if the subject is *singular* (one person or thing), the verb must be singular; if the subject is *plural* (more than one), the verb must be plural.

With most verbs, this is pretty easy to figure out.

	Singular	**Plural**
First Person	I write poems	We write poems.
Second Person	You write poems.	You write poems.
Third Person	She writes poems.	They write poems.

The verb *to be* is a little more complicated.

	Singular	**Plural**
First Person	I am a poet.	We are poets.
Second Person	You are a poet.	You are poets.
Third Person	She is a poet.	They are poets.

Words in the Way

Words between the subject and the verb in a sentence can give you false clues about whether the subject is singular or plural. In the following example, there is only one collection, so the verb must be singular.

Not in Agreement	**In Agreement**
A collection of poems are called an *anthology*.	A collection of poems is called an *anthology*.

✔ *Agreement check*: If you're not sure about singular or plural, try saying the sentence aloud, removing all words between the subject and the verb.

4. Using Personal Pronouns

A *pronoun* is a word in a sentence that replaces a noun, another pronoun, or group of words in the same or an earlier sentence. The word or words the pronoun is replacing is called the *antecedent*. Pronouns are useful because they help the writer avoid repeating words.

Without Pronouns	**With Pronouns**
Aisha kept a logbook so Aisha could record Aisha's television-viewing hours.	Aisha kept a logbook so she could record her television-viewing hours.

In a sentence, the antecedent must be clear to the reader. In the first sentence of the following pair of examples, you can't tell which boy became nervous.

Unclear Antecedent	**Clear Antecedent**
When Conrad interviewed Jim, he became nervous.	Conrad became nervous when he interviewed Jim.

✔ *Pronoun check*: If there is more than one noun before the pronoun, make sure the reader can tell which noun the pronoun refers to.

Forms of Personal Pronouns

Personal pronouns are pronouns that we use to refer to people. These pronouns take different forms depending on what they refer to and whether they are subjects or objects of the verb. Here's a summary of the different forms of personal pronouns.

	As Subject	**As Object**
Singular		
First Person	I	me
Second Person	you	you
Third Person	he, she, it	him, her, it

Plural

First Person	we	us
Second Person	you	you
Third Person	they	them

Pronouns as Subjects and Objects of Sentences

A pronoun takes a different form depending on whether it is the *subject* of the sentence (the person or thing that performs the action) or the *object* of the sentence (the person or thing that receives the action). A *direct object* answers the question *what* or *whom* after an action verb.

In this sentence, *camera* is the direct object.

Clara dropped the camera.

An *indirect object* answers one of: *to what, for what, to whom,* or *for whom.*

In this sentence, *I* is the subject, *camera* is the object, and *her* is the indirect object.

I gave the camera to her.

Most of the problems with personal pronouns come up when there are two parts to the subject or object.

What People Often Say	**The Correct Way**
• Wrong form for the subject of the sentence: Santok and me have different opinions about violence on TV.	Santok and I have different opinions about violence on TV.
• Wrong form for the object of the sentence: She gave the data to Truda and I.	She gave the data to Truda and me.

✔ *Pronoun check:* When there is more than one part to the subject or object, remove all the parts except the verb and the pronoun. Read the sentence aloud to see if it sounds right, then check your choice of pronoun against the pronoun chart.

5. Paragraphs

A paragraph is a collection of sentences on a single topic. A paragraph might be a complete piece of writing on its own, or part of a longer piece.

There are three parts to an effective paragraph.

- A paragraph starts with a *topic sentence* that clearly states what the paragraph is about.

- The middle of the paragraph consists of *supporting sentences* that discuss the topic. These sentences include information that communicates your main idea, such as explanations, examples, and specific details.

- A paragraph ends with a *concluding sentence* that states the topic in a new way and sums up the main idea of the paragraph.

Organizing Your Ideas

The ideas in the middle of the paragraph should follow an order that suits the topic and your main idea. Some choices are:

- Describe a sequence of events in the order in which they occurred.

- Describe a place by setting the scene with a general image, then adding details.

- Pose a question and then answer it.

- Build up to your main idea through a series of facts and examples.

Use linking words and phrases to help the reader understand how your ideas are related. Some useful linking words and phrases are: *therefore, because, secondly,* and *as a result.*

Helpful Hints

- Keep it simple. Use only your best ideas, facts, or examples.

- Write from one point of view throughout the whole paragraph.

✔ *Paragraph check*: Read your paragraph slowly, thinking of every sentence as a point in a list. Look for and remove any points that aren't directly related to the topic and main idea.

Punctuation, Capitalization, and Underlining

This is an alphabetical listing of topics to help you know when to use each punctuation mark, when you need a capital letter, and when to use underlining.

Apostrophes '

Use an apostrophe to form the possessive of a noun. A possessive form indicates ownership.

That is the cat's dish.

That is Lois's hat.

That is the girls' changing room.

Beware: If the noun is singular, you add an apostrophe and an *s*, even if the noun ends in *s*. If the noun is plural, you only add an apostrophe. Also be sure not to use an apostrophe for the possessive form of *its*.

The group did its best.

Use an apostrophe to show where letters have been left out in contractions.

I can't remember that rule!

Capital Letters

Capitalize proper nouns. A proper noun is the unique name of a person, place, thing, or idea.

The Red River flooded.

I'm now in Grade 7.

Beware: A common noun is a general name and does not take capital letters.

This river often floods.

Capitalize the first word of every sentence and the first word of a direct quotation.

There is no reason to quit now.

He shouted, "Don't quit now!"

In titles, capitalize the first and last words, and the other important words. Don't capitalize conjunctions, articles (for example a *or* the*), prepositions (for example* to *or* on) *unless they are five letters or longer.*

"Bodies and Bones"

"The Sales Formula"

Beware: On book covers or in illustrated works, the designer might break these rules to make the title more attractive. When you write titles, follow the rules.

Colon :

Use a colon to introduce a long list that is introduced by a main clause. The clause can end with the phrase "the following."

Each Readers' Theatre participant will need to bring the following: a chair, a script, props, and a glass for water.

Use a colon between numbers that show hours and minutes.

She came at 4:45 p.m.

Commas ,

Use a comma after every item in a series except the last, whether the items are single words or clauses.

The students made posters, tickets, and programs for the play.

In our group, we divided the tasks as follows: Sandy collected props, Arjeet arranged for the rehearsal space, and Leila made copies of the script.

Use commas between two or more adjectives of equal importance that modify the same noun. (An adjective gives you additional information about a noun.)

It was a long, boring movie.

Use a comma to separate an introductory word, phrase, or clause from the rest of the sentence.

In this parody, the main character resembles Robin Hood.

However, there were good reasons for not going.

If you insist on shouting, people are going to stare.

Use commas to set off the speaker's tag in direct quotation. The speaker's tag tells you who is talking.

"I think it looks good," he said.

"It looks good," he said, "but you could add another row of pompoms."

Use a comma before a conjunction that joins the main clauses in a compound sentence.

Arlo took many notes, and then he compiled them on a data sheet.

Beware: You don't need a comma if the conjunction is actually joining the parts of the predicate. If there isn't a second subject, it isn't a complete clause.

Arlo took many notes and compiled them on a data sheet.

Double Quotation Marks " "

Use double quotation marks to set off direct quotations. Periods and commas go inside the quotations in all cases. Exclamation points and question marks only go inside the quotation if they are part of the quotation.

The story ended with the narrator saying, "and they all live happily ever after."

The poem began, "Hark! The birds sing!"

Use double quotation marks for the titles of shorter works such as short stories, poems, essays, articles, chapters, songs, and television episodes.

The first chapter of *Sun in the Morning* is called "Daybreak."

Beware: Sometimes, people break this rule so that they can use text features in a way that makes sense for a particular book. In your work, make sure you are consistent. It is safest to follow the standard rules.

Exclamation Points !

Use an exclamation point to intensify a sentence or a single-phrase expression.

I won't do that again!

Yoiks!

Periods .

Use a period at the end of a sentence that makes a statement or gives a command.

Charlie walked the dog.

Walk the dog.

Use a period after most abbreviations and initials.

Dr. A. Schug-Smythe-Marquez

S.P.C.A.

Beware: Symbols for measurement are not abbreviations, so they don't need periods.

km (kilometre)

g (gram)

In standard usage, some abbreviations do not take periods. Examples include *URL* (universal resource locator — information needed to access a web site) and the post office abbreviations for the provinces of Canada.

Question Marks ?

Use a question mark at the end of a sentence that asks a direct question.

Will you go with us?

Semicolon ;

Use a semicolon to join the two parts of a compound sentence if there is no coordinating conjunction.

It rained all day; the fields were flooded.

Underlining

Underline titles of longer works, such as novels, television series, movies, and plays. If you are using a word processor, use italics.

We watched *The Incredible Journey* when we worked on the theme of animal heroes.

Identities 7

Abbreviations used: (t) top, (c) centre, (b) bottom, (l) left, (r) right, (bkgd) background.

PHOTOS:

UNIT 1: Page 4-6, Canapress Photo Service; 7(tr), Alexandra Boulat/Sipa Press; 8,9(l), Michael Alberstadt; 9(tr), Canapress Photo Service/Santiago Lyon; 9(cr), Canapress Photo Service/Jacqueline Arzt; 10, Alexandra Boulat/Sipa Press; 14(t), National Archives of Canada PA74583; 15(tr), Toronto Sun; 17(tl), Toronto Sun/Silvia Pecota; 17(tr), Doug MacLellan/Hockey Hall of Fame; 20, Michael Alberstadt; 22-24, Dave Starrett; 25, Courtesy of Random House; 29, Robert Haddock/Tony Stone Worldwide; 33, Ian Crysler; 36, Stephen Homer/First Light. **UNIT 2:** Pages 48,53, Dave Starrett; 54(bl), Canapress Photo Service/Paul Chiasson; 54-55(t), Dimension Films; 55(tr), Everett Collection; 57(tl), Pronk&Associates; 64(cr),64(b), Gail Harvey; 65(bl),66,67(tl)(tr), Dave Starrett; 68, Corel Photo Library. **UNIT 3:** Page 111(l), Columbia Pictures; 111(r), Paramount Pictures. **UNIT 4:** Page 128, O. Louis Mazzatenta/NGS Image Collection; 129,130(tl), Cheryl Nuss/NGS Image Collection; 130(tr), Jonathan Blair/NGS Image Collection; 142-143, Illustration from "I Am the Mummy Heb-Nefert" by Eve Bunting. Copyright ©1997 by David Christiana, reproduced by permission of Harcourt Brace & Company; 145, Sygma; 146(t), Paul Hanny/Pono Presse Internationale; 148-149(t), Sygma; 149(b), G. Hinterleitner/Pono Presse Internationale; 150(l), Kenneth Garrett/NGS Image Collection; 152-153(b), Sygma; 156-160, Copyright©1996 by Charlie Fellenbaum. Reprinted by permission. **UNIT 5:** Page 168-171, all photos courtesy of The Banff Centre for the Arts except top banner photo from the Corel Stock Photo Library; 169(#1), Peter C. Wylde (period consultant) in a masterclass for the Advanced Actors Workshop preparing the company for the 1993 Banff Arts Festival production of The School for Scandal by Richard Brinsley Sheridan; 169(#2), Andrew Dolha, Sharon Heldt and Ted Atherton prepare for the 1992 Banff Arts Festival Production of Twelth Night by William Shakespeare; 169(#3), Jay Tuttle and Jenny Such in a training session during the 1996 Song Integration program at the Banff Centre for the Arts; 170(#4left), Costume designer John Pennoyer and a design participant plan the costumes for the 1989 Banff Arts Festival production of Jules Massent's Cendrillon; 170(#4r), Jerry Longboat (Lightning Spirit) works on his own costume for the 1995 production of The Sun Raiser for the Banff Arts Festival. Written and directed by Yves Sioui Durand; 170(#5r), A scenic carpenter welds a prop for the Banff Arts Festival; 170(#5b-left), Josef Svoboda leads a scenography masterclass at the Banff Centre for the Arts; 170(#5br), Wulf and Stephanie Tjelios prepare a prop for the 1994 Banff Arts Festival production of Igor Stravinsky's The Rake's Progress; 171(#6left), Technicians set the sound boards into the mixing positions for a production in the Eric Harvie Theatre, Banff Centre for the Arts; 171(#6r), Michelle Dias prepares a prop for the 1995 Banff Arts Festival production of 'Oh My Baby'; 171(#7), Laurie Levier as Jenny Donnelly in James Reaney's Sticks & Stones, The Donnellys Part I at the Banff Arts Festival; 192, (19642.7C#). **UNIT 6:** Page 200(tl), Ken Marschall Collection; 200(bl), Brown Brothers; 200(br), Harland&Wolff; 200(cr), Ken Marschall Collection; 201(bl), Ken Marschall Collection; 201(bc), University of Pennsylvania Archives and Records Center; 201(br), Harland&Wolff; 205(tl),(tc),(tr), Ken Marschall Collection; 205(tr-insert), Denver Public Library/Don Lynch Collection; 208(t), White Star Publications; 208(cr), Copyright ©1912 by The New York Times Company. Reprinted by Permission.; 208(br), Southampton City Heritage Services; 209(tl), Bill Sauder Collection; 209(tr), ©Woods Hole Oceonographic Institution; 210, Corel Stock Photo Library; 214(t), National Archives of Canada C46350; 214(b), National Archives of Canada C26386; 215(tl), National Archives of Canada PA103542; 215(tr), Taken from A Child in Prison Camp ©1971 Shizuye Takashima published by Tundra Books; 215(b), 219, Vancouver Public Library 1380; 220(t),224, National Archives of Canada C24452; 220-221(b), Taken from A Child in Prison Camp ©1971 Shizuye Takashima published by Tundra Books; 221(t), courtesy of Keiko Orida Yamashita; 222, Corel Stock Photo Library; 225, Keiko Orida Yamashita; 227,229, Canapress Photo Service (Ron Poling). **UNIT 8:** Page 258, Jessica Marshall; 259, NASA; 262(t), Dave Starrett; 262(b), Pronk&Associates; 265, Dave Starrett; 267(b), The Lifecycles Project; 269-270(bkgd),270(bl), Dave Starrett; 273, Pronk&Associates; 274, Dave Starrett.

ILLUSTRATIONS:

Attoe, Steve pages 190, 236-239, 268

Day, David pages 69-70

Dover Publications, Inc page 126

Gauthier, Don page 193

Ghiglione, Kevin pages 88-97

Harris, Stephen pages 263-266

Herman, Michael pages 64-70(t), 65(tr), and logos on Unit Opener pages 2,40,74,124,166,198,234,256

Hunt, Tom pages 112-119

Kolacz, Jerry pages 76-84

Lau, Bernadette pages 243-245, 269-270

Marshall, Ken pages 200-201(t), 201(cr)-Illustration©1996 by Ken Marshall from I WAS THERE: ON BOARD THE TITANIC, a Scholastic/Madison Press Book; page 209(b)-Illustration by Ken Marshall ©1988 from EXPLORING THE TITANIC, a Penguin/Madison Press Book.

Mazierski, Dave pages 130(lc),(lb), 131

McKay, Dave pages 7(br), 35(l), 146(inset)

McMaster, Jack page 147-Illustration by Jack McMaster ©1996 The Madison Press Limited, from "I WAS THERE: DISCOVERING THE ICEMAN, a Scholastic/Madison Press Book; page 150(r), pages 204,208(bl)-Illustrations by Jack McMaster ©1996 the Madison Press Limited, from I WAS THERE: ON BOARD THE TITANIC, a Scholastic/Madison Press Book

Nasmith, Ted page 27

Pariseau, Pierre-Paul pages 134-140

Park, Jun pages 14-15(b), 67(b), 205, 206,207

Porter, Clarence pages 12-13

Power, Stephanie pages 49-51

Pronk&Associates page 44, 163, page 205(b)-Illustration by Pronk&Associates ©1988 from EXPLORING THE TITANIC, a Penguin/Madison Press Book.

Sealock, Rick pages 175-186

Springett, Martin pages 100-109